Teaching the Tiger

A Handbook for Individuals Involved
in the Education of Students with
Attention Deficit Disorders,
Tourette Syndrome or
Obsessive-Compulsive Disorder

Marilyn P. Dornbush, Ph.D.
Sheryl K. Pruitt, M.Ed.

The tiger symbolizes the ADHD/ADD/TS/OCD students. Just as the tiger cannot control its natural instincts, neurologically impaired students often cannot control their unpredictable, impulsive behavior. These students easily become overaroused and unable to perform at an optimum level.

One cannot corner a tiger without expecting an agitated, uncooperative animal. Likewise, one cannot always place demands on these students to perform and behave without expecting a similar reaction. In a structured, rule-governed world, inflexible, unrealistic demands often precipitate behaviors that do not meet the expectations of teachers and parents.

This book is an attempt to give teachers and parents the tools they need to alter the environment and to "teach the tiger."

Teaching the Tiger

A Handbook for Individuals Involved in the Education of Students with Attention Deficit Disorders, Tourette Syndrome or Obsessive-Compulsive Disorder

by
Marilyn Dornbush, Ph D.
Sheryl K. Pruitt, M.Ed.

Published by: **Hope Press**
                       P.O. Box 188
                       Duarte, CA 91009 U.S.A.

For other books by Hope Press see **www.hopepress.com** or insert at the back.

Copyright © 1995 by Marilyn P. Dornbush, Ph.D. and Sheryl K. Pruitt, M.Ed.
2nd Printing - April 1996
3rd Printing - January 1997
4th Printing - September 1997
5th Printing - July 1998
6th Printing - May 1999
7th Printing - July 2000

Library of Congress Cataloging-in-Publication

Dornbush, Marilyn Pierce, 1993 -
        Teaching the tiger: A handbook for individuals involved in the education of students with attention deficit disorders, Tourette syndrome, or obsessive-compulsive disorder.
Marilyn P. Dornbush, Sheryl K. Pruitt.
                p. Cm.
        Included bibliographical references.
        ISBN 1-878267-34-5
        1. Attention-deficit-disordered children–Education–United States–Handbooks, manuals, eta. 2.Attention-deficit hyperactivity disorder–United States–Handbooks, manuals, etc. 3. Tourette syndrome in children–United States–Handbooks, manuals, etc. 4. Obsessive-compulsive disorder in children–United States-Handbooks, manuals, etc. I.
Pruitt, Sheryl K., 1944 -
II. Title.
LC4713.D67 1995   95-2018
371.94—dc20   CIP

Disclaimer

This book is designed to provide information regarding the subject matter covered. It is sold with the understanding that the authors and publisher are not engaged in rendering medical, psychiatric, psychological, legal or other professional services to the reader. If such are required, the services of a competent professional in the appropriate field should be sought.

Every effort has been made to make this book as complete and accurate as possible. However, there may be mistakes both typographical and in content. Therefore, this text should be used only as a source of general information and specifics relating to a given individual should be obtained from the services of a professional. Furthermore, this book contains only the information available to the authors at the time of printing.

The purpose of this book is education. Neither the authors nor the publisher shall have or accept liability or responsibility to any person or entity with respect to loss or damage or any other problem caused or alleged to be caused directly or indirectly by information contained in this book.

This book is dedicated to the ADHD/ADD/TS/OCD students with whom we have worked. All recommendations we offer in this book were derived from the incredible experiences that these students shared with us.

Preface

Tourette syndrome, Attention Deficit Hyperactivity Disorder and Obsessive-Compulsive Disorder are extremely complex, interrelated behavioral problems that can devastate both the affected child and the child's family. The medical community has increasingly come to recognize that these are genetic disorders, that much of the behavior is biochemically driven, and that a variety of medications can be extremely helpful in modulating the behaviors toward normal. Despite this, an equal and sometimes more than equal degree of improvement can come from an educational and psychoeducational approach. I have had many hundreds of parents tell me that their child had a "good year" when they had a teacher who understood their disorder and was willing to be flexible and use innovative approaches to help the child, and had a "horrible year" when this was not the case. Teachers (and others) who are not familiar with these disorders often label the behavior problems as "psychological problems," "parenting problems," "not working to their potential," "laziness," "severe emotional disturbance" or "out-and-out delinquency."

While these disorders clearly do not exclude children from also having some of these labels occasionally be correct, in most cases the behaviors rapidly improve when the medication is right, the educational program is right or especially when both are right. While other books on these conditions help us to understand the clinical aspects, neurochemistry, genetics and medical treatment of these disorders, **Teaching the Tiger** is uniquely designed to help teachers, parents, students and relatives maximize the educational plans necessary to help these children. This can be so effective that for some children this understanding of their condition and appropriate help in the classroom is all that is necessary. For the others who require medication, it can make the difference between whether the problems are largely eliminated or remain a major impediment to progress. An understanding teacher and an appropriately designed educational plan is a critical part of treating all of these children.

David E. Comings, M.D.
Department of Medical Genetics
City of Hope Medical Center
Duarte, California

i

Acknowledgements

We wish to express our gratitude to the following individuals:

Marcia D. Rothschild, M.Ed., who unselfishly gave professional time to edit the first and second documents and to provide valuable information regarding computer use.

Betsy Richards, our editor, who has ADHD, TS and OCD, and therefore brought personal insights and knowledge to our project.

Teddi Rae Erickson, Gale Swanson and **Heath Romer** for completing the final copy.

The members of the Scientific Advisory Board of the Tourette Syndrome Association of Georgia, who reviewed and constructively commented on the handbook.

The staff at Parkaire Consultants for their assistance in preparing this handbook, in particular Jewell McClure for her administrative support and kindness, Jory Bush and Lori King, who on a moment's notice, typed and prepared text and graphics for this project. Jewell and Lori also were willing to read the final text.

Parents Educating Parents, who allowed us to include information prepared by the organization for use in training parents to be advocates for their handicapped children.

Darin and Jory Bush, Sherry Pruitt's sons, for their personal insights which have helped us know what is valid and how it feels to have these neurological impairments.

Daniel G. Pruitt and **John Harne** for the cover illustration, and Dan for reading the final text and going anywhere, anytime to make this project work.

Kirk Dornbush, who provided invaluable feedback and helped us keep this book from being too technical.

Leslie Seeley, who thoughtfully gave her time to read and critique the final copy.

Donna Cherry, who went beyond any reasonable expectation of a friend and gave her spring to read, edit and ensure the quality of the final copy.

Columbia Jones, for reading the final copy.

****

*We especially wish to thank our husbands, **Dan** and **Terry**, who understood the importance of imparting this information to individuals involved in the education of students with ADHD, ADD, TS or OCD, provided unwavering moral support and exhibited extraordinary patience which allowed us to pursue this endeavor.*

Contributors

Barbara Black, M.S., Speech and Language Pathologist and Learning Disability Teacher; Atlanta, Georgia.

Sharon Cargill, M.A., Speech and Language Pathologist; Atlanta, Georgia.

Donna M. Cherry, M.Ed., Educational and Computer Consultant, Parkaire Consultants, Inc.; Director of Resource Program, Mt. Paran Christian School; Marietta, Georgia.

Sue Conners, M.A., President of the Western New York Chapter of the Tourette Syndrome Association, Educational Chairman of the National Tourette Syndrome Association, Teacher; Snyder, New York.

John Harne, Hummingbird Studios; Atlanta, Georgia.

Patricia H. Herzog-Jacobs, M.S., Occupational Therapist; Atlanta, Georgia.

Mary Kay Jennings, Learning Therapist, Parkaire Consultants, Inc.; Atlanta, Georgia.

Gerald V. Kroetsch, Ph.D., Psychologist, Parkaire Consultants, Inc.; Atlanta, Georgia, and Ottawa, Canada.

Dottie Pettes, M.Ed., Educational Consultant, Parkaire Consultants, Inc.; Atlanta, Georgia.

Daniel G. Pruitt, Pruitt Construction Services, Artist and ADHD/TS/OCD parent; Atlanta, Georgia.

Vickie Rhinehart, Handwriting Specialist and Reading Tutor, Parkaire Consultants, Inc.; Atlanta, Georgia.

Marcia D. Rothschild, M.Ed., Learning Therapist and Computer Consultant for Families, Rothschild Learning Services; Atlanta, Georgia.

Leslie Seeley, Educational Consultant, Parkaire Consultants, Inc.; Atlanta, Georgia.

Jeanie D. Taylor, Founder of the Tourette Syndrome Association of Georgia; Atlanta, Georgia.

Tourette Syndrome Association of Georgia; Atlanta, Georgia.

List of Figures

Table of Contents

Section I: Toward an Insider's Point of View
Helping Those Without Neurological Impairments Understand
What Neurological Impairments Are All About

Section III: Computer Use

Section IV: Evaluation/Assessment

Section V: IEP—Individualized Education Plan

Section VI: Modifications for College Admissions Testing

Section VII: Federal Laws Pertaining to Handicapped Students

Section VIII: Appendices

Section I
Toward an Insider's Point of View

*Helping Those Without Neurological Impairments Understand
What Neurological Impairments Are All About*

Definitions

Attention Deficit Disorders

Attention Deficit Disorders are clinically diagnosed neurological syndromes that affect 3 to 5 percent of students. Research suggests that there are at least two subtypes: Attention Deficit/Hyperactivity Disorder (ADHD) and Attention Deficit Disorder without the hyperactivity component (ADD).[1] ADHD involves developmentally inappropriate impulse control and motor activity whereas ADD involves poorly focused attention, disorganization, slow cognitive processing and decreased fine motor speed.

■ *Attention Deficit/Hyperactivity Disorder, Predominately Hyperactive, Impulsive Type—ADHD*

Impulsive Behaviors
(poor cognitive/thinking and physical impulse control)

Acting before thinking

Answering before questions are completed

Beginning work before directions are completed

Difficulty delaying gratification (I have to have it NOW!)

Difficulty following oral and written directions

Difficulty predicting consequences and sequencing behavior

Difficulty self-monitoring classwork (making careless mistakes)

Difficulty self-monitoring vocal, motor, emotional or sensory behavior

Difficulty waiting turn in games/group activities

Engaging in risk-taking behaviors

Grabbing things from other students

Interrupting adults/peers

Interrupting or intruding on other students' games/activities

Responding without waiting to be called on

Rushing through assignments

Shoplifting (particularly young adolescents)

Talking to other students during quiet classroom activities

Hyperactive Behaviors
(vocal, motor, emotional, sensory)

Becoming physically uncomfortable when bored

Being irritable

Difficulty playing quietly

Difficulty remaining seated

Excessive running/climbing

Excessive talking

Experiencing rapid/unpredictable mood changes

Feeling angry

Fidgeting (tapping pencil, fingers, feet)

Having a low tolerance for frustration

Hypersensitive (overreacting) to auditory, visual, tactile, olfactory, gustatory input

Hypersensitive to pain

Overreacting to situations

Repeatedly shifting positions in seat

Shifting from one uncompleted activity to another

Throwing things

---

[1] Goodyear, P. and Hynd, G.W. (1992). Attention-deficit disorder (AD/HD) and without (ADD/WO) hyperactivity: Behavioral and neuropsychological differentiation. <u>Journal of Clinical Child Psychology</u>, 21, 273-305.

Other Behaviors

Acting aggressively towards others

Being immature (functioning similarly to a student who is two-thirds the chronological age)[2]

Cognitively "clueless"[3] (failing to perceive, utilize, benefit from primary information being presented)

Difficulty feeling satisfied

Difficulty following rules of behavior

Difficulty learning from experience

Difficulty using appropriate social skills

Difficulty attending due to fatigue from sleep deprivation

Enuretic (bedwetting) or encopretic (soiling)—not related to a physical problem

Lacking metacognitive skills (failing to learn strategies to store, manipulate, retrieve information)

Lacking problem-solving skills

Morally "clueless" (failing to comprehend abstract moral principles needed to respond in appropriate manner)

Overfocusing, especially on TV, computer/video games

Socially "clueless" (failing to perceive, understand, express correct social behaviors)

Using intentional belligerent/disrespectful language

◼ *Attention Deficit/Hyperactivity Disorder, Predominately Inattentive Type—ADD*

Inattentive Behaviors

Appearing to lack energy, be lethargic or sleepy

Avoiding tasks requiring sustained attention (schoolwork, homework, reading)

Being hypoactive (underreacting to auditory, visual, tactile input)

Daydreaming (tending to free-associate, stare into space)

Delaying initiation of tasks/assignments

Difficulty finishing tasks/assignments

Difficulty following instructions

Difficulty listening

Difficulty paying close attention to details

Displaying inconsistent academic performance

Experiencing auditory, visual, tactile distractibility

Forgetting/losing materials needed for tasks/activities

Forgetting recently learned material

Having difficulty organizing tasks/activities

Having difficulty sustaining attention

Performing timed handwritten tasks slowly

Responding slowly on cognitive tasks

Seeming "lazy" or "unmotivated" when confronted with goal-oriented activities

---

[2]   Barkley, R.A. New ways of looking at ADHD. (Lecture. 1991). Third annual CH.A.D.D. Conference on Attention Deficit Disorders, Washington, D.C.

[3]   "Clueless" is a term developed by Sheryl K. Pruitt to mean literally "not having any clue." This means the student either does not have the obvious information or does not know when it is appropriate to utilize it.

■ *Attention Deficit/Hyperactivity Disorder, Combined Type*

Although ADHD and ADD are considered to be two separate disorders, some students display behaviors associated with both categories.

■ *General Information - ADHD/ADD*

O **Gender Frequency.** During the childhood years (6 - 11 years), research suggests that ADHD is manifested by 9.4 percent of males and 2.8 percent of females, while ADD is exhibited by 1.4 percent of males and 1.3 percent of females. In adolescence, the percentage of students having ADHD is 2.9 for males and 1.4 for females. The percentage of adolescent students having ADD is 1.4 for males and 1.0 for females.[4]

O **Age of Onset.** The onset of ADHD/ADD typically occurs between 2 and 7 years.[5] However, many above average ADHD/ADD students, particularly those with ADD, may not display symptoms that interfere with school performance until later childhood when the demand for focused and sustained attention and self-control increases. ADD students tend to be referred for diagnosis 6 months to 1 year later than ADHD students.[6]

O **Associated Disorders.** ADHD/ADD can have a significant impact on the student's academic progress, social interactions and emotional functioning.

    ■ 40 percent are placed in special education classes
(ADHD students tend to be served in behavior disorder programs, while ADD students are served in learning disability programs.)

    ■ 19 to 26 percent are diagnosed as learning disabled

    ■ 52 percent have poor fine motor skills

    ■ 23 to 35 percent repeat at least one grade

    ■ 50 percent have impaired social relationships

    ■ 45 percent have a conduct disorder
(Conduct Disorder is diagnosed more frequently in ADHD students than ADD students.)

    ■ 10 to 30 percent have Obsessive-Compulsive Disorder[7]

---

[4]   Satterfield, J.H., Satterfield, B.T. and Cantwell, D.P. (1981). Three-year multimodality treatment study of 100 hyperactive boys. Journal of Pediatrics, 98, 650-655.

[5]   Barkley, R.A. (1990). Attention deficit hyperactivity disorder: A handbook for diagnosis and treatment. New York: Guildford Press.

[6]   Goodyear, P. and Hynd, G.W. (1992). Attention-deficit disorder (AD/HD) and without (ADD/WO) hyperactivity: Behavioral and neuropsychological differentiation. Journal of Clinical Child Psychology, 21, 273-305.

[7]   Comings, D.E. Personal Communication, 1995.

- ADD students display symptoms of anxiety, depression and low self-esteem.

○ **Prognosis.** Research studies have shown that, although the primary symptoms of Attention Deficit/Hyperactivity Disorder tend to diminish during the adolescent years, the following problems persist:

- 70 percent experience restlessness, inattention, impulsivity, emotional volatility, poor self-esteem, low self-confidence, academic under-achievement and impaired social interactions

- 25 to 35 percent engage in antisocial behaviors

- 58 percent fail one or more grades in school

- 10 percent drop out of school

- 59 percent meet the criteria for Oppositional Defiant Disorder

- 43 percent qualify for a diagnosis of Conduct Disorder (lying, stealing, fire setting)[8]

   ☙ *The severity of ADHD predicts academic achievement, but does not predict adolescent outcome.*

Symptoms continue to be exhibited by 50 to 60 percent of the ADHD adults. The general level of educational attainment and employment is lower than might be expected.

- 30 percent do not finish high school

- Only 5 percent receive a university degree

- ADHD adults, although usually employed and self-sufficient, have lower job status than family members, change jobs frequently, have difficulty in their relationships with their employer and tend to quit or be fired from their jobs.

- 75 percent have social interaction problems

- 79 percent report anxiety, sadness and physical complaints

- 12 percent have a Substance Abuse Disorder

- 25 percent exhibit antisocial behaviors

- 25 percent are diagnosed with an adult Antisocial Personality[9]

   ☙ *Similar statistics are not available for ADD adolescent and adult outcomes.*

---

[8]   Barkley, R.A. (1990). <u>Attention deficit hyperactivity disorder: A handbook for diagnosis and treatment</u>. New York: Guildford Press.

[9]   Barkley, R.A. (1990). (ibid)

The results of research suggest that an ADHD student who receives a multimodal approach to treatment (p. 24) has a significantly better adjustment than a student who receives no treatment or only one form of treatment.[10]

---

[10]   Barkley, R.A. (1990). <u>Attention deficit hyperactivity disorder: A handbook for diagnosis and treatment</u>. New York: Guildford Press.

Tic Disorders[11]

Tic disorders are neurological conditions composed of involuntary movements (**motor tics**) or sounds (**vocal tics**).

The classification of tic syndromes typically separates the disorders into two categories:

Transient tic syndromes—history of tics for less than 12 months

Chronic tic syndromes—history of tics for more than 12 months

■ *Transient Tic Disorder*

For a diagnosis of **Transient Tic Disorder**, the following criteria must be met:

○ Age of onset: before 21

○ Presence of multiple, involuntary motor tics (*usually* eyeblinking and facial movements) and, at times, vocal tics (typically throat clearing or sniffing)

○ Tics occur many times a day, almost every day or intermittently for *less* than 12 months

○ Symptoms may *change* in type and location and may *wax and wane* in number, frequency, complexity and severity

■ *Definite Tic Disorder, Diagnosis Deferred*

Definite Tic Disorder, Diagnosis Deferred meets all criteria for **Chronic Tic Disorder** *except* the tics have been present less than 12 months.

■ *Chronic Multiple Tic Disorder*

For a diagnosis of **Chronic Multiple Tic Disorder** (Motor or Vocal), the following criteria must be met:

○ Age of onset: before 21

○ Presence of multiple, involuntary motor tics or, less often, vocal tics, *but not both*

○ Tics occur many times a day, almost every day or intermittently for *more* than 12 months

○ Symptoms may remain *constant or fluctuate* in location, number, frequency, complexity, type and severity

---

[11]   Singer, H.S. and Walkup, J.T. (1991). Tourette syndrome and other tic disorders: Diagnosis, pathophysiology, and treatment. <u>Medicine</u>, <u>70</u>, 15-32.

■ *Chronic Single Tic Disorder*

The criteria for a diagnosis of **Chronic Single Tic Disorder** is the same as for Chronic Multiple Tic Disorder, except that the individual has only *one* motor or vocal tic that does *not change*.

■ *Tourette Syndrome (TS)*

<u>My Curse</u>

Imagine if you will
    A clean and clear night,
And then it comes upon you
    And sets you in a state of fright.

Sometimes it's mild
    Sometimes it's bad,
But whenever it happens
    It might make you mad.

It won't stop
    Until you are dead,
But this is no reason
    To put a bullet through your head,

The PAIN you can feel is all too real
    And when it goes by,
You may think,
    WOW! What an ordeal.

Corey, age 18

The prevalence of TS is estimated to be 1 in 100 boys and 1 in 600 girls.[12]

The criteria for a diagnosis of **Tourette syndrome (TS),** is similar to those for other tic disorders. A TS diagnosis requires tics that last more than a year. The criteria for diagnosis follows.

O Age of onset: before 21

O Presence of multiple involuntary motor tics *and* one or more vocal tics

O Tics occur many times a day, almost every day or intermittently for *more* than twelve months

O Symptoms may *change* in location and type and may *wax and wane* in number, frequency, complexity, severity

[12] Comings, D.E., Himes, J.A. and Comings, D.B. (1990). An epidemiological study of Tourette's syndrome in a single school district. <u>Journal of Clinical Psychiatry</u>, <u>51</u>, 436-469.

TS symptoms are different for each student and may include any movement or sound.

The most common motor symptoms are eyeblinking, head jerking and shoulder shrugging.

Motor Symptoms

Abdominal jerking

Ankle flexing/moving

Arm flailing/flapping

Arm flexing/jerking

Blowing on hands/fingers

Body jerking/tensing/
posturing

Chewing clothes/paper/
hair

Clapping

Eyeblinking

Eye rolling/squinting

Eye twitching

Facial contortions

Facial grimacing

Finger tapping

Finger moving

Foot dragging

Foot shaking/tapping

Hair patting/tossing/
twisting

Hand clenching/
unclenching

Head jerking/rolling

Hitting - others/self

Hopping

Inhaling/exhaling

Jaw/mouth moving

Joint cracking

Jumping

Kicking

Kissing - hand/others

Knee, deep bending

Knee knocking

Knuckle cracking

Leg bouncing

Leg jerking

Lip licking/smacking

Lip pouting

Muscle flexing/unflexing

Muscle tensing/untensing

Nose twitching

Picking at lint

Pinching

Pulling clothes

Scratching

Shivering

Shoulder shrugging/rolling

Skipping

Smelling fingers/objects

Spitting

Squatting

Stepping backwards

Stomping

Stooping

Table banging

Tapping objects

Tearing books/paper

Teeth clenching/unclenching

Throwing things

Toe walking

Tongue thrusting

Twirling in circles

Twirling objects

Trichotillomania (pulling hair out)*

Copropraxia (making obscene gestures)*

*   Clinical experiences of the authors suggest that these symptoms may be manifestations of Obsessive-Compulsive Disorder (OCD) in the TS student.

The most common vocal symptoms are sniffing and throat clearing.

Vocal Symptoms

Barking

Belching

Blowing noises

Calling out

Clicking/clacking

Coughing

Gasping

Grunting

Gurgling

Hiccuping

Hissing

Honking

Humming

Laughing

Making animal noises

Making "tsk," "pft" noises

Making guttural sounds

Making motor/jet noises

Making unintelligible noises

Moaning

Noisy breathing

Saying "hey hey," "ha ha"

Screaming

Screeching

Shouting

Shrieking

Sniffing

Snorting

Squealing

Syllables: "hmm," "oh," "wow," "uh," "yeah"

Talking in character voices

Throat clearing

Whistling

Yelping

Unusual speech patterns (Accenting words peculiarly/stammering or stuttering/using unusual vocal rhythms)

Coprolalia (uttering obscene words)*

Echolalia (repeating others' words)*

Palilalia (repeating own words)*

*   Clinical experiences of the authors suggest that these symptoms may be manifestations of Obsessive-Compulsive Disorder (OCD) in the TS student.

■ *General Information - TS*

○ **Gender Frequency.** TS is six times more common in males than in females.

○ **Age of Onset.** The average age of onset of Tourette syndrome is 6.5 years. The average age of onset of coprolalia is 13.5 years; however, only 10 to 15 percent of individuals with TS develop coprolalia.

○ **Symptom Control.** Tics can be suppressed or controlled by the student for seconds to hours, depending on the severity of the case and the psychological and environmental factors. Excessive control can produce an explosive build-up which must be released. Anxiety, anger, excitement, fatigue, physical illness and stress significantly increase symptoms, thereby reducing the ability to suppress tics.

○ **Diagnosis.** Today, the correct diagnosis of TS is often delayed for more than 5 years. Sixty percent of the diagnoses are made by students with TS, parents, relatives or friends who discover information about the disorder in the media.

TS is often misdiagnosed or not diagnosed by professionals because there is a lack of knowledge regarding TS. Some professionals mistakenly consider:

- TS symptoms as a psychological problem

- eye tics as a visual problem

- sniffing, snorting, noisy breathing, nose wiping, nose twitching, throat clearing, coughing as symptoms of allergies and upper respiratory disorders

- coprolalia as a necessary symptom of TS

- suppression or control of symptoms during office visits to negate presence of TS

  ☙ *For decades, TS was little understood, and false information (if any) circulated through the medical, psychological and educational fields. Although certainly some individuals with TS have the following problems, they are not required for a diagnosis of TS:*

  Coprolalia (utterance of obscene words)
  Echolalia (repetition of other person's words)
  Intellectual deterioration

○ **Associated Neurological Disorders**. An individual with TS may also have one or more of the following disorders: ADHD, ADD, OCD (Obsessive-Compulsive Disorder), LD (learning disability).

- Research studies suggest 50 to 70 percent are affected by an Attention Deficit/Hyperactivity Disorder. (Clinical observations suggest that there is a correlation between the frequency and severity of the symptoms of TS and those of ADHD/ADD.)

- Clinical experience suggests that 85 percent are referred for behaviors associated with ADHD/ADD rather than for tics. (It is generally agreed that ADHD/ADD has a more significant impact on the student's life than TS.)

  ☙ *Comings (1985) found that the symptoms of ADHD were more severe in the TS patient even when the tics were too mild to treat with medication. The ADHD symptoms included: difficulty listening, concentrating and thinking; distractibility; trouble sitting still; running about; calling out in class; impatience; impersistence; needing supervision; and problems organizing and finishing work.*[13]

○ **Prognosis.** TS is considered a chronic, lifelong disorder. The course and duration of the disorder varies in individuals as much as the symptoms.

- 30 to 40 percent have symptoms that disappear by late adolescence

- 30 percent have symptoms that decrease by late adolescence

- 50 percent have symptoms that persist in adulthood[14]

---

[13] Comings, D.E. and Comings, B.G. (1985). Tourette syndrome: Clinical and psychological aspects of 250 cases. American Journal of Human Genetics, 37, 435-450.

[14] Comings, D.E. (1990). Tourette syndrome and human behavior. Duarte, CA: Hope Press.

Obsessive-Compulsive Disorder—OCD

Obsessive-Compulsive Disorder (OCD) is a neurological disorder that affects approximately 2 percent of the population[15] and 0.5 percent of school-age children.[16] Ten to 30 percent of the students with Attention Deficit Disorders[17] and 40 to 60 percent of the students with Tourette syndrome[18] have OCD.

OCD is characterized by involuntary, recurrent obsessions and compulsions that consume time, provoke anxiety and interfere with normal school functioning. Obsessions are persistent thoughts, images, ideas or feelings that enter the student's thinking and are experienced as unreasonable, meaningless and excessive. Compulsions are repetitive, ritualistic behaviors that are usually associated with an obsession and are performed to relieve the tension and anxiety associated with the obsession. Obsessive-compulsive behaviors share the chronic waxing and waning course of ADHD, ADD and TS. They may be precipitated by environmental, emotional and physical events and are exacerbated by stress. Some students are able to suppress the symptoms during school.

While involved in obsessions and compulsions, the OCD student experiences anxiety and has the feeling of being "stuck." Typical manifestations include:

- Difficulty delaying gratification ("I have to have it NOW!")

- Inability to change tasks or to let go of a subject to the point of harassing other students, school personnel or self

- Perfectionism (erasing until tearing a hole in the paper; writing numbers and letters over and over again)

- Perseveration on feelings or routines

When an OCD student feels "stuck," an interruption often increases anxiety until the task is completed. Anxiety may be exhibited as fearfulness, agitation, aggression, irritability, restlessness, indecisiveness or somatic complaints (headaches, stomachaches).

---

[15]   Flament, M.F., Whitaker, A., Rapoport, J.L., Davies, M., Berg, C.Z., Kalikow, K., Sceery, W. and Shaffer, D. (1988). Obsessive compulsive disorder in adolescence: An epidemiological study. Journal of the American Academy of Child and Adolescent Psychiatry, 27, 764-771.

[16]   Adams, G.B. and Torchia, M. School personnel: A critical link in the identification, treatment and management of OCD in children and adolescents, Milford, CO: The Obsessive Compulsion Foundation.

[17]   Comings, D.E. Personal communication, 1995.

[18]   Comings, D.E. (1990). Tourette syndrome and human behavior, Duarte, CA: Hope Press. p. 113.

■ *Obsessions*

Common obsessions may include, but are not limited to, contamination, harm, illness, death and constant doubt.[19]

Being afraid of losing things

Being concerned about dirt/germs/ illness (AIDS)

Being concerned with colors of special significance

Being concerned with symmetry, exactness, cleanliness, order

Being preoccupied with knives, scissors, blood, fire

Body Dysmorphic Disorder (needing perfect body)

Counting letters, steps, objects, breaths

Focusing on a movie, TV show, computer/video game, music, sounds

Focusing on minute details

Focusing on moral issues (right/wrong, fairness)

Focusing on sensory input (noises made by fluorescent lights, textures of clothing, computer games, pain)

Focusing on specific numbers/words

Having aggressive thoughts, images, impulses

Having sexual thoughts, images, desires

Needing to know or remember things

Obsessing about obsessions[20]

Performing mental rituals (counting, reciting, spelling)

Ruminating on one idea, action, feeling (hurt feelings, embarrassing event, angry encounter)

Scrupulosity (thinking about religion)

Thinking about food and eating

Thinking about forbidden behaviors

Thinking about hoarding/collecting

Thinking macabre or gory thoughts

Worrying about harming self/others

Worrying that something terrible might happen (fire, burglary, divorce, death of relative/friend)

---

[19]   Adams, G.B. and Torchia, M. <u>School personnel: A critical link in the identification, treatment and management of OCD in children and adolescents</u>, Milford, CO: The Obsessive Compulsion Foundation.

[20]   Johnston, H.F. and March, J.S. (1993). Obsessive-compulsive disorder in children and adolescents. In W. Reynolds (Ed.), <u>Internalizing disorders in children and adolescents</u> (pp. 107-148). New York: John Wiley and Sons.

■ *Compulsions*

Common compulsions may include washing, cleaning, checking, repeating, touching and counting rituals.[21]

Adjusting/readjusting clothes (socks, sleeves) to feel just right

Asking the same question repeatedly

Avoiding people/objects

Biting (nails, arms, objects, others, self)

Checking/rechecking (doors, locks, windows, stoves)

Constantly fiddling with objects, clothes

Coprolalia (uttering obscene words)

Copropraxia (making obscene gestures)

Counting/grouping objects repeatedly

Cracking joints/knuckles

Echolalia (repeating the words of others)

Echopraxia (repeating the actions of others)

Erasing repeatedly

Evening-up (socks, touching with one hand and then the other)

Excessive handwashing, bathing, cleaning

Excessively ordering/arranging objects

Having to respond with a verbalization even when unnecessary

Hoarding

Licking/biting objects

Needing to engage in rituals for good luck

Needing to experience sensations (pinch, cut or burn self)

Needing to finish verbalizations if interrupted

Needing to start over if interrupted

Needing to say/do what told not to say or do

Not being able to change to a new task/activity

Palilalia (repeating aloud one's own words)

Perseverating on a task

Picking skin/sores

Playing computer/video games over and over in the mind

Reading/rereading, reading backwards

Reciting sequence of statements/series of numbers

Repeating actions (in/outdoor, up/down from chair

Repeating sounds, words, numbers, music, movies to oneself

Seeking reassurance

Sexually touching others (breasts, buttocks, genitals)

Sexually touching self (sometimes masturbation)

Sniffing or smelling hands/objects

Stealing

Sucking thumb

Touching objects exact number of times

Touching objects, self, others, wounds

Trichotillomania (pulling hair out)

Visualizing a particular image

Vomiting

Writing/rewriting until paper looks perfect or has hole in it

---

[21]   Adams, G.B. and Torchia, M. School personnel: A critical link in the identification, treatment and management of OCD in children and adolescents, Milford, CO: The Obsessive Compulsion Foundation.

■ *General Information - OCD*

○ **Gender Frequency**. Research suggests that the sex differences in OCD may vary during childhood. Boys are more often affected than girls. However, in adolescence males and females are equally affected.[22]

○ **Age of Onset.** Although the onset of OCD typically occurs during adolescence and early adulthood, studies indicate that 15 percent of the cases begin in childhood.[23] The usual age of onset is 5 to 8 years for males and adolescence for females.[24]

○ **Associated Disorders.** Approximately 75 percent of OCD children have other diagnosed disorders. Research identifies the following disorders:

■ 10 percent have Attention Deficit/Hyperactivity Disorder

■ 12 percent meet the criteria for Tourette Syndrome

■ 24 percent have developmental disabilities

■ 11 percent are diagnosed with an Oppositional Defiant Disorder

■ 40 percent have anxiety disorders (phobias, overanxious disorder and separation anxiety)[25]

○ **Prognosis.** OCD is considered a chronic, life-long disorder. The course and duration of the disorder varies in individuals as much as the symptoms.

■ 85 percent of OCD individuals experience a chronic life-long disorder.

■ 5 percent of the people have periods when the symptoms are mild or absent.

■ 5 to 10 percent suffer a progressive deterioration.[26]

[22]   Goodman, W.K., Rasmussen, S.A., Foa, E.B. and Price, L.H. (1994). Obsessive-compulsive disorder. In R.F. Prien and D.S. Robinson (Eds.), <u>Clinical evaluation of psychotropic drugs and guidelines</u> (pp. 431-466). New York, Raven Press.

[23]   Goodman, W.K. (1994). (ibid)

[24]   Adams, G.B., and Torchia, M. School Personnel: A critical link in the identification, treatment, and management of OCD in children and adolescents, Milford, CO: The Obsessive Compulsive Foundation.

[25]   Swedo, S.E., Rapoport, J.L., Leonard, H., Lenane, M. and Cheslow, D. (1989). Obsessive-compulsive disorder in children and adolescents: Clinical phenomonology of 70 consecutive cases. <u>Archives of General Psychiatry</u>, <u>46</u>, 335-341.

[26]   Rasmussen, S.A. and Eisen, J.L. (1990). Epidemiology and clinical features of obsessive-compulsive disorders. In M.A. Jenike, L. Baer and W.E. Minichiello (Eds.), <u>Obsessive-compulsive disorders: Theory and management</u>. Littleton, MD: Year Book Medical.

Deregulated Arousal System

Arousal

A student's state of arousal (alertness) significantly affects the ability to function in school and at home. **Optimal arousal** enhances school performance, behavioral control and socialization. The adequately aroused student demonstrates the following characteristics:

- Alertness/availability for learning
- Focused/sustained attention
- Attention to details
- Efficient organization
- Task initiation
- Task persistence
- Task completion
- Ability to retrieve information

- Ability to reason abstractly
- Ability to make inferences
- Ability to draw conclusions
- Ability to solve problems
- Behavioral self-control
- Appropriate socialization
- Awareness of feelings of others
- Awareness of needs of others

The neurologically impaired student's arousal, however, fluctuates unpredictably between underarousal and overarousal. Functioning can vary from minute to minute, hour to hour, day to day and even week to week. Fluctuating arousal produces inconsistent learning, variable test scores, erratic behavior and impaired socialization. Teachers often report:

"He knew the multiplication facts yesterday, but has forgotten them today."

"His handwriting was neat this morning, but messy this afternoon."

"He was happy one minute, but something as insignificant as demanding eye contact produced an angry outburst!"

The student who is **underaroused** is not sufficiently alert to perform adequately in the classroom. The underaroused student lacks physical and mental energy, often appears fatigued and sleepy and exhibits the following behaviors:

- Decreased effort and motivation
- Difficulty attending to details
- Difficulty completing tasks
- Difficulty focusing/sustaining attention
- Difficulty initiating behavior

- Difficulty performing timed tasks
- Difficulty persisting on tasks
- Impaired academic performance
- Inefficient problem solving
- Slow information processing

The student who is **overaroused**, on the other hand, is too stressed or overstimulated to function effectively. Excessive arousal, which is precipitated by anxiety, frustration, fear, anticipation, emotional excitement or stress, impacts behavior and performance and may be manifested as the following:

- Anger and aggression
- Difficulty retrieving information
- Difficulty thinking clearly
- Impaired academic performance
- Inability to complete homework

- Irritability
- Low frustration tolerance
- Sensory overload
- Temper outbursts
- Test anxiety

■ *Shark Theory of Arousal*[27]

The Shark Theory of Arousal was developed in response to two ADHD/TS/OCD students, both named Michael (p. 197), to illustrate how a deregulated arousal system affected their school performance, ability to control behavior and social competency.

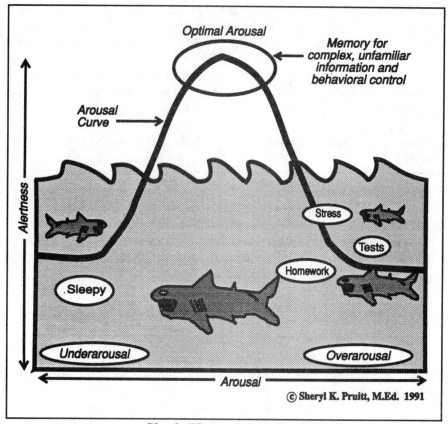

Shark Theory of Arousal

○ *The arousal curve[28] above the water line represents behavioral control, age-appropriate social interactions and successful academic achievement (remembering the answer to a fill-in-the-blank question, even recalling the letter "a").*

○ *The circled area at the top of the curve depicts the ability to learn and recall complex, unfamiliar information (answering questions on a science test).*

○ *The area below the water line illustrates the inability to function adequately. The lower left section of the arousal curve represents the hypoactive, underaroused state (lacking energy and feeling fatigued); the lower right section represents the hyperactive, overaroused state (feeling stressed).*

○ *The shark is the negative consequence of an impaired arousal system (failing a test, being rejected by peers for inappropriate behavior). The students stated, "The shark eats the answers to our tests even when we have studied."*

---

[27] Developed by Sheryl K. Pruitt, M.Ed., Parkaire Consultants Inc., 1991.

[28] Hebb, D. (1955). Drives and the C.N.S. (conceptual nervous system). Psychological Review, 62. 243-254.

○ **Shark Theory of Normal Arousal**

The student wakes up when the alarm rings and quickly moves up the left side of the arousal curve. The student dresses and hurries to breakfast. When the school bus arrives, the student remembers to take the bookbag, which was organized and packed with the homework the previous night. Most of the day is spent above the water line learning, retrieving information, solving problems, producing correct answers to tests, controlling behavior and being aware of the feelings and needs of others. After returning home and completing homework without argument, the student reads a book, slowly slides down the left side of the curve and goes to sleep. This routine is usually predictable and enables the student to feel in control of behavior and to be able to predict performance. The only time the student falls down the right side of the curve is when a traumatic event, such as the illness of a parent or a car accident, occurs.

○ **Shark Theory of Underarousal**

> *I remember the arrival of the baby in our family. The first weeks home from the hospital, everyone was up late at night, had restless sleep and got up earlier than usual. During this time adult tempers flared, thinking was foggy and normal functioning was inefficient in some areas and non-existent in others. No one considered us "lazy" or "stupid" when we could not perform according to normal expectations at home or work. Everyone around us, the new parents, understood our exhaustion, irritability and inability to function.*
>
> Sherry, adult

Common Adult Experience of Underarousal

The ADHD/TS student frequently has difficulty going to sleep and stays up late to read, watch television or engage in an interesting activity. Sleep is marked by restlessness and irregular sleep patterns such as enuresis (bedwetting), sleepwalking and night terrors[29]. The TS student may also tic during sleep or experience drowsiness upon waking due to medication side effects. The student then has difficulty getting up in the morning, dressing and going to breakfast. With each reminder to hurry, the student becomes increasingly irritated. When the school bus arrives, the bookbag and homework cannot be located. The student often cannot achieve sufficient arousal until mid morning, if at all, and spends most of the day submerged in the shark-infested waters.

The underaroused ADD student remains below the water line, underreacting both mentally and physically, and sometimes does not achieve full arousal. The student lacks drive and motivation, is slow to initiate and complete assignments and avoids tasks requiring sustained attention. Failing to pay close attention to details and using inefficient problem-solving skills, the student's school performance is compromised.

---

[29]   When experiencing night terrors, the student awakens, screaming from fright. (Fear can only be inferred from body and facial expressions.) The student remains in a semiconscious state, cannot be awakened, cannot be reassured or calmed and continues to experience the frightening event. The fear persists for a time until the student falls into a deep sleep. The next morning there is no memory of the event.

> *I get so tired of waking up every morning with everyone yelling at me to get up. Although I am tired, my body refuses to go to sleep at night. I wish my family understood how hard it is to wake up in the morning. Some days my body is awake, but my brain does not turn on until almost noon.*
>
> Sheryl, age 13

○ **Shark Theory of Overarousal**

> *Imagine me having no control over my arousal system. I am unable to predict where I will be on the curve day or night. While other kids in my class drop down a little on the right side of the curve because they are nervous about a test, I fall down into shark infested waters where the sharks eat the answers to my test questions. One time, I failed a geography test. When the teacher saw my test, she accused me of not studying and said she was going to call my parents and tell them how lazy I was. Luckily my parents knew the truth because they quizzed me the night before and were aware that I knew all the answers to my study guide questions. Sometimes, I find it hard to keep trying when I do not get credit for the work I do. I feel like giving up!*
>
> Cookie, age 10

The neurologically impaired student is easily overaroused by many situations that other students take in stride. The following events may precipitate overarousal and plunge the student down the right side of the curve into dangerous waters:

- Being lightly touched
- Criticism in front of peers
- Crowded/noisy hallways
- Lengthy handwritten assignments
- Homework
- Insistence on eye contact
- Requirement to listen to speaker over background noises
- Restrictions on movement
- Several people talking at the same time
- Teasing and ridicule
- Tests
- Unpredictable rules and expectations
- Work assigned at a frustration level

Anxiety and stress produce overload which impacts performance. The overaroused student is unable to solve problems or to respond appropriately. Anger, aggression and loss of self-control are common outcomes.

Effort does not predict success; that is, the level of success achieved is seldom in proportion to the amount of effort put forth. This is analogous to an adult who goes to work, and works hard every day, but does not always receive a paycheck.

> *A rookie police officer approaches the victim of a car accident moments after the collision and starts asking for a name and license number. The accident victim cannot retrieve his name or license number and responds with a temper outburst, pushing at the officer. The officer does not understand the victim's agitation and misinterprets it as unruliness. Fortunately, at this moment a more experienced police officer approaches.*
>
> *The senior officer tells the younger officer to encourage the victim to sit down and allow his arousal system time to calm down. She explains that the victim will then be more capable of retrieving the information and controlling his behavior. Although still somewhat excited, the victim relaxes, and, as predicted, is able to answer the questions and control his emotions and behavior.*

Common Adult Experience of Overarousal

■ *Storms*

> *Having raised two sons with ADHD, tics and OCD, the term "storm" evolved as I often witnessed my nine-year-old child lose control over minute issues. He would become so out of control that he would break furniture and put holes in walls. When I tried to intervene, it was like cornering a caged tiger. Ten minutes later, he would not be able to remember the event. I was shocked that he could not recall what happened because we were so stunned and scared during those tornado-like "storms."*
>
> Sherry, parent

A *storm*[30] occurs when the ADHD/TS student is at the height of overarousal and is out of control. During overarousal, access to abstract knowledge becomes impaired and problem solving ability deteriorates. The ability to comprehend and sequence the consequences of abusive attitudes, actions and verbalizations is impaired. Any verbal, visual or tactile input increases the storm and leads to a more violent outburst. When the storm subsides, the student is as surprised as everyone else and may feel remorse for behavior that others interpret as "bad," "stupid" or "crazy."

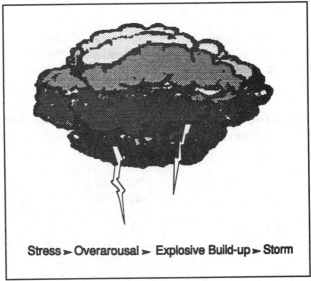

Stress ➤ Overarousal ➤ Explosive Build-up ➤ Storm

ADHD/TS Storm

---

[30]   The term *Tourette storm* to describe this neurological loss of control was developed by Sheryl K. Pruitt, M.Ed.

Psychological Consequences

Imagine, if you will, living in my world of mental and physical chaos. The sensation is similar to being in a room with eight televisions, all of them turned on and tuned to a different program and the volume turned up. I frequently must put forth huge amounts of mental effort to filter out numerous sensations, noises and other external and internal stimuli and to concentrate on the one thing at hand. Now imagine that at the end of the eight simultaneous television programs, you will be tested on what you saw, heard and learned on one particular station.

Here's how it would be for me. Just as I get a mental fix on the desired station, I have the sensation of someone or something tickling my throat or the back of my neck, causing me to jerk my head and want to strike back at the "intruder." I turn, but there is no intruder there. However, my action drew the attention of others in the room, who have turned to look at me. Feeling silly, I stretch my arms, yawn and say, "Gee, this show is boring!" I hope my yawn disguised my "tic" reaction to the tickling sensation.

Not wanting to disappoint my family with another bad grade, I dig in and try to concentrate on the show once more. The TV host talks about wood working and mentions saw horses, which immediately triggers the thought in my mind that I forgot to feed and water my horse the previous night, and with temperatures in the 100's today he could die without water!

I will have no opportunity to leave the room for several hours. I am trapped in school. By the time I get home or have an opportunity to call my family about the horse, he may already be dead from heat exhaustion. When it comes time to take the quiz, the only thing I remember about the show is that the host looked like my Uncle Sam and mentioned saw horses. I feel a bad headache coming on and spend the rest of the day anxious, frustrated and depressed. I hyperventilate from stress and suffer from a headache that is so intense I can't pay attention to much of anything.

Betsy, adult

This story may sound contrived; however, to the ADHD, ADD, TS or OCD student, it is all too familiar. The neurological chaos that is part of these disorders creates continual and stressful situations that can easily turn into frustration, failure, embarrassment and criticism from self or others.

The following psychological problems are common as secondary consequences of having to cope with ADHD, ADD, TS and/or OCD:

- Anger
- Depression
- Discouragement
- Excessive anxiety
- Feeling/acting self-destructive
- Feeling "bad"
- Feeling "crazy"
- Feeling hopeless/discouraged
- Feeling rejected/unloved
- Feeling "stupid"
- Feeling suicidal
- Frustration
- Impaired peer relationships
- Inability to understand/respond to feelings of others
- Inability to regulate responses to peers
- Low self-esteem
- Oversensitivity
- Social embarrassment
- Social withdrawal

Research has found that teachers considered 58 percent of the ADHD/TS students to feel tense and anxious, 38 percent to act timid and shy, 23 percent to be unhappy, 46 percent to fear failure and 31 percent to give up easily. Statistically lower self-concepts were found in the students' attitudes toward themselves, relative to their peers, and their ability to be successful in school.[31]

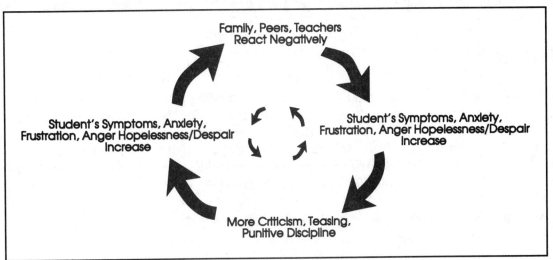

Psychological Consequences of Stress
Developed by TSA of Georgia

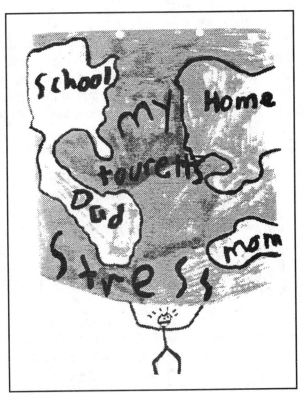

"My World With Tourette Syndrome"
Painted by Buddy, age 14

---

[31]   Research conducted by Marilyn P. Dornbush, Ph.D.

Treatment

ADHD, ADD, TS and OCD can produce significant educational, behavioral and social handicaps for the student. An appropriate treatment program must be an interdisciplinary and coordinated team effort.

Medication

The use of medication is a decision made between the treating physician and parents. A decision to initiate drug therapy is typically based upon the severity of the symptoms and the extent to which they are affecting the student's academic, behavioral, social and emotional adjustment. When needed, medication makes the student neurologically available for learning and functioning in the home, school and social environment. However, medication cannot remedy the academic, social or psychological complications of the disorder(s).

> ♥ *Pharmacological treatment is most effective when prescribed in conjunction with other supportive interventions, not as the only means of therapy.*

Counseling and Therapy

■ *Parent Education and Counseling*

It is essential that parents become familiar with and understand the various manifestations of the neurological disorder(s). Some parents need help dealing with their reactions to the diagnosis such as denial, anger, frustration, sorrow, depression, blame and guilt. Parents often need assistance in setting realistic expectations and in managing behavior. Parents need to be knowledgeable advocates with doctors, family members, school personnel and peers.

■ *Parent Support Group*

A mother at a parent support group shared the following story.

My son and I went to a toy store to buy a birthday present for one of his friends. He wanted to buy a toy for himself. I told him he could not have the toy he wanted and that it was time to leave. He got very angry and proceeded to have a storm (p. 21), yelling, "I hate you! I hate you!" I was so angry at him—I went to my van angry and crying.

As I waited, I mentally measured the width of my van with the entrance to the store. I thought if I could get my van in the store, I would hunt him down and roll over him once or twice. The fantasy allowed me to defuse my anger and regain control of myself. Then I was able to go back in the store, handle my son's behavior appropriately, get what we needed and go home.

(The parent support group decided that fantasizing or visualizing that which cannot happen in reality was an acceptable means of decreasing intense emotions.)

Parents of the ADHD/ADD/TS/OCD child experience more stress than normal. Neurologically impaired children can be very difficult to live with and to raise. At least once a month, it is crucial that parents have a setting in which they can be heard by an empathetic group that will understand their anger, frustration and hurt.

■ *Family Therapy*

The cognitive and behavioral characteristics of ADHD, ADD, TS and OCD students can cause serious problems within the family. Family therapy alleviates the problems by helping the family understand the interactions between the family members and the impact those interactions have on the family's functioning. Through family therapy, parents and other family members learn how to create a more positive family environment and to more effectively relate to the child. For example, the family therapist may identify family situations in which the child reacts aggressively and help the parents and siblings modify the way they respond when the behaviors occur.

■ *Group Therapy*

Group therapy provides an environment in which the neurologically impaired student can meet others with similar problems. The students share experiences, become knowledgeable about the symptoms associated with the disorder(s) and learn how to deal with people's reactions. The group setting restores a sense of normalcy and provides a safe environment to practice age-appropriate social skills and to receive realistic feedback from peers. Receiving support and acceptance alleviates feelings of loneliness and isolation. The therapists are able to monitor school and family problems and intervene before a situation escalates out of control.

■ *Behavior Therapy*

Exposure and response prevention therapy has been found to be an effective method of behavior therapy for some children and adolescents with OCD. The goal of therapy is to lengthen the time between the obsession and the compulsion. The student is encouraged to confront and remain in contact with the feared object or idea (contamination, doubt) that prompts the obsession and refrain from engaging in the compulsive response (handwashing, questioning). Exposure to the fear decreases the anxiety associated with the obsession, while response prevention lessens the time spent carrying out the compulsive ritual.

🐾 *Clinical observations suggest that the TS student with OCD does not respond as well to exposure and response prevention.*

■ *Individual Child/Adolescent Therapy*

Individual therapy is most beneficial when a student is unresponsive to other forms of treatment (parent counseling, educational modifications and interventions, group therapy or social skills training) or when the emotional and behavioral problems are too severe to be handled in group therapy (severe anxiety, depression). Individual psychotherapy allows the student to meet on a one-to-one basis with a warm and impartial adult. The focus of therapy is to enable the student to cope with the feelings and psychological conflicts caused by the disorder(s). The therapist helps the student recognize and understand problems and find solutions to those problems.

☙ *Traditional psychotherapy aimed at helping the individual gain insight into his or her problems by accessing unconscious thoughts and feelings generally is not effective. The student with ADHD as one of the co-existing disorders may have difficulty with task initiation and not know how and where to begin. On the other hand, the student may be continually bombarded by extraneous thoughts and associations and become distracted and lose track of the primary issue.*

School Interventions

■ Teacher and Peer Education

ADHD, ADD, TS and OCD are complex neurological disorders with unusual symptoms that are impacted by environmental factors. It is important that all school personnel and peers be educated about the disorder(s) and the symptoms manifested by the students. Ineffective and/or inappropriate management, teasing and ridicule can be minimized. Teacher and student in-services (school awareness workshops) effectively reduce stress and create a more positive environment. The student can assist in the peer in-service, if the student chooses.

■ Educational Modifications

The school environment must challenge the ADHD/ADD/TS/OCD student's intellectual capacities and promote self-esteem while accommodating special needs. The neurologically impaired student has the same intellectual potential as the unimpaired student. The student is capable of learning and experiencing success if the educational environment and teaching strategies are modified. Comprehensive recommendations are included in Section II.

■ Academic Remediation

Approximately 25 percent of the ADHD/ADD/TS students have co-existing learning disabilities, a percentage much greater than the 4 to 5 percent in the general population. Another 25 percent have significant school-related problems. The OCD student's academic performance is impacted by sequencing problems, perseveration and stress. Academic remediation needs to be individualized according to the student's unique learning needs.

■ Computer Competency Training

Graphomotor (handwriting) problems are present in the majority of ADHD/ADD/TS students. The TS student often has hand and arm tics which interfere with writing. The OCD student may have the compulsion to write, erase and rewrite words. Direct instruction in computer skills and word processing is a necessity.

■ Home-School Management Program

A home-school management program fosters communication between parents and teachers. Cooperation then enables the student to view the parents and teachers as respected authority figures working together for the good of the student. A behavior management program that is consistent between the home and the school teaches responsibility and the value of hard work and promotes respect for self and others. Rewards/privileges or consequences at home and at school are based on work completion and appropriate behavior.

■ *Social Skills Training*

The neurologically impaired student often does not learn age-appropriate social skills. Failure to successfully develop and maintain relationships usually results from problems expressing ideas and feelings, understanding and responding to the ideas and feelings of others, recognizing the effect and consequence of behavior and resolving conflict situations. Social skills must be directly taught and practiced in a safe environment such as in the home or in a therapy group.

Section II
In The Classroom

*Effectively Educating a Child Whose Inherent Neurology Confounds
and Is Confounded By Traditional Classroom Techniques*

Teacher and Peer Education _____

Disability Awareness

> Tic To Me
>
> "How did school go today?"
>
> "**I** tic tic **wish** fidget scratch **I** tic **were** scratch twitch **more** wink tic wink **like the** swallow tic twitch **other** fidget **kids** tic swallow scratch **at** wink fidget tic tic pop **school** sigh blink tic."
>
> "I know you do, dear."
>
> Dedicated to "Touretters" everywhere.
>
> Darin, Adult Reflection

Encourage all individuals involved in the education of the ADHD, ADD, TS and OCD student to become familiar with the disorder(s) and its many manifestations. ADHD, ADD, TS and OCD are complex neurological disorders with unusual, frequently changing symptoms. These symptoms are affected by medication, as well as environmental, emotional and physical factors.

■ Request that representatives from the local chapters of organizations such as the Children and Adults with Attention Deficit/Hyperactivity Disorder (CH.A.D.D.), the Tourette Syndrome Association (TSA) or Obsessive-Compulsive Foundation provide in-service programs designed to foster understanding and thereby reduce ineffective or inappropriate management. There are many resources (films, tapes, publications) available from local and national organizations for use by schools or other groups. Names, addresses and phone numbers of organizations are included in the appendix (p. 259).

■ Educate classmates about the behaviors associated with the disorder. Have an advocate from the local association present an age-appropriate program about the disorder so that teasing and ridicule are minimized. Emphasize that teasing is immature and a trait associated with younger students.

✤ *Always ask the student and parents for permission prior to discussing the disorder with peers.*

○ Sponsor a science fair. Have the students gather information regarding various physical disorders such as ADHD, ADD, TS, OCD, epilepsy, muscular dystrophy, cerebral palsy, diabetes, asthma and learning disabilities.

■ Promote empathy by simulating a typical problem associated with the disorder(s). For example, ask the teachers or peers to try to read a passage for a few minutes and, each time signaled, blink their eyes five times. This allows teachers and peers to experientially feel the stress and frustration caused by an eyeblinking tic.

■ Help the student's peers understand and accept the importance of individual differences and the needed modifications. For example, some students cannot see well and need glasses; others cannot hear well and need to sit at the front of the room. Emphasize the special contribution each student can make.

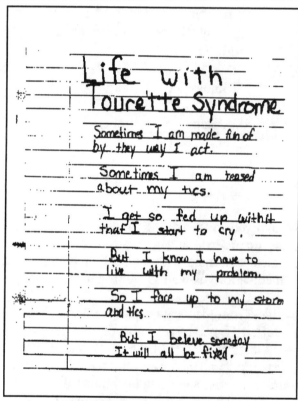

Life with Tourette Syndrome
Susan, age 12

■ Explain the differences between "fairness" and "equality." Fair does not mean equal. All students are not the same; everyone is unique and must be treated according to individual needs. For example, a student should not be told to stop wearing glasses because the other students do not wear glasses. Frequently parents and teachers become over-involved in wanting students to be treated equally. Work toward a level playing field; not everyone needs to be treated exactly the same way.

Classroom Modifications

This section of the handbook provides classroom and individual intervention strategies that will help both the neurologically impaired student and the teacher experience success. These modifications will decrease anxiety and stress, maximize structure and predictability, enhance the student's receptivity for learning and reduce undesired incidents between the impaired student, peers and teacher. The strategies recommended for the student with Tourette syndrome also apply to other tic disordered students.

Specific interventions presented may apply to several categories. So the reader does not have to cross-reference more than necessary, interventions are repeated when appropriate.

Emotionally Safe Environment

> *"I've come to the frightening conclusion that I am the decisive element in the classroom. It's my personal approach that creates the climate. It's my daily mood that makes the weather. As a teacher, I possess a tremendous power to make a child's life miserable or joyous. I can be a tool of torture or an instrument of inspiration. I can humiliate or humor, hurt or heal. In all situations, it is my response that decides whether a crisis will be escalated or de-escalated and a child humanized or dehumanized."[32]*
>
> Dr. Haim G. Ginott

■ Create an educational environment that challenges the student's intellectual capabilities and builds self-esteem while accommodating special needs.

■ Maintain a supportive and stress-free environment so that the student can learn. A negative school and classroom environment significantly affects the performance and behavior of the student with ADHD, ADD, TS and/or OCD. If the student does not feel emotionally safe to make mistakes and display a handicap, the student experiences anxiety, frustration, anger and/or stress. These feelings decrease attention and concentration, interfere with learning, exacerbate hyperactive and tic behaviors and impair self-esteem.

    ☙ *A visual cue can be used in the classroom to symbolize it is okay to make mistakes.*

© Daniel G. Pruitt, 1988

---

[32]   Ginott, H.G. (1993). <u>Teacher and child: A book for parents and teachers</u>. New York: Collier Books, 15-16.

■ Establish predictable rules and expectations.

○ Set clear and explicitly stated rules and expectations. If the student does not understand the teacher's rules and expectations or if the rules and expectations change frequently, the student will remain in a constant state of anxiety and hyper-vigilance which affects attention and thereby learning.

○ Always state rules positively because the ADHD/TS/OCD student is suggestible. If a rule is phrased negatively, the TS student may have an uncontrollable urge to do the action stated in the rule. The ADHD student may have a milder, but similar, suggestibility and response. The OCD student may perseverate on the negative rule.

○ Post rules at eye level in the front of the room.

○ Repeat the rules often.

○ Provide a structured routine for the student to follow. An anxiety reaction followed by aggression or withdrawal may follow unexpected changes in routine: for example, changes in class schedule, disruptions, teacher absences, assemblies, fire drills, field trips and vacations.

○ If the routine must change, give the student as much notice as possible and as many cues as needed to afford a smooth transition. For example, give the student several warnings at 30-minutes, 15-minutes and 5-minutes prior to a transition. A timer can be used to remind the student of impending change.

   ♣ *The OCD student often cannot change tasks, and the previous activity may have to be completed.*

■ Be flexible and adjust expectations.

   ♣ *The severity and intensity of the symptoms wax and wane. Be flexible and adjust expectations. When the symptoms are more noticeable, performance and behavior may deteriorate. The student may not be neurologically available to learn new information.*

○ Have the student review previous skills towards increasing mastery. Prepare and keep a packet of materials ready for use when the student experiences an increase in symptoms.

○ Have the student work on the computer to reinforce previously learned skills when symptoms are interfering with learning. The neurologically impaired student is often able to focus on the computer when focusing on other types of learning activities is impossible.

○ Understand that the OCD student is unable to stop rituals once begun in the classroom (checking, lining up, arranging, counting, erasing, rewriting and other perfectionistic behaviors).

■ Promote respect for the student.

○ Model respectful behavior. Any student who is treated disrespectfully by the teacher will be less able to experience personal, academic or social success. If the teacher is intolerant of the symptoms, the student's peers will react negatively. If the teacher shows empathy for the student, peers will manifest the same behavior.

○ Respect the student's limitations so that the student is not embarrassed and rendered unavailable for learning. However, do not limit the expectations of the student.

🐾 *There was a TS outfielder in the World Series, and a successful one-armed pitcher in major league baseball!*

○ Instill in the student the realization that the student is fundamentally a good person. Many students feel that they are "bad," "stupid" or "crazy" because of their unusual behaviors.

○ Separate behavior from the self-worth of the student.

○ Remain aware that the student is being bombarded by internal stimuli. Reported experiences have included the following statements:

ADHD student: "I need an OFF switch because my mind is racing and I can't listen to what the teacher is saying."

ADD student: "The teacher is talking and all I can think about is the ball game I am going to play this afternoon."

TS student: "My neck is jerking and my eyes are blinking. Then the teacher calls on me and gets mad because she thinks I'm not listening."

OCD student: "I keep seeing a movie over and over again in my head and can't remember what is happening in class."

○ Grade work on the student's abilities rather than disabilities. For example, grade the content of the history exam, not the handwriting, punctuation or spelling.

■ Understand the purpose of the student's behavior.

> *"Children often misbehave when they have difficulty with an assignment. They are afraid to ask for assistance. Their experience has taught them that to request help is to risk rebuke. They would rather be punished for acting up than ridiculed for ignorance. A teacher's best antidote to misbehavior is a willingness to be helpful."[33]*
>
> Dr. Haim G. Ginott

○ Try to discern the underlying reason for the student's behavior. Ask the who, what, when, where, how and why questions regarding this behavior.

🐾 *Many times the responsibility for the behavior is incorrectly placed on the student.*

---

[33]   Ginott, H.G. (1993). Teacher and child: A book for parents and teachers. New York: Collier Books, 60.

- The behavior may have been caused by the student's neurological impairment(s). For example, the TS/OCD student might have a neurologically based tic or compulsion that produces hitting, kicking or pinching. The neurochemical imbalance may lead to such a low frustration tolerance that trivial things often set the student off.

- The behavior may have been a side effect of medication. Inappropriate reactions such as anger, aggression or school phobia are often side effects of medication.

- The problem may have been caused by the teacher(s), parent(s) or peer(s).

  ☙ *Behavior is a form of communication.*

The following questions might be utilized to find out the meaning of the behavior:

- Was the behavior elicited by the need for:

  - more structure?
  - more strategies?
  - more emotional support?
  - obsessive reassurance?
  - more movement?
  - more personal space?
  - more stimulating and interesting work?
  - less stimulation?
  - leaving the situation to calm down?
  - cleanliness?
  - perfectionism?

- Was the behavior caused by:

  - insistence on eye contact?
  - being touched lightly?
  - listening to loud noises in the cafeteria?

- Was the behavior a reaction to:

  - mentioning the student's handicap in front of the class without the student's permission?
  - criticizing the student in front of other students?
  - insisting on a response before the student had time to access the needed information?
  - sitting near inappropriate models?
  - teasing and ridicule by peers?
  - being penalized for inherent disorganization (loss of books, pencils, papers, homework, materials)?
  - assigning a boring task (too easy, too short, too repetitive)?
  - giving work at the frustration level (too hard, too long)?
  - assigning too much handwritten work?
  - giving an unclear direction?
  - handing out an illegible ditto with too many problems poorly spaced on the page?

■ Enhance a sense of mastery and control over events.

> *"The teacher listens to the problem, rephrases it, clarifies it, gives the child credit for formulating it, and then asks, 'What options are open to you?', 'What are your choices in this situation?' Often the child himself comes up with a solution. Thus, he learns that he can rely on his own judgement. When a teacher hastily offers solutions, children miss the opportunity to acquire competence in problem-solving and confidence in themselves."[34]*
>
> Dr. Haim G. Ginott

○ Learned helplessness is a concept introduced by Seligman[35] which states that some individuals learn that there is no relationship between what they do and their ability to master and control their environment. They become discouraged, give up and respond passively. The ADHD/ADD/TS/OCD student who is confronted with constant failure often learns that no response or behavior will impact a situation or alleviate a problem. The perceived inability to influence and control events causes the student to place responsibility for learning and behavior on others and to respond as though "helpless." Learned helplessness leads to a lack of persistence, impaired academic performance and low self-esteem.

○ Structure a learning experience that reduces the chance of failure.

○ Present teacher-directed and teacher-monitored lessons at the instructional level. Assign unmonitored seatwork and homework at the independent level. No work should be at the frustration level.

○ Grade work on the student's abilities rather than disabilities. For example, grade the content of the science exam, not the handwriting, punctuation or spelling.

○ Use some ungraded assignments to evaluate the student's knowledge and provide feedback.

○ Emphasize what the student does right by marking the number of correct answers, rather than the number of incorrect answers.

○ Provide the student with acceptable choices to encourage success and active involvement in learning.

○ Teach the student strategies for efficient learning and how to use these strategies to demonstrate mastery and control of academic tasks.

     🐾 *The student often cannot generate strategies or solve problems.*

     ■ Have the student or teacher record the strategies in a list or chart and add them to the strategy (trick) book.

---

[34] Ginott, H.G. (1993). <u>Teacher and child: A book for parents and teachers</u>. New York: Collier Books, 112.

[35] Seligman, M.E. (1974). Depression and learned helplessness. In R.J. Friedman and M.M. Katz (Eds.), <u>The psychology of depression: Contemporary theory and research</u>. Washington, D.C.: Winston-Wiley.

Strategy Book: A strategy book is a collection of metacognitive strategies or thinking and learning "tricks" that the student accumulates from year to year. The strategy book solves the following problems. First, the book itself introduces a physical reminder of the student's need to collect and use strategies to solve problems. Second, the student who has been repeatedly unsuccessful when attempting to solve problems independently learns to respond passively. This is a particularly difficult habit to break. The student needs constant cuing and supervision to learn a new "active" habit of responding. The teacher can cue the student to use the "trick" book as an active, independent method for solving problems. Third, parents and teachers do not have to continually recreate strategies each time they help the student. Some examples include:

- When the student develops a "trick" for recognizing when to ask for help, place the strategy in the book.
- When the student finds a solution for organizing the notebook, write the "trick" in the strategy book.
- When the student learns a successful strategy for organizing a term paper, record the strategy in the book.

🐾 *Do not forget to add a section for socialization and diplomacy strategies.*

■ Encourage the student to refer to the strategy book when the steps are not readily remembered.

○ Encourage the student to assume responsibility for success. Overprotective teachers and parents who do too much for a student interfere with the development of a sense of personal achievement. Having others solve all the student's problems teaches the student that all events are outside his or her control.

■ Praise the student, no matter how small the success.

> *"Praise consists of two parts: what we say to the child and what he in turn says to himself."*[36]
>
> Dr. Haim G. Ginott

■ When the student experiences success, offer an enthusiastic, clearly stated comment about the student's ability to succeed. ("You organized your time well and worked on your report 15 minutes every day. Your report is ready on time!")

■ Have the student describe and record the steps to success.

○ Encourage the student to assume responsibility for failure.

🐾 *Prohibiting the occurrence of natural consequences or pain will prevent the student from learning how to function as an adult. Mistakes are valuable learning experiences.*

---

[36] Ginott, H.G. (1993). Teacher and child: A book for parents and teachers. New York: Collier Books, 126.

Individual Modifications

☙ *When designing modifications, clinical experience suggests that the student's cognitive, behavioral, social and emotional age equivalents are approximately 2/3 the student's chronological age.[37] For example, a neurologically impaired 12-year old may have a functional age of 8.*

■ Place the student in a classroom with an understanding and flexible teacher who sets clear and consistent limits.

■ Establish daily communication between teachers and parents through an assignment notebook. The most important element necessary for the success of the student is positive communication between the home and school.

    ○ Frequent phone conversations between teachers and parents may be necessary to keep everyone informed regarding new symptoms, changing circumstances and medication adjustments.

    ○ Encourage good work and appropriate school behavior by writing notes that compliment the student, rather than contacting the parents only when the student has done something wrong.

■ Allow the student to choose as a mentor one of the school's personnel with whom problems can be shared.

■ Assign the student a buddy—a capable peer who will assist the student by either doing a task that the student cannot do (note-taking buddy, work-completion buddy) or modeling and supporting appropriate behavior (hall buddy, cafeteria buddy, playground buddy, bus buddy).

■ Allow the student opportunities throughout the day for physical activity. This time should be in addition to P.E. and recess. Suggested activities include getting a drink of water or delivering a note.

☙ *Punishing an ADHD/TS/OCD student by taking away recess or P.E. creates additional stress and anxiety and exacerbates symptoms.*

■ Permit the student who is easily distracted by noises to use a headset with white noise or music of the student's choice. If the student elects to use music and works appropriately, the music can be used. If the student abuses the privilege, the privilege is lost.

■ Report all observations of medication side effects to the student's parents and doctor. Report both positive side effects (improved attention and concentration, reduction of tics and obsessions/compulsions, increase in work completion) and negative side effects (fatigue, sleepiness, thirst, nausea, irritability, increased aggression, school phobia).

☙ *Obtain written permission from the parents before calling the doctor.*

---

[37] Barkley, R.A. New ways of looking at ADHD. (Lecture, 1991). Third Annual CH.A.D.D. Conference on Attention Deficit Disorders, Washington, D.C.

■ Do not ask the TS student to suppress tics. Suppression diverts attention and concentration from learning. Suppression also produces stress, and stress exacerbates tics. Prolonged stress can result in an explosion or "storm" (p. 21).

■ Provide the student with a safe place to go when the tics become severe or must be released (resource room, nurse's office, counselor's office, school psychologist's office). Privately prearrange with the student a hand signal that indicates the need to leave the room, or agree to allow the student to leave when necessary.

🐾 *Remember that the student is sometimes too overaroused to ask for permission to leave the room. Earlier meetings must cover this contingency.*

■ Teachers and parents need to work together sharing the problems and enjoying the successes that result from cooperative effort. Too often teachers and parents move into adversarial positions and feel frustrated, unappreciated and angry.

🐾 *Teachers must listen to parents and try to understand the problems they are experiencing in trying to help their handicapped child become a successful adult with an intact ego.*

🐾 *Parents must listen to teachers and praise them for the time and caring they devote to their child with special needs.*

A Parent's Point of View

Always having to constantly be on your guard with the people who come in contact with your son. Making sure they aren't going to say or do anything to hurt your child.

Trying to soothe your other children's feelings because they don't understand why their friends won't come over to play if their brother with Tourette is home.

Trying to get other family members (aunts, uncles, cousins, grandparents, etc.) to get involved in the education of other people about Tourette, instead of sitting there saying, "I feel so sorry for him." They don't need your pity. They need your support, prayers, understanding, and a tremendous amount of patience. But mostly, they need your love.

Cringing inwardly when you hear footsteps on the stairs, is it going to be Dr. Jekyl or Mr. Hyde? Will the real child please stand up!!!!!

Always having to explain to others why your son has to walk in a certain pattern. Why he has to use a computer to do school work because he has difficulty with writing and reading even though there is not a physical handicap.

Explaining things over and over and over again because your child can't remember from one moment to the next what is expected of him. Or to control his actions or his movements.

Telling your child a thousand times to quit twitching and him telling you a thousand times back, "I can't, Mom, I'm retarded."

Always being upbeat and positive for your child because one of you has to be strong enough for the both of you. And when are you allowed the tears for this beautiful child from God who has to suffer so much hurt and humiliation from the outside world?

Trying not to crawl under the table when you have taken the family out to eat at a nice restaurant and your child with Tourette has decided to make a spectacle out of himself and sobbing when you get to the car because, "I am so sorry, Mom, I just can't help myself."

Some think that the child with Tourette syndrome is the only one to suffer, but it affects the whole family. Brothers are constantly trying not to be embarrassed by their brother's actions and behavior and trying to love him at the same time. It makes it very difficult to have a normal relationship with your brother and not to constantly be referred to as the STRANGE brother.

The sleepless nights when your child with Tourette tells you that if it wasn't for you and his Dad he would have already committed suicide and you're thinking, "My gosh, you're only 11 years old. How could things be so horrible when you haven't even experienced all the things in life yet?"

The new medications and the old medications, what a nightmare. Always looking for the magical pill that will cure it all or always having to adjust the dosages everyday. Finding out which ones work best for your child, and which ones make your child a zombie. Which ones are compatible with others to control different things. Which ones make him too drowsy and which ones make him bounce off the walls. And trying to convince the doctor that you know your child better than he does. And the child who is finally sleeping upstairs after all his rituals is not your son, but some drug induced weirdo, with suicidal tendencies and pendulum mood swings.

"I love you, son!" "I know you do, Mom, but do you love me enough for both of us? I need for you to, you know."

Carolyn Campbell, Parent

■ Brainstorm possible solutions with parents and school personnel if the student has a socially inappropriate tic (spitting, swearing, touching self and others in inappropriate places). For example, a student whose tics include spitting might carry a box of tissues; a student who feels the urge to swear or touch might be allowed to go to a prearranged location without needing to ask permission each time the strategy is needed.

■ Recognize that the OCD student may be experiencing anxiety because of unwanted thoughts and images which cannot be controlled or eliminated. Although the student understands that the thoughts are unreasonable or excessive, the student cannot stop the behavior without becoming physically distressed. Preoccupation with obsessions renders the student unable to concentrate on learning activities and class assignments. Adjust assignments and expectations when this occurs.

■ Recognize that the OCD student's work may be interrupted by a strong urge to engage in a compulsive act such as erasing and rewriting letters and words or starting a writing assignment over every time a mistake is made.

   🐾 *Remember that the student cannot modify the behavior.*

   ○ Recommend that the parents notify the physician if the behavior is excessive.

   ○ Have the student complete written work on a computer.

■ Design tasks that the OCD student can complete within the allotted time period. The student often feels "stuck" and unable to change sets or tasks. An anxiety reaction may be induced when a task has to be left unfinished. If the student cannot be redirected, allow the student to complete the task.

■ Allow the OCD student who is compelled to check and recheck answers on assignments and homework to submit the work after the due date. The OCD student who is "stuck" in a checking loop often does not finish the assignment on time or takes several hours to complete a short task.

■ Provide preferential seating in the classroom.

   ○ Place the student's desk in a location near the teacher, but still included as part of the regular classroom seating. This allows the teacher to monitor the student's work and behavior so that more frequent feedback can be provided.

      🐾 *If the TS student's tics are severe enough to cause embarrassment in front of the class, the student may need to be seated in the back of the classroom.*

   ○ Surround the student with peers who model appropriate behaviors and who will not encourage or stimulate inappropriate behaviors.

   ○ Place the student's desk in proximity to the door so that an unobtrusive exit can be made when necessary.

   ○ Provide as an option a carrel for the hyperactive or tic-disordered student, when needed. Reward the student for going to the "office."

■ Organize the classroom to promote independent functioning. Organization allows the student to gain confidence in the ability to control the environment. The more competence a student exhibits in the environment, the more motivation the student brings to each task.

     ○ Create an interesting environment. When a classroom is stripped, the student often self-stimulates in response to the need for input.

     ○ Choose materials that the teacher prefers and is comfortable using. Research studies suggest that the most successful teaching programs are those which the teacher likes.

     ○ Establish learning centers, labs or stations that offer a variety of materials and methods of instruction. Such diversity helps maintain interest and attention to task and provides freedom of movement for the hyperactive student.

     ○ Post daily work, schedules, duties and homework assignments at eye level in front of the class.

     ○ From grades three and up, use a syllabus to assist the student with planning and organization.

■ Teach the student how to organize and maintain a neat and readily accessible notebook.

     ○ Recommend that the student purchase a three-ring notebook of business quality (metal rings) that is wide enough to hold materials for all classes and that has pockets inside both covers.

     ○ Suggest that the student use one of the newer notebooks with velcro fasteners on the outside to prevent materials from falling out of the notebook.

     ○ Obtain agreement from each teacher that will allow the student to use only one notebook.

     ○ Have the student place a three-ring school supply pouch in the front of the notebook. The pouch should contain:

         ■ Several mechanical pencils

         ■ Erasable pens (not for left-handed student because left hand and arm will smear the ink)

         ■ Extra erasers (students erase frequently)

         ■ Colored markers in several basic primary colors

         ■ Small calculator (large enough for accurate key strokes)

         ■ Scissors

         ■ Small hole punch or a 3-hole punch designed to fit on the binder rings behind the pouch.

- Ruler

- Self-adhesive hole reinforcements for notebook paper (ADHD/TS/OCD students often tear holes in notebook paper)

○ Have the student place an assignment sheet or book in the front of the notebook. Make sure it is attached securely to the notebook.

- Allow the student to choose the type of assignment book. The student is less likely to use it if the system feels awkward.

- Have the student design assignment sheets on a computer. List the subjects in the order in which they occur during the day.

○ Use the assignment sheet as a communication log between the parents and teachers.

- Have the teachers initial that homework assignments have been noted correctly, and that the homework was received by the teachers.

- Have the parents initial that assignment has been completed. This prevents unfair accusations if the work itself is misplaced between home and school.

- Use a log as a means of providing an accurate record if weekend privileges are being awarded for completion of work. A Friday report can determine what rewards a student can earn (watching television, playing arcade games, using the computer, driving, staying up late, receiving an allowance).

- Use the log as a convenient way to send messages between parents and teachers.

○ Have the student label subject dividers in the order of the student's schedule.

○ Have the student place a tabbed divider for each class.

○ Have the student color code tabbed dividers and book covers with the same color.

○ Have the student place a photocopy of the teacher's daily notes or notebook paper for taking notes behind each divider. Have the student date all notes and place them in chronological order.

○ Have the student place a double manilla folder with horizontal pockets at the end of each section. Use one side for class handouts and the other side for homework papers.

○ If teachers absolutely insist on a separate notebook for each class, have the student attach the assignment book to the bookbag with a shoe lace or other long cord so that it will not be lost.

■ Recommend that the parents purchase a heavy-duty bookbag because the student often has difficulty organizing and keeping track of belongings, assignments and materials. Sturdy hiking day packs that are guaranteed for life are frequently available through wilderness outfitters. The bag should have two strong zippers that work in both directions and straps with cushioned shoulders.

■ Circumvent the student's disorganization and forgetfulness.

    ○ Have an extra supply of materials, such as paper and pencils, available. Ask the parents to provide a large supply of materials at the beginning of each quarter. Keep the supplies in a box labeled with the student's name. Allow the student to get whatever is needed. This expedites completion of the task and prevents the student from feeling like a failure when supplies are misplaced.

    ○ Suggest that the parents keep an extra set of books at home to alleviate worry and failure due to forgetting books. If necessary, purchase the books so that the student can underline during lectures or reading assignments.

        🐾 *Teachers and parents are more readily able to understand an external handicap than an invisible handicap such as ADHD, ADD, TS or OCD. An extra set of books is similar to having an extra set of crutches for the physically handicapped student.*

    ○ Provide time throughout the day for the student to organize materials.

    ○ Help the student keep the desk and other possessions organized. For example, periodically help the student clean out the desk and locker and reorganize the notebook, its pockets and dividers.

        🐾 *Periodically means at least once a week.*

    ○ Provide an extra transition time between classes.

    ○ Allow the student to leave class with an aide two to three minutes early at the end of the day to go to the locker. Fine motor impairment, sequencing problems and/or the need to repeat or do an act perfectly make opening the lock a very difficult task in a noisy, crowded hallway. The extra time also enables the student to calmly pack the school bag without the distraction of other students. This helps insure that the required items go home.

        🐾 *Have the parents purchase a lock with a key or a combination lock that requires no reverse sequencing to open the lock. If the lock is built into the locker, provide the student with an alternative place to store books and materials.*

    ○ Have an aide or resource teacher check the student's school bag to make sure the necessary items are included.

    ○ Color code textbooks, notebooks and folders so that each subject is color coordinated. For example, the blue book cover for the science book corresponds with the blue notebook and the blue folder.

■ Have the student make a strategy ("trick") book (p. 38).

    🐾 *The neurologically impaired student often cannot generate strategies or solve problems by accessing previously acquired knowledge.*

Attention

To learn, the student must be mentally available. Research has found the following behaviors exhibited by ADHD/TS students to be significantly different from those manifested by the students' peers.[38] (See table below).

Percent	Characteristics
65	short attention span
62	difficulty concentrating
58	daydreaming
65	difficulty sitting still
46	difficulty following directions
77	need for extra explanations from teacher
68	difficulty completing work on time
88	difficulty assuming responsibility for work
58	tension and anxiety
78	dislike for school

Characteristics Exhibited by ADHD/TS Students

The ADHD/ADD/TS/OCD student does not intentionally fail to "pay attention," and may in fact be exerting more effort to pay attention than the other classmates. Failure to attend is due to the student's neurological impairment. With patience, the student can learn techniques to help stay "tuned in."

■ Be sure the student is attending appropriately before presenting information or giving instructions. Strategies for obtaining the student's attention might include saying the student's name or using a hand gesture or signal.

■ Keep the following guidelines in mind when trying to get the student's attention:

○ Use an introductory sentence before giving instructions.

○ Do not require eye contact. Requiring eye contact is often overstimulating to the visually defensive student and produces academic and behavioral problems.

🐾 *Just because the student is not looking at the person delivering information does not mean the student is not listening. Sometimes the student avoids looking at the person talking to concentrate on the words.*

○ Touch the tactilely defensive student firmly. A light touch can sometimes overarouse the student and produce irritability and an inability to focus and use self-control.

---

[38] Research conducted by Marilyn P. Dornbush, Ph.D.

■ Tell the student what to listen for prior to delivering directions or information.

■ Present verbal information slowly and concisely, giving one direction at a time.

■ Provide directions and instructions in a variety of modalities: verbal and written instructions, cognitive cues, demonstrations, etc.

■ Have the student mark directions with a highlighter or underline with a mechanical pencil with a grooved grip and dark, strong lead. Younger students can add visual cues to specific words in directions by putting a circle around the word "circle," underlining the word "underline" or drawing two dots (eyes) over the word "read."

■ Have the student demonstrate knowledge of instructions by restating directions, doing the first step of the task or working through one example and having it checked before continuing.

■ Make the student feel comfortable about asking for repetition or assistance. Many of the students will not ask for help because they are too embarrassed. Model the appropriate way to ask for repetition and assistance.

■ Use a calm, reassuring voice when repeating information and directions.

Task Initiation

Failing to initiate tasks and activities is behavior associated with the student's neurological problems rather than purposeful behavior. The student fluctuates constantly on the arousal curve (p. 18) and may have trouble changing and initiating a new task.

■ Give the student demanding tasks during optimum arousal time to avoid classroom frustration. When possible, schedule academic lessons in the late morning. The student usually is not fully aroused at the beginning of the day and experiences a decline in energy and attention in the afternoon.

■ Always provide learning activities with which the student can experience success. A student learns to initiate a task with repeated success.

■ Assign work at the appropriate instructional level. Teacher-directed and teacher-monitored lessons should be presented at the instructional level. Unmonitored seatwork and homework should be at the independent level. No work should be at the frustration level.

■ Determine whether the student feels capable of performing the assigned task. Often the teacher is unaware that the student is not willing to admit simple tasks are sometimes too difficult to perform.

■ Make sure the student understands the directions needed to initiate a task. Use a comprehension check before allowing the student to begin working.

■ Break assignments into 10-minute segments. The student tends to become discouraged and frustrated when confronted with long assignments and is then unable to overcome the inertia caused by feeling overwhelmed. Gradually increase the length and difficulty of the assignments as the student demonstrates success.

■ Cue the student to initiate the task. A hand signal or previously agreed-upon verbal cue might be used.

■ Positively reinforce task initiation.

   ♨ *Point systems are frequently too abstract and nonmeaningful to many ADHD/TS students. Use concrete, meaningful reinforcers to increase on-task behaviors.*

   ○ Give the student five chips (baseball cards, coins, etc.) at the beginning of the day. Each time the student initiates a task, give the student another chip. Feedback must be immediate and consistent. A reward should be given at the end of the day in exchange for the chips earned.

   ○ Always provide extrinsic rewards (baseball cards) rather than expect the student to get adequate reinforcement from an intrinsic feeling of accomplishment. The neurologically impaired student frequently does not internalize intrinsic rewards (praise, smile or nod). Earned chips can be spent on special classroom privileges or rewarding activities. Suggested activities include leading the line, collecting or passing out materials, taking a note to the office, enjoying five minutes of free time or being exempt from homework.

   ○ Make sure the reinforcement is appropriate for the individual student. What is rewarding for one student may not be rewarding for another. Interview the student or observe the student's choice of free-time activities to determine which activities might be used as rewards.

   ○ Change rewards frequently. The ADHD/TS student tends to become quickly satiated with a reinforcer.

   ○ Accompany the reward with an enthusiastic, clearly stated comment about the student's initiation to task ("I was very impressed with how well you started your work today, and look what happened—you finished all your work!").

   ♨ *Praise the student, no matter how small the success.*

   ○ Ignore off-task behavior. Paying attention to off-task behavior increases the likelihood that the student will continue the off-task behavior to get the help needed to initiate the work. When the teacher's attention is removed, the student typically stops working; therefore, the teacher must remain present or provide repeated intervention until the assignment is started. The simultaneous use of reinforcing the positive and ignoring the negative improves initiation.

■ After an absence, initiate a meeting with the student to schedule make-up work. Direct teacher intervention and monitoring are required. The student may feel overwhelmed by the amount of work missed and therefore be unable to initiate getting and completing make-up assignments. The neurologically impaired student works harder than usual just to keep up. The student may feel it is an impossible challenge to complete all the unfinished work.

   ○ Break the work into manageable units.

   ○ Check with and support the student at regular intervals until the work is completed.

On-Task Behavior and Work Completion

Difficulty remaining on-task and thereby finishing a class assignment is a behavior related to the student's neurological disorder. Task requirements and the classroom environment must be modified to improve the student's ability to stay on task and complete work.

🐾 *Note that the strategies for task initiation, on-task behavior, work completion and self-control are frequently repeated. The teacher and parent do not have to have a different strategy for each area if one is successful across several targeted behaviors.*

■ Check to see that the student knows appropriate on-task behavior. Frequently the neurologically impaired student has not learned on-task behavior.

■ Model on-task behavior and reinforce other students in the classroom who demonstrate the appropriate behavior. Always define the on-task behavior during reinforcement ("I like the way John is sitting quietly at his desk and concentrating on his work.").

■ Surround the student with peers who model appropriate on-task behavior and who will not encourage or stimulate inappropriate behaviors.

■ Assign a peer who is compatible with the student to act as a work buddy.

■ Provide a carrel for the student who is easily distracted by objects, movements and events. The student needs to be rewarded for going to the "office" when necessary.

■ Permit the student who is easily distracted by noises to use a headset with white noise or music of the student's choice. (Some students prefer headsets without any noise.) If the student elects to use music and works appropriately, music can be used. If the student abuses the privilege, the privilege is lost.

■ Privately prearrange with the student a nonpunitive hand gesture or signal to be used during listening and work periods as a reminder from the teacher to refocus attention to the task.

■ Teach the student the steps needed to complete a task.

   O Have the student or teacher record the steps in a list or chart and add them to the strategy "trick" book (p. 38). The neurologically impaired student often cannot generate strategies or solve problems.

   O Encourage the student to refer to the book when the steps are not readily remembered.

■ Modify the presentation, requirements and length of academic tasks.

   O Alternate seatwork with other kinds of learning activities by creating learning centers, labs or stations in the classroom.

   O Offer a variety of materials and methods of instruction through different modalities (auditory, visual, motor, tactile and cognitive).

   O Use games and hands-on projects.

○ Vary the pace and change tasks frequently. The ADHD/ADD/TS student needs the stimulation of new, different and exciting assignments to help maintain arousal and attention. Follow less interesting work with more interesting work. Have the student complete the first, less interesting, task before being allowed to perform the second, more interesting, task.

○ Assign the student short tasks so accuracy and quality can be required.

○ Divide assignments into several parts. Give only one paper or ditto at a time. Have the student turn in each portion as it is completed, allowing the student the opportunity to move before continuing.

○ Break work periods into several short segments with breaks between tasks.

■ Have the student use cognitive strategies to assist on-task behavior.

○ Provide the poor readers with visual cues for the directions on written work so the student knows how to complete the assignment.

○ Allow the student to quietly recite the instructions or to think aloud while following through on tasks. Provide the student a place to work where subvocalizations will not disturb other students. Using self-directed speech helps the student focus on the assignment and remain on task.

○ Tape a cognitive strategy with visual cues to the desktop or inside the notebook to remind the student to pay attention to the task and to finish the assignment.

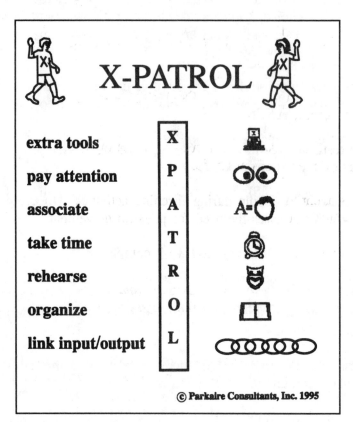

The X-Patrol strategy is a reminder of a previously agreed-upon system the student uses to decrease the effect of his neurological disorders on classroom performance.

○ Extra tools: reminds the student to use electronic aides to assist with accuracy and production.

○ Pay attention: reminds the student to return to task.

○ Associate: reminds the student to associate abstract, difficult to learn concepts to meaningful information.

○ Take time: reminds the student to take the time needed for appropriate work.

○ Rehearse: reminds the student to practice and review to increase chances for successful learning.

○ Organize: reminds the student to use the organizational strategies that have been taught.

○ Link input/output: reminds the student to use strategies for retrieval of information learned.

■ Allow frequent opportunities for physical movement. This decreases the ADHD/TS student's restlessness and overactivity.

○ Use interactive teaching activities, such as class discussions, group projects, board work.

☙ *Allow extra time for the transition back to quiet activities. Sometimes a student may not be able to handle transitions.*

○ Allow the student to make a trip to the office, sharpen a pencil, take a note to another teacher, get a drink, etc.

○ Provide the restless student with a small squeeze toy or an eraser with which to fidget during times of needed concentration.

○ Permit the student to doodle during listening activities. Doodling allows fine motor movement which decreases the need for physical movement.

■ Positively reinforce on-task behavior and work completion.

☙ *Point systems are frequently too abstract and nonmeaningful to many ADHD/TS students. Use concrete, meaningful reinforcers to increase on-task behavior and work completion.*

○ Give the student five chips (baseball cards, coins, etc.) at the beginning of the day. Each time the student displays on-task behavior or completes work, give the student another chip. Feedback must be immediate and consistent. A reward should be given at the end of each day in exchange for the chips earned.

○ Always provide extrinsic rewards (baseball cards) rather than expecting the student to get adequate reinforcement from an intrinsic feeling of accomplishment. The neurologically impaired student frequently does not internalize intrinsic rewards (praise, smile or nod). Earned chips can be spent on special classroom privileges or rewarding activities. Suggested activities include leading the line, passing out or collecting materials, taking a note to the office, enjoying five minutes of free time or being exempt from homework.

○ Make sure the reinforcement is appropriate for the individual student. What is rewarding for one student may not be rewarding for another. Interview the student or observe the student's choice of free-time activities to determine which activities might be used as rewards.

○ Change rewards frequently. The ADHD/TS student tends to become quickly satiated with a reinforcer.

○ Accompany the reward with an enthusiastic, clearly stated comment about the student's attention to task ("I was very impressed with how well you stayed on task today, and look what happened—you finished all your work!").

    ✊ *Praise the student, no matter how small the success.*

○ Ignore off-task behavior. Paying attention to off-task behavior increases the likelihood that the student will continue the off-task behavior to get the help needed to complete the work. When the teacher's attention is removed, the student typically stops working; therefore, the teacher must remain present and provide repeated intervention until the assignment is completed. The simultaneous use of positive reinforcement and ignoring negative behavior improves on-task performance.

○ Always provide learning activities with which the student can experience success. A student learns on-task behavior by repeated success.

■ When off-task, acting-out behavior interferes with the rest of the class, use the following progression of interventions:

○ Cuing—give the student a previously agreed upon signal to jump-start attention and increase persistence.

○ Redirection—use the student's own distractibility to switch from off-task to on-task behavior. Refocus the student's attention with a change of physical location or a change of activity.

○ Time-Out (opportunity to regain self-control)—prearrange with the student a safe place to go to regain control. Three time-out procedures are:

    ■ Student voluntarily goes to time-out without being prompted.

        ✊ *Reward the student for initiating time-out rather than losing control.*

    ■ Teacher signals the student to go to time-out.

    ■ Teacher directs the student to go to time-out.

○ Natural Consequences—a student learns best from consequences related to the behavior. After the incident has ended and calm has been restored, hold the student responsible for any damage done during the episode. (If the student marks on the walls, have the student stay after school or come early to clean the walls. If the student must be removed from the room because others are being disturbed by a behavior within the student's control, have the student complete unfinished assignments during free time or after school. If other students have their feelings hurt or feel angry or resentful, encourage the student to repair damaged relationships).

🐾 *The school cannot legally give the student consequences for behaviors associated with the neurological disorder (impulsivity, hyperactivity, inattention, tics, obsessions, compulsions).*

■ Avoid sending unfinished class assignments home. It is not productive and is frequently psychologically harmful to the student. Finishing school work at home creates astonishing and terrifying power struggles between the students and parents.

🐾 *The student who is unable to finish classwork at school will not be able to complete it at home due to a decrease in physical and cognitive energy.*

○ Evaluate the appropriateness of the assignments and modify expectations until the student can be successful. Gradually increase expectations for work completion.

○ If the teacher is certain the workload has been reduced to a level at which the student can be successful, have the student stay after school to complete unfinished classwork. It usually takes only a few episodes of remaining after school to ensure work completion. However, this consequence must occur consistently, even when inconvenient for the parents or teacher.

Self-Control

The ADHD/ADD/TS/OCD student is often impulsive, failing to think before acting or speaking. This is called the "Ready! Fire! Aim!" phenomena.

© Parkaire Consultants, Inc. 1989

Poor impulse control is neurologically based. Impulsivity may be manifested by one or more of the following behaviors:

- Acting before thinking
- Answering before questions are completely asked
- Beginning work before directions are completed
- Constantly touching others or objects
- Difficulty learning from consequences of behavior
- Difficulty listening to or following verbal directions
- Difficulty reading or following written directions

- Difficulty playing quietly
- Difficulty waiting turn in games or group activities
- Engaging in risk-taking behaviors
- Grabbing things from other students
- Interrupting or intruding on activities of others
- Interrupting teacher or peers
- Making careless errors
- Responding without waiting to be called on
- Rushing through assignments
- Talking to others during quiet activities

■ Positively reinforce behaviors that reflect appropriate impulse control

    🐾 *Point systems are too abstract and nonmeaningful to many ADHD/TS students. Use concrete, meaningful reinforcers to increase on-task behavior.*

○ Ignore impulsive behaviors as much as possible. Do not expect perfection. An expectation for perfect behavior makes the student more frustrated and exacerbates impulsivity.

○ Give the student five chips (baseball cards, coins, etc.) at the beginning of the day. Each time the student shows self-control, give the student another token. Feedback must be immediate and consistent. A reward should be given at the end of each day in exchange for the chips earned.

○ Always provide extrinsic rewards (baseball cards) rather than expect the student to get adequate reinforcement from an intrinsic feeling of accomplishment. The neurologically impaired student frequently does not internalize intrinsic rewards (praise, smile or nod). Earned chips can be spent on special classroom privileges or rewarding activities. Suggested activities include leading the line, passing out or collecting materials, taking a note to the office, enjoying five minutes of free time or being exempt from homework.

○ Make sure the reinforcement is appropriate for the individual student. What is rewarding for one student may not be rewarding for another. Interview the student or observe the student's choice of free-time activities to determine which activities might be used as rewards.

○ Change rewards frequently. The student tends to become quickly satiated with a reinforcer.

○ Accompany the reward with an enthusiastic statement about the student's impulse control ("I liked the way you were able to wait before answering the question.").

■ Teach the student cognitive strategies to decrease impulsive behavior.

○ Teach the student to verbalize thoughts. Using self-directed speech helps the student focus on assignments and reduces impulsivity.

○ Tape a simple visual cue, such as a picture of the reward, to the desktop or inside the notebook to remind the student to stop and think before acting (p. 50).

Overactive Behaviors

Hyperactivity may be exhibited by one or more of the following behaviors.

- Constantly shifting position in seat, moving desk
- Drumming fingers, tapping pencil
- Excessive running and climbing
- Excessive talking

- Failing to remain seated when required
- Fidgeting: shaking leg, tapping foot
- Playing with objects
- Shifting from one uncompleted activity to another
- Throwing things

■ Ignore minor motor movements which allow the student to release hyperactivity. Minor motor movements include drumming fingers, doodling, playing with small objects or moving papers on desk.

   ☙ *The ADHD/TS student has great difficulty following rules that restrict movement.*

■ Allow the student to stand, shake legs or reposition self in chair while completing class assignments.

■ Periodically give the class breaks for physical activity. For example, have the class stand up, reach for the sky, touch toes, twist waist and pat each other on the back.

■ Privately prearrange appropriate mobility options.

   ○ Assign the student two seats in different locations in the classroom. Allow the student to move from one seat to another when movement is needed.

   ○ Place a table with three or four chairs at the back of the room. Permit the student to change chairs at the table when the need for movement is experienced.

   ☙ *Do not use these procedures if the student feels embarrassed by them.*

■ Provide the ADHD/TS student with frequent opportunities to leave the classroom to release hyperactivity. Suggested opportunities include taking a note to the office, running an errand for the teacher, getting a drink or using the restroom.

■ Allow the overly hyperactive ADHD/TS student opportunities throughout the day for physical activity. This should be in addition to regularly scheduled P.E. and recess. Suggested opportunities include running around the track or throwing a ball in the gym.

■ Establish learning centers, "labs" or "stations," which offer a variety of materials and methods of instruction. Such diversity helps maintain the student's interest and attention to task and also allows freedom of movement for the restless student.

■ Maintain a position close to the student during less structured activities such as walking in the halls, eating in the cafeteria, participating in P.E. and riding the bus. Hyperactive behaviors tend to increase at times such as these.

Aggressive and Oppositional Behavior

> *"Ethical concepts such as responsibility, respect, loyalty, honesty, charity and mercy cannot be taught directly. They can only be learned in concrete life situations from people one respects. One grows into virtue; one cannot be forced by punishment."*[39]
>
> Dr. Haim G. Ginott

The neurologically impaired student lives day in and day out with symptoms that infrequently remit. The ADHD/TS student's body is rarely still and is constantly making unwanted movements. Persistent tics may cause intense pain. The OCD student may become highly anxious and scared when obsessions and compulsions are present. It takes very little stimulation to arouse feelings of anxiety, frustration and anger and precipitate aggressive behaviors. It is essential that the teacher create a classroom environment that enhances the student's ability to maintain emotional control.

🐾 *Loss of control is not an expression of bad behavior or emotional problems; it is a manifestation of the neurological disorder.*

■ Create a positive relationship with the student. Before the student will allow the teacher to help during difficult times, the student must sense the teacher's respect and concern.

■ Respond to the child inside the student. Within each individual is a small child. This seems like an obvious statement, but it is all too often forgotten by significant people in the student's life. So often the aggressive behaviors become the primary focus. It is important to see and make contact with the "inner child" to have a positive experience with the student.

■ Model controlled behavior by expressing anger without blame. Say, for example, "You asked for extra time after school to complete the test. I agreed to give you the time. You did not keep the appointment, nor did you ask to cancel. When I do things to help you, I feel angry when you are not considerate of my time and my feelings." Validate the feelings of the student, teacher and parent.

■ Allow the student to choose a compatible buddy. A buddy helps alleviate stress and diminish the impact of the student's handicapping condition. Examples might include a work-completion buddy, note-taking buddy, homework buddy, playground buddy, hall-walking buddy, cafeteria buddy or bus buddy. Make sure that the student is comfortable having a buddy assigned and that the buddy wants the job.

■ Hold class meetings. The first class meeting should occur as soon as possible after the beginning of the school year. This meeting is a vehicle for discussing the need for rules and for developing mechanisms for problem solving. Other meetings can be held when crises occur. At these meetings, the teacher assists by mediating and offering solutions to the problems occurring within the social context of the class.

---

[39] Ginott, H.G. (1993). Teacher and child: A book for parents and teachers. New York: Collier Books, 152.

■ Modify classroom procedures to reduce stress and prevent the occurrence of frustrating, anger-provoking situations.

> 🐾 *The ADHD/TS student is very easily over-aroused by disorganization in the classroom, loud noisy situations and large crowds. Some of the most difficult situations may occur in the hallways between classes, in the cafeteria, at P.E. and on the school bus. These are not only noisy, less structured times, but they also offer limited, if any, adult supervision. Students often complain about being teased, embarrassed and touched by other students in these unstructured situations.*

○ Seat the student near the teacher.

> 🐾 *If the teacher's desk is at the front of the room, the TS student with severe tics should be seated in a less conspicuous location.*

○ Allow no unstructured time.

○ Provide consistency. The predictability of consistent routines decreases stress and allows the student to direct more energy to self-control and learning.

○ Privately prearrange appropriate mobility options. Stress occurs naturally and its effects wax and wane inside the body. Frequent movement allows this natural build-up of energy to be modulated or alleviated. This not only decreases stress, but also increases attention, provides release for tics and helps the student calm down.

> ■ Assign the student two seats in different locations in the classroom. Allow the student to move from one seat to another when movement is needed.

> ■ Place a table with three or four chairs at the back of the room. Permit the student to change chairs at the table when the need for movement is experienced.

> > 🐾 *Do not use these procedures if the student is embarrassed by them.*

> ■ Provide the ADHD/TS student with frequent opportunities to leave the classroom to release hyperactivity. Suggested opportunities include taking a note to the office, running an errand for the teacher, getting a drink or using the restroom.

○ Notify the student of impending changes to facilitate readjustment (five minutes prior to the end of an activity, several days before a teacher's absence and each day thereafter).

> 🐾 *Changes in routine increases stress and can produce overarousal, anger, anxiety and the feeling of being "stuck." The neurologically impaired student often does not adjust and respond in a rapid, integrated fashion.*

○ Arrange the environment to prevent aggressive behavior from occurring rather than reacting to it after it has occurred. For example, if the student has a touching or hitting tic, move the student's desk far enough away from the neighboring desks to provide room for the tic. A tactilely defensive student may become agitated or aggressive when another student accidentally touches the body.

○ Minimize academic failure. Always give the student tasks at the appropriate instructional level. Teacher-directed and teacher-monitored lessons should be presented at the instructional level. Unmonitored seatwork and homework should be at the independent level. No work should be at the frustration level.

> *"Teachers often ask psychologists how to motivate children to learn. The answer is 'Make it safe for them to risk failure.' The major obstacle to learning is fear; fear of failure, fear of criticism, fear of appearing stupid. An effective teacher makes it possible for each child to err with impunity. To remove fear is to invite attempt. To welcome mistakes is to encourage learning."[40]*
>
> Dr. Haim G. Ginott

○ Assign the student short tasks that can be easily completed. The student tends to become frustrated and agitated when confronted with long assignments. Gradually increase the length and difficulty of the assignments as the student demonstrates success.

○ Do not allow the OCD student to start any activity that cannot be finished in the allotted time frame. The student may be unable to change tasks or sets without subsequent anxiety which can produce inappropriate behaviors. If the student cannot be redirected, the action must be completed. A lengthy assignment can be broken up to appear as several independent assignments.

○ Structure social situations so they do not simulate inappropriate behavior.

○ Allow the student to leave the classroom two to three minutes early to avoid crowded hallways.

○ Have an adult remain in close proximity to the student in the hallways or cafeteria. This prevents a possible confrontation.

○ Intervene when the student has a problem on the bus.

   ■ Educate the bus driver about the student's needs.

   ■ Assign a bus buddy (a compatible peer who models appropriate bus behavior).

   ■ Require the student to sit at the front of the bus.

   ■ If modifications in the regular bus situation do not alleviate the problem, assign the student to a special education bus. These buses are smaller and frequently have monitors in addition to the drivers.

   ☙ *Use this procedure as a last resort. The student is usually embarrassed by the special education bus.*

---

[40] Ginott, H.G. (1993). <u>Teacher and child: A book for parents and teachers</u>. New York: Collier Books, 242.

■ If the symptoms appear to be temporary, suggest that the parents drive the student.

■ Teach the student how to verbalize feelings before losing control ("This is too much work." "I do not understand this work." "Please leave me alone, I'm beginning to feel angry.").

■ Acknowledge the student's feelings. Do not confuse the student's behavior with the feelings being expressed. Remember, feelings are always valid even if the behavior is inappropriate. Be sure to provide consequences for the behavior, not the feeling.

■ Teach the student strategies for releasing anger and aggression. Intervention must focus on helping the student understand that, although it is difficult to control aggressive impulses caused by neurological problems, aggression is unacceptable, and appropriate strategies for releasing anger and aggression must be learned.

   ○ Provide a safe place to which the student may go to regain control. This area might be supplied with a plastic bat with which to beat a pillow, a heavy cylinder-shaped punching bag or other nonbreakable items. The student should be reinforced for using these objects to release anger.

   ☙ *Do not use a light, pear-shaped punching bag. It fights back and tends to make the student even angrier.*

   ○ Teach the student how to make a graceful exit. A graceful exit is effected when the student, anticipating or experiencing an ADHD/TS "storm" (p. 21) leaves the room according to a previously agreed upon procedure.

      ■ Privately prearrange a set of options which delineate how to exit and where to go because the student often will not be able to ask to leave the room during the "storm" (p. 21).

      ■ Privately prearrange cues for saving face. These cues may be auditory, visual, motor or tactile or may represent a cognitive frame that has been established previously. For example, the student agrees that when the teacher notices that loss of control is imminent, the student is given a colored pass to leave the room and perform an errand. (Allow the student to choose the color of the pass. Color choice promotes a positive feeling about using the pass which enhances the ability to leave gracefully. Some students are calmed by certain colors.)

      ☙ *The student often saves face by muttering and grumbling while exiting. Understand this is in fact a compliant response. A better exit might be a future expectation and goal.*

      ■ Reinforce the student for exiting rather than allowing the situation to escalate, even if the exit is less than graceful.

   ○ <u>Never</u> enter into a power struggle or try to add input to the student's sensory system. Once the "storm" (p. 21) begins to build, further input increases the overstimulation already occurring in the body and leads to an automatic escalation of the event. Sensory input includes requiring eye contact, saying "no," arguing, insisting on an immediate response and touching the student.

■ Redirect the student's anger when loss of control is imminent.

    ○ Learn to recognize the signs of impending loss of control. Watch for an increased activity level, angry facial expression, hostile tone of voice, use of angry words, exacerbation of movements and vocalizations or heightened anxiety and stubbornness.

    ○ Change the ADHD/TS student's focus of attention by encouraging physical movement from one place or activity to another.

    ○ If an ADHD/TS student displays signs of frustration while working on an assignment, have the student take a break and check the appropriateness of the task. If the task is consistent with the student's ability level, change activities until calm is restored. The student's own distractibility possibly can be used to redirect attention to another task.

■ Teach the student how to recognize signs indicating imminent loss of control (tightening of the stomach, flushing of the face and ears, racing heart, anxiety).

■ Use humor to defuse tension. Power struggles with the student cannot be won. The use of humor distracts the student and deflects an impending impasse.

■ Use the ADHD/ADD/TS student's need for diversity to control behavior. For example, the student can use computer time or learning centers to break up seatwork.

■ Explore alternative solutions to resolve conflicts. The student under stress is unable to easily or spontaneously generate options.

    ○ Hold a class meeting. Have the group generate nonaggressive alternatives to hypothetical or real problems that occur within the social context of the class. For example, the group can decide that a student should fight with words rather than fists or walk away when becoming angry.

    ○ Have the student discuss with an adult effective strategies to use in problem situations.

    ○ Use a previously agreed-upon cue to remind the student to think about an alternative solution when a real problem occurs.

■ Use nonjudgmental correction procedures. Correction procedures should leave the dignity of both the student and the teacher intact.

    ○ Remain calm and avoid giving long sermons and logical reasons. Do not debate or argue with the student.

    ○ Talk about feelings and behavior, but not the student's self-worth. Some students need specific information ("I feel _____ when you behave like this. Your actions hurt my feelings.").

    ○ Provide feedback as clearly and dispassionately as possible, rather than in a passive-aggressive manner (angry tone of voice, angry facial expression, sarcasm).

    ○ Provide nonjudgmental corrective feedback on the student's performance ("I asked you to do _____. You did not do _____. I want you to do _____ now.").

■ Eliminate public hangings.

> ☙ *Everyone can remember being the victim of a public hanging at the hands of a teacher.*

○ Do not discipline the student in front of the class. This focuses the other students' attention on the misbehavior and wounds the student's self-esteem.

○ Do not embarrass the student in front of the class. Pain and embarrassment are not appropriate management tools.

■ Use contingency management known as "Grandma's Rule" (source unknown).

Child: "I don't want to eat my spinach!"

Grandma: (without anger) "As soon as you finish your spinach, you can eat your chocolate cake."

Child: "But I want my cake now!"

Grandma: (calmly and sympathetically) "Of course you do, and, as soon as you finish your spinach, you can have your chocolate cake."

> ☙ *Avoid the temptation to be sarcastic when giving this response.*

■ When a student misbehaves, try to discern the underlying reason for the student's behavior. The following questions might be utilized:

> ☙ *Many times the responsibility for the behavior is incorrectly placed on the student.*

○ Ask the who, what, when, where, how and why questions regarding the behavior.

   ■ Was the behavior caused by the student's neurological impairment(s)?

   > ☙ *The TS/OCD student might have a neurologically based tic or compulsion that produces hitting, kicking, spitting and pinching.*

   ■ Was the behavior a side effect of medication?

   > ☙ *Some medications increase anger and aggression.*

   ■ Was the problem caused by the teacher(s), parent(s) or peer(s)?

- Was the behavior elicited by the need for:

  - more structure?
  - more strategies?
  - more emotional support?
  - obsessive reassurance?
  - more movement?
  - more personal space?
  - more stimulating and interesting work?
  - less stimulation?
  - leaving the situation to calm down?
  - cleanliness?
  - perfectionism?

- Was the behavior caused by:

  - insistence on eye contact?
  - being lightly touched?
  - listening to loud noises in the cafeteria?

- Was the behavior a reaction to:

  - mentioning the student's handicap in front of the class without the student's permission?
  - criticizing the student in front of other students?
  - insisting on a response before the student had time to access the needed information?
  - sitting near inappropriate models?
  - teasing and ridicule by peers?
  - being penalized for inherent disorganization (loss of books, pencils, papers, homework, materials)?
  - assigning a boring task (too easy, too short)?
  - giving work at the frustration level (too hard, too long)?
  - assigning too much handwritten work?
  - giving an unclear direction?
  - handing out an illegible ditto with too many problems poorly spaced on the page?

- Follow the general principles of behavior management when dealing with angry, aggressive and oppositional behaviors.

  ○ Develop a set of explicit limits and rules. The rules should be clearly defined so the student knows exactly what is expected.

    - Post the rules at eye level in the front of the classroom.

    - Always state the rules positively. If the rule is phrased negatively, the TS student may have an uncontrollable urge to do the action stated in the rule. The ADHD student may have milder, but similar, suggestibility and response. The OCD student may perseverate on the negative role.

    ■   Restate the rules often.

○ Pre-arrange natural, logical consequences for misbehaviors and communicate those consequences to the class and/or the student during a time when no emotional problems are occurring. Prearranging consequences allows the student to make choices ("If I ____, the consequence will be ____.").

    ■   Choose an appropriate consequence.

    ■   Do not impose a major consequence for a minor offense. Be fair and consistent. The student must learn to be accountable for misbehavior.

○ Do not punish the student for behavior caused by the neurological impairment (impulsivity, impersistence, hyperactivity, short attention span, tics, obsessions or compulsions).

○ The consequence should be imposed immediately after the inappropriate behavior occurs. Similarly, when rewards are promised, give them immediately after the appropriate response is exhibited.

○ Do not spend excessive time consequating inappropriate behavior at the expense of encouraging appropriate behavior. Reward good behavior frequently to build self-esteem.

○ Do not threaten consequences that are not intended to be carried out.

○ Always respond the same way to the same specific misbehavior.

○ Reward the student for remaining in control. Allow the student to earn chips that can be used for extra free-time, being excused from a homework assignment, etc.

    🐾 *Do not give the student additional consequences for a "storm" (p. 21).*

○ After a "storm" (p. 21) has passed and the student has regained self-control, hold the student responsible for cleaning up or correcting any problems that may have resulted from the incident. (If the student marks on the walls, have the student stay after school or come early to clean the walls. If the student must be removed from the room because others are being disturbed by a behavior within the student's control, have the student complete unfinished assignments during free time or after school. If other students have their feelings hurt, feel angry or resentful, encourage the student to repair damaged relationships.)

■ Teach the student how to cognitively control angry, aggressive and oppositional behavior.

    🐾 *Traditional behavior management techniques, except for positive reinforcement and time-out, are usually ineffective in modifying the behavior of a student with neurological impairments. These methods rely on the student's ability to attend, concentrate and neurologically remain in control. Cognitive techniques are more effective.*

○ Help the student learn how to identify the problem and state it orally.

> Teacher: "What is the problem?"
> Student: "I keep hitting my classmates."

○ Have the student recognize the controlling factors in a situation that cause the problem.

> Teacher: "Do you know why you hit them?"
> Student: "They keep teasing me and calling me names."

○ Encourage and assist the student to think about the consequences of an inappropriate response.

> Teacher: "What happens when you hit other children?"
> Student: "I'm the one who gets in trouble and gets sent to the principal's office or gets detention."

○ Teach the student to identify an appropriate goal.

> Teacher: "What will you gain by solving the problem?"
> Student: "I won't get in trouble and I'll get along with people better."

○ Help the student generate alternative responses or solutions to the problem.

> Teacher: "Can you think of some things you could do instead of hitting?"
> Student: "I don't know."
> Teacher: "What about fighting back with words instead of fists?"
> Student: "Sure, but my mother and father get upset when I say certain words."
> Teacher: "What if you and your parents look at our list of acceptable words and add some of your own. Then you can use the words they approve."

○ Help the student evaluate the alternative solutions generated.

> "Will it work?"
> "Will you be able to do it?"
> "Have you ever tried that before?"
> "Will you break any rules?"
> "What will be the effect on you and others?"

○ Teach the student how to evaluate the results of the student's change in behavior.

> Teacher: "Did it work? Are you satisfied? Are there any new problems?"
> Student: "It works! The kid was so surprised he left me alone! I didn't get in trouble!"

○ Show the student how to make self-directed positive statements about the results of the change in behavior.

> Student: "I did very well at not getting into a fight when I was teased. How do I feel about that? Great! Proud!"

Academic Interventions _____

School Personnel

Most school systems have personnel who provide help or special education services when needed. These specialists are valuable assets when a classroom teacher needs intervention strategies or recommendations for day-to-day management. The following specialists might be consulted:

Educational Support Team (EST)

🐾 This committee has different names in different states. For instance, in California, it is the Child Study Team (CST).

The educational support team in each school meets on a regular basis to consider the needs of a student having problems in the regular classroom. The EST may be composed of an administrator, one or two teachers, a special education teacher, school psychologist, counselor and other support personnel as needed. EST members brainstorm with the classroom teacher to develop modifications and strategies to help the student circumvent problems and remain in the regular class. If those modifications do not help the student make sufficient progress, the team considers whether a psycho-educational or other evaluation is warranted.

Learning Disabilities Teacher (LD)

The learning disabilities teacher is trained to provide services to a student experiencing academic problems. The classroom teacher might consult with the LD teacher to obtain strategies for accommodating the student's cognitive style and special learning needs. The resource room might be made available on a flexible basis to the student who requires additional academic support, a quiet place to finish assignments and take tests or a respite from the pressures of the classroom. This can be accomplished by qualifying the student for service through the Other Health Impaired placement category (p. 177).

Speech and Language Therapist (SL)

The speech and language therapist evaluates and provides therapy for a student who is having difficulty processing or expressing language. The SL therapist is specifically trained to remediate problems in the areas of articulation, auditory processing, verbal comprehension, expressive and receptive vocabulary development, word retrieval, sentence formulation, verbal pragmatic language and effective retrieval, sequencing, organization and expression of information. The SL therapist also works with the student who is having difficulty organizing and expressing ideas in writing due to organizational and language problems.

Occupational Therapist (OT)

An occupational therapist evaluates and remediates problems affecting the motor and perceptual skills required by the activities of daily living and school functioning. These skills include correct posture, body positioning, gross and fine motor coordination, graphomotor functioning, visual perception and organization, visual-motor integration, motor planning and problem solving and sensory integration. An OT can also help a student overcome sensory defensiveness. The OT uses special exercises and activities to remediate deficit areas. In addition, the OT can provide adaptive methods and equipment if needed for successful use of writing implements and computers, adaptive living skills and academic functioning in the school environment.

School Counselor

The school counselor is available to provide emotional support to students and conduct social cognition and therapeutic groups. The counselor leads awareness workshops which help classmates understand the nature of a handicapping condition and the needs of the neurologically impaired student. In addition, the counselor provides assistance in student scheduling and programming decisions and assists in large and small group testing.

School Psychologist

The school psychologist is trained in the areas of assessment, academic instruction, classroom management, social interaction, family structure and parenting. The school psychologist conducts a psycho-educational evaluation to assess the intelligence, learning style, academic achievement and emotional functioning of a student with learning problems. The obtained information is then used to develop an appropriate educational plan. The school psychologist consults with teachers, principals and other educators to provide them with information regarding ADHD, ADD, TS and OCD.

Neuropsychologist

The neuropsychologist applies knowledge pertaining to brain-behavior relationships, as well as information from the other areas of psychology, to the evaluation and treatment of a student with a neurological disorder such as Attention Deficit Disorder, Tourette syndrome, Obsessive-Compulsive Disorder, closed head injury, seizure disorder or learning disability. The neuropsychologist assesses intelligence, language, verbal and visual memory, fine motor and graphomotor performance, auditory and visual processing, sensory perception, academic achievement and emotional functioning. The neuropsychologist also evaluates behaviors associated with brain dysfunction (deficits in attention and concentration, reasoning and judgment, social skills) and recommends intervention strategies.

Impact on Learning and Recommended Interventions

> *"Labeling children only shifts the burden of failure to them. Perhaps a better label under which academic underachievers might be placed is "teaching disabled." This term more adequately describes the situation. We are not faced with children who cannot learn, but with children who need instruction somewhat different from that provided in regular classrooms. These children can learn; it is teaching that needs modification.*"[41]
>
> Richard Allington

Research studies suggest that approximately 19-26%[42] of the students with Attention Deficit Disorders and 35% of students with Tourette syndrome have co-existing learning disabilities. Most of the learning disabilities are diagnosed in written expression and math calculation. Other problems relate to hyperactivity, disorganization, impaired fine motor skills when using a pencil and an inability to complete assignments. Seventy percent of ADHD/ADD students experience restlessness, inattention, impulsivity, poor self-esteem, low self-confidence, academic under-achievement and impaired social interactions. Fifty-eight percent of students with ADHD/ADD fail at least one grade in school. In spite of these statistics, the ADHD/ADD/TS/OCD student is capable of learning when teaching strategies are modified.

The following information is organized around the seven areas of learning as used by many school systems to identify learning disabilities. Please note that specific interventions presented in this section may apply to several categories and have been repeated to eliminate cross-referencing by the reader. In the following sections, the professional noted in the parentheses should be consulted when a student has that particular problem.

> 🐾 *Hearing and vision screening tests should be administered prior to the implementation of any academic intervention.*

Oral Expression

Difficulty Maintaining Prosody (SL)

Prosody is the rhythm and modulation of speech (too fast/too slow, too loud/too soft).

■ Provide nonjudgmental corrective feedback on student's performance.

■ Ask the student to breathe when searching for words, rather than filling the time with additional rapid verbalizations.

■ Determine whether the stuttering of a TS student is a true stuttering problem or a vocal tic.

---

[41] Allington, R.R. (1975). Sticks and stones . . . but, will names never hurt them? The Reading Teacher, 28, 364-369.

[42] Comings, D.E. and Comings, B.G. (1987). A controlled study of Tourette syndrome I, attention deficit disorder and school problems. American Journal of Human Genetics, 91, pp. 707-741.

☙ If remedial interventions designed for stuttering do not improve the stuttering, it is most likely a tic. Sometimes a student is articulate enough to describe a sensation that is like an electrical charge or pressure that builds up prior to the stutter. The tic occurs to relieve the presence of the sensation. The pressure will then begin to build again.

Neglecting Needs of Listener (SL)

■ Teach the student to cue listener to topic of discussion.

   ○ Teach the student to verbalize the new topic when changing subjects.

   ○ Teach the student to state the main idea of a sentence rather than focusing on details.

■ Teach the student to communicate intent.

   ○ Ask the student to clarify what the student wants or needs.

   ○ Teach the use of complete sentences as opposed to meaningless, disconnected fragments of a story or request (who, what, when, where, how and why).

   ○ Determine whether the affect of the student is consistent with the feelings stated in the verbalizations. Provide feedback if content and feeling are not congruent.

■ Teach the student to follow turn-taking routines.

   ○ Point out other students in the classroom who demonstrate appropriate turn-taking behavior. Always define the turn-taking behavior ("I like the way John waited his turn before speaking.").

   ○ Practice turn-taking in a structured, teacher-directed lesson.

   ○ Use gestures to cue turn-taking.

■ Teach the student to use clarification strategies when misunderstood.

   ○ Let the student know that being misunderstood is very common.

   ○ Teach the student the importance of accurate self-expression to get needs met.

   ○ Teach the student to clarify statements: "I might not have made myself clear. Let me try again."

Problems Maintaining Topic (LD/SL)

■ Conference with the student privately to establish a verbal or visual cognitive cue. For example, use a verbal cue such as "I-285" or a hand signal to indicate rambling.

All major cities have perimeter highways such as I-285 in Atlanta. To get from the north part of the city to the baseball or football stadium on the south side during five o'clock traffic, people must enter I-285 at northern entrances, go around the city until they get to the correct exit on the south side and exit to the stadium. If they miss the exit, they have to go around the city again before arriving at the stadium.

When telling a story, the ADHD/TS student often goes around in circles (on I-285) before getting to the point of the story (the stadium). Sometimes the student will get distracted by another thought (wanting a drink at a fast food restaurant at another exit) and forget the main idea of the story (getting to the baseball game). This inability to maintain the topic is frustrating for the listener as well as the student who is trying to communicate.

© Sheryl K. Pruitt, 1984

■ Limit the student to responding to the primary stimuli (who, what, when, where, how, why).

■ Model and rehearse appropriate topic maintenance.

■ Make a flow chart or mind map (see following figure) as the student speaks to illustrate inappropriate changes of topic. A mind map is a verbal, reading comprehension or prewriting organizational technique which allows ideas to be linked appropriately regardless of the order in which they were generated. Have the student write the main topic in a circle in the center of a piece of paper. Then have the student connect subtopics in other circles to the main circle by "spokes" and add details relating to each secondary idea, and so on. Use outline numeration to organize, prioritize and sequence events.

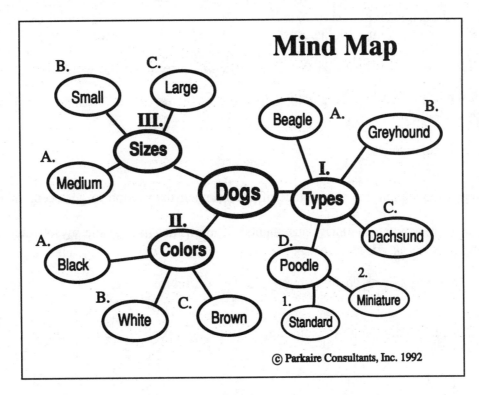

© Parkaire Consultants, Inc. 1992

Trouble Organizing Narrative Logically and Sequentially (LD/SL)

■ Help the student develop organizational strategies. Begin in a hierarchical fashion.

    🐾 *Identifying the primary stimulus is very difficult for the neurologically impaired student.*

■ Help the student learn how to use sequential time concepts when expressing ideas: "first, second, third," or "first, next." Have the student tell about a movie using these words.

■ Use picture cues to teach the student how to tell story sequences.

■ Have the student tell a personal story on tape and then have the student listen to the tape and evaluate the organization of the story.

■ Have the student or teacher use a mind mapping strategy (p. 69).

■ Monitor the student's organization by indicating an illogical sequence: "You told me first you _____, but then you said _____."

Difficulty Retrieving Words (LD/SL)

    🐾 *The student often pauses, repeats words, talks in circles or uses filler words, such as "thing," "stuff" or "um."*

■ Provide phonetic cues.

    ○ Say the beginning consonant sound of the intended word as in saying "p" to elicit "pie."

    ○ Use phonetic placement, that is, the position of the beginning sound of the intended word, as in pursing the lips for the "sh" sound to elicit the word "shoe."

    ○ Give a rhyming word such as "sing" to facilitate recall of the word "ring."

    ○ Provide a word fragment containing one or more of the beginning syllables of a polysyllabic word, such as "hippo" for "hippopotamus."

■ Provide associative cues.

    ○ Use an associated word which belongs to the same semantic (conceptual) class as a cue, such as "bread and _____" to elicit the word "butter."

    ○ Use the name of a semantic (conceptual) category to elicit the name of a member of a group, such as, "It's an insect," for "ant," or, "It's a fruit," for "apple."

■ Provide multiple-choice cues, as in saying, "Is it a house, a tree or a chair?" to elicit the word "tree."

■ Provide sentence completion cueing, as in saying, "I went to the fire station and climbed up on the big red _____."

Difficulty Expressing Emotions Appropriately (LD/SL)

■ Determine whether the student can identify feelings in self.

■ Determine whether the student understands the vocabulary of the basic feelings (mad, sad, glad, scared).

■ Determine whether the student can identify the facial expressions of the basic feelings (mad, sad, glad, scared).

■ Teach the student to identify and respond to the feelings of others from their words, tone of voice, body language and facial expressions.

■ Teach the student how to give affective feedback as a listener.

Difficulty Changing Topic (LD/SL)

■ Use a visual cue to let the student know the topic has changed.

■ Cue the new topic by mentioning the topic change when involved in a conversation with the student.

🐾 *A student who frequently perseverates (is "stuck") on a subject may have OCD and be unable to change topics.*

Listening Comprehension

Deficits When Processing Auditory Information (LD/SL)

■ Avoid unclear, rapid verbalizations.

■ Decrease level of vocabulary.

■ Define vocabulary.

■ Decrease extraneous details.

■ Use more concrete examples.

■ Use verbal, visual, tactile and cognitive mediation cues.

■ Provide single-step instructions.

Difficulty Maintaining Focus on Verbal Details and Prolonged Listening Activities (LD/SL)

■ Announce important information before actually imparting the lesson.

■ Have the student listen for key information (who, what, when, where, how and why).

■ Present oral directions in small concrete steps and, if necessary, check for comprehension at each step.

■ When presenting a series of directions, pause after each step to allow the student to process the information.

■ Repeat verbal directions and check for comprehension.

■ Use fewer abstractions in verbalizations.

■ Use cognitive, visual, motor and tactile cues when providing verbal information.

■ Check to determine comprehension at intervals.

Fatigue and Distractibility When Listening in Highly Verbal Settings (LD/SL)

■ Use cognitive, visual, motor and tactile cues when providing verbal information.

■ Give oral directions in small concrete steps.

■ Use fewer abstractions in verbalizations.

■ Repeat verbal directions if necessary.

■ Chunk (break into small sections) verbal information. Follow with short breaks to review or resummarize.

■ Check for comprehension at intervals.

■ Schedule short periods of verbalizations. Then follow them with less demanding activities.

Difficulty Following Oral Directions (LD/SL)

■ Look for cues other than eye contact to determine if the student is attending. A student looking out the window or at another student may in fact be paying attention. Use a signal that can be used to attract the student's attention before giving directions. For example, say to the class in general or the student in private, "Listen to the following directions," or use a prearranged hand signal.

■ Whenever possible, accompany oral instructions with visual stimuli.

■ Have the student restate oral directions. This strategy helps maintain the verbal information in short-term memory until the instructions can be completed.

■ When a complex or lengthy direction is given, have the student repeat the instruction prior to initiation of the task.

   ☙ *Avoid using this approach in front of a group.*

■ State oral directions one step at a time. Say, "Take out your math book. (pause) Turn to page 5. (pause) Do column 1." Avoid saying, "Now take out your math book, turn to page 5 and do column 1."

■ Present verbal directions at a slower rate to ensure that the student has time to process all of the information.

■ Control vocabulary and syntax (grammar) to make the directions easier to understand.

Difficulty Detecting Pragmatic Language Cues (LD/SL)

🐾 *Pragmatic language is the ability to utilize practical communication skills.*

■ Teach the student to detect, read and understand verbal feedback cues (tone of voice).

■ Suggest that the parents enroll the student in an on-going therapy group which specializes in the remediation of pragmatic skill deficits.

Difficulty Interpreting Abstract Language Concepts (LD/SL)

■ Translate abstract concepts into more concrete, meaningful examples. For example, explain that "I am pulling your leg" means "I am teasing you."

■ Directly teach figurative language (idioms, proverbs, metaphors and teenage expressions).

🐾 *Remember that teenage language is the most changeable and difficult figurative language.*

Difficulty Sequencing Oral Information (LD/SL)

■ Have the student or teacher use a mind mapping strategy (p. 69).

■ Have the student think about the beginning, middle and end of the information.

Basic Reading Skills

The ADHD/ADD/TS/OCD student is eligible to borrow taped texts. Recordings can be used when the student cannot sit still long enough to read or to supplement reading until the student is able to read independently. A student may request a book from a general area of interest. Special equipment is required because the books are recorded on 4-track cassette players, which are available on extended loan at no charge. To receive an application, contact the Library for the Blind (a public service). There are federal and state departments, such as:

National Library Service for the Blind
and Physically Handicapped
Library of Congress
Washington, D.C. 20542
1-800-248-6701

Georgia Department of Education
Library for the Blind
1150 Murphy Avenue, S.W.
Atlanta, Georgia 30310
404-756-4619

For information about 4-track cassette players and recorders which can be purchased, ask for the publication "Fact: Sources for Purchase of Cassette and Disc Players Compatible with Recorded Materials Produced by the National Library Service."

For recordings of textbooks and unabridged books:

> Recorded Books (also called Recording for the Blind)
> 20 Roszel Road
> Princeton, NJ 08540
> 1-800-221-4792

There is a nominal registration fee for Recorded Books.

Difficulty Attending (LD/SL)

■ Reduce impulsivity

    ○ Encourage the student to use a finger to correct tracking problems (losing place, skipping lines, omitting or repeating words).

    ○ Have the student use a bookmark or other appropriate guide.

    ○ Have the student underline directions with a mechanical pencil that has finger grip grooves and dark, strong lead.

    ○ Have the student mark directions with a highlighter. Allow the student to choose the color.

■ Decrease distractibility during the reading activity.

    ○ Encourage the student to use earphones to block out auditory distractions. Allow the student to select either white noise or music of his or her own choice. (If the use of music decreases production, the student loses the privilege and must use white noise or earphones without sound.)

    ○ Provide a carrel for the visually distractible student. The student needs to be rewarded for going to the "office" to avoid distractions.

    ○ Limit the size of the reading group.

    ○ Allow the student to read in a comfortable position, for example, lying down, sitting on the floor, in a bean bag or in a rocking chair.

    ○ Allow the student to act as a peer tutor to another student.

    ○ Before reading, have the student preview the questions that will be asked after reading is completed. This allows the student to know what information is important.

■ Promote sustained attention to the reading task.

    ○ Use verbal, visual, tactile and cognitive cues. For example, use colored chalk on the board or colored markers on the overhead.

    ○ Positively reinforce sustained attention to task. Accompany the reward with an enthusiastic statement about the student's attention to task.

○ Provide extrinsic rewards (special classroom privileges or activities) rather than expecting the student to get an intrinsic feeling from praise, a smile or a nod. Many neurologically impaired students do not get positive reinforcement from intrinsic feelings. Make sure the reinforcement is appropriate for the individual student. What is rewarding for one student might not be rewarding for another. Observe the student's choice of free-time activities to determine which activities might be used as rewards.

Difficulty Acquiring Decoding and Sound-Blending Skills (LD/SL)

🐾 *The severe OCD student tends to have difficulty with sound blending due to sequencing problems.*

■ Link the letter-sound combinations to meaningful stimuli (pictures, stories or rhymes).

■ Use color coding to aid recognition (consonants—black; vowels—red; blends—green).

■ Use backward chaining (source unknown) to imprint sight words.

Example: If a student is having difficulty learning a sight word such as "who," write the word on a chalkboard, in shaving cream spread on a formica surface or a desk top, with a dry erase marker on a whiteboard, with an overhead marker on a transparency or with an erasable magic marker on a window. (The tactile and visual input provided by these media increases attention to task and improves both storage and retrieval.) Erase the last letter. Have the student rewrite the "o" and say and spell "who." If the student is successful, erase the last two letters. Have the student rewrite the "h" and "o" and say and spell "who." If successful, continue erasing backwards until the student has learned the word. Have the student say the word and spell it orally during each step. Once the student can write the entire word from memory, introduce the next sight vocabulary word. Once mastered, ask the student to spell the previous word. Recheck each week thereafter.

■ Use a cognitive strategy to teach decoding skills. A cognitive decoding approach to teaching phonics is "Mother Vowel."

The Story of Mother Vowel[43]

Mother Vowel and her five babies live on a farm. The babies' names are "a," "e," "i," "o" and "u." The babies are too young to talk; and they only make sounds. Poor Mother Vowel does not always know what they want.

One day Baby "a" was hungry and saw an apple tree. Pointing to the apple tree with her arm raised up in the air, Baby "a" began to shout, "Aaaaaaaaaaaa" as in the beginning sound of apple. Mother Vowel was thrilled to know that each time Baby "a" raised her hand and shouted, "Aaaaaaaaaaaaaa," she wanted an apple. [A mirror is helpful to allow the student to see the mouth pull way back when making the (short) baby "aaaaa" sound.]

Hand signal: Raise hand and wave as if trying to reach an apple.

(The complete story of Mother Vowel is in the appendix, p. 199.)

---

[43]   Mother Vowel is a cognitive strategy developed by Sheryl K. Pruitt, M.Ed., and Vickie Rhinehart, 1988.

Problems With Tracking (LD/OT)
(losing place, skipping lines, omitting or repeating words)

■ Teach the student to use a finger to assist tracking.

■ Teach the student to use a tachistoscope (a reading window) to reduce the amount of page available to the eye.

■ Provide a bookmark, ruler, paper strip or index card for the student to use while moving down the page.

■ Have the student use a colored plastic overlay. These can be cut from plastic report covers and used as bookmarks. Allow the student to choose the color.

　　🐾 *If a student's eye tics interfere with reading, try recorded textbooks. (p. 73).*

Difficulty Reading at the Appropriate Rate (LD/SL/OT)
(too fast, too slow)

■ Teach the student how to read at a slower pace.

　　○ Have the student use a finger to track the words.

　　○ Provide a bookmark, ruler, paper strip or index card for the student to use while moving down the page.

　　○ Highlight punctuation marks. Use yellow for commas to represent "yield signs" and red for periods to represent "stop signs."

　　○ Ask the student to take a short breath at each comma and a regular breath at the end of each sentence.

　　○ Ask the student to silently count to one after a comma and to two after a period. Or, depending on the learning style and interest of the student, relate commas and periods to half rests and whole rests from music.

　　○ Cue the student to wait after the period by raising a hand and to continue by putting the hand down.

　　○ Have the student use a tape recorder to provide feedback and comparison.

　　　　🐾 *If the student has a poor self-concept, this may be too threatening to self-esteem.*

　　○ Provide corrective feedback indicating that the teacher cannot listen and understand that quickly.

■ Encourage the student to read faster.

　　🐾 *The student most likely has a specific reading skill or processing deficit.*

    ○ Evaluate reading skills, including the ability to decode words, blend sounds together, and use word families. Assess mastery of sight vocabulary words and the reading level.

    ○ Evaluate speech and language skills, such as word retrieval.

    ○ Determine whether the student can read better silently than orally.

    ○ Model reading at an appropriate rate.

    ○ Provide oral reading practice on a lower skill level.

    ○ Allow the student to silently preview a passage before reading aloud.

    ○ Have the student read short passages several times and record the number of words per minute. Graph the student's progress.

Reading Comprehension

Trouble Controlling Impulsivity (LD)

■ Have the student read comprehension questions before starting passage.

■ Have the student read short passages.

■ Encourage the student to use a mind mapping strategy (p. 69).

■ Require the student to indicate where an answer is found in a passage by underlining the text or indicating the page number.

Difficulty Persisting (LD)

■ Positively reinforce the student for remaining on task.

■ Allow the student to physically move after reading each section.

■ Permit the student to walk or sit in a rocking chair while reading.

■ Allow the student to quietly read aloud.

Problems Attending to Important Details (LD)

■ Teach the student how to read and follow directions at the beginning of the school year and in every course of study.

    ○ Give directions that are clear and specific.

    ○ Make sure knowledge of the subject is assessed rather than understanding of the directions.

    ○ Provide directions and questions in the same format.

     ○ Have the student highlight key action words in directions, such as "read," "underline" or "write."

     ○ Have the student number the order of the directions.

■ Read any review questions before reading the text.

■ Provide the student with an outline of the chapter and ask the student to complete the outline as the material is read.

■ Encourage the student to focus on the who, what, when, where, how and why details.

■ Teach the student graphic reading skills including:

sequential (flow charts, time lines, organizational charts and process charts)
quantitative (number lines, bar graphs, line graphs, pictographs, pie charts)
maps (political, physical, special purpose)
diagrams (cross sections, blueprints, machine drawings)
tables and charts (row-by-row column matrices)

     ○ Draw the student's attention to the graph and help with interpretation.

     ○ Provide direct instruction in reading and interpreting graphs.

          ■ Determine what graphic information is contained in the text; what information is in the graphs; how the information in the graph relates to the text; what other information in the text could be graphed.

          ■ Discuss whether the graphs are clear or confusing.

          ■ Have the student determine whether the main ideas in the text can be displayed graphically.

          ■ Have the student move away from traditional graphic display forms and create mind maps (p. 69) and other visual illustrations.

     ○ Connect interpretation to the student's experiences.

Difficulty Using Organizational Strategies (LD/SL)

■ Have the student use mind mapping (p. 69).

■ Encourage the student to organize information to be learned into categories or chunks (memory units). For example, names, dates and places are easier to remember if they are grouped together into small, meaningful groups, rather than one long list. The size of the chunk should match the length of the student's verbal and nonverbal memory span. The ability to remember information decreases significantly when the student is trying to recall more than the memory span can retain.

■ Have the student organize information into a written chart, table, flow chart or diagram. Most of the information will be memorized by the time the chart is completed. Teach the student to make charts and diagrams independently as a study method. Have the student place charts or diagrams that work best in the "trick" or strategy book (p. 38).

Difficulty Learning Memory Strategies (LD/SL/OT)

■ Determine whether an inability to retrieve information is a true memory problem rather than an inability to demonstrate knowledge verbally or motorically. For example, a first grader might not be able to verbally name the letter "A" or write the letter "A," but might be able to point to the letter "A."

○ Use multiple-choice tests to evaluate content knowledge.

○ Provide a word bank for fill-in-the-blank tests.

　　🐾 *The format of a fill-in-the-blank test is very difficult for the neurologically impaired student with word retrieval problems.*

■ Do not expect mastery too soon after introducing new skills and information. Provide adequate repetition and drill to ensure overlearning and mastery. Require mastery before moving to the next skill. Mastery is defined as knowing the information 90 percent of the time over an extended period of time.

■ Distribute periods of intense concentration, as the student can only memorize small amounts of information at a time. Schedule several short sessions with breaks between tasks rather than scheduling one long session.

■ Present only a limited amount of information so that the student can store, retain and retrieve the material.

■ Teach strategies for associating the information to be remembered with other information.

○ Have the student create acronyms by combining the first letters of each word to be learned. For example, an acronym for the names of the Great Lakes would be HOMES—Huron, Ontario, Michigan, Erie, Superior (source unknown).

○ Have the student create a mnemonic device by using the first letter of each word to be learned to make a sentence or rhyme. For example, a mnemonic for E, G, B, D, F, the lines in the treble clef music staff, would be "Every Good Boy Does Fine" (source unknown).

○ Teach the student to associate information with current knowledge and personal life experiences.

○ Encourage the student to use a strategy to link an abstract concept with a previously learned, meaningful experience. For example, relating the Shakespearean play *Romeo and Juliet* with Stephen Sondheim's musical *West Side Story* places the play in the vernacular, both culturally and linguistically.

　　🐾 *Abstractions are more difficult for the neurologically impaired student to memorize and retrieve.*

■ Teach the student how to visualize the information to be learned. Multi-sensory input reinforces learning and provides a variety of modalities in which to recall the material.

○ Have the student create a mental image or a series of pictures about the information. The pictures should be absurd or unusual to enhance recall.

🐾 *Before starting, check to make sure the student can visualize (make mental pictures). This skill can be taught.*

○ Have the student underline or highlight the key words in material for emphasis. Translate the key word into a familiar sounding word that can be easily pictured.

○ Have the student draw pictures that illustrate important information to be recalled.

○ If the student must memorize visual material such as diagrams or maps, divide the diagrams into several sections, make meaningful shapes out of the diagrams, or color code sections and related items.

■ Encourage the student to subvocalize and rehearse (recite, repeat) the material to be learned. After the information has been read, have the student quietly describe it aloud with attention focused on listening to the content again.

○ Have the student recite often during a study session (after each paragraph, each section of a chapter, etc.).

○ Encourage the student to spend at least as much time reciting as reading.

○ Have the student recite while covering or looking away from the material.

○ Have the student recite aloud. Encourage the use of inflection to enhance memory.

■ Encourage the student to spend extra time studying the middle sections of study material, textbook chapters, lectures and presentations. Beginnings and endings are more easily remembered. Middle sections need extra study and emphasis.

■ Have the student review new information immediately, even if just for 5 minutes.

🐾 *Research suggests that most forgetting occurs in the first few minutes after the information is learned. This quick review helps ensure learning is permanent and saves time. Studying the material at a later time requires relearning, not just reviewing.*

■ Have the student role-play or pantomime stories or procedures to strengthen recall of the information.

■ Have the student extract and write down key information to be remembered, such as who, what, when, where, how and why.

■ Have the student do something different each time the material is studied. For example, reading notes over and over is an ineffective and inefficient means of transferring information into long-term memory. A better approach would be to reorganize or outline the notes, color code the material or transcribe the notes on a word processor.

Difficulty Sequencing Information (LD/SL/OT)

■ Divide the task into steps.

■ Present and discuss only one step of the sequence at a time.

■ Present part of a sequence and have the student finish the sequence. Increase the length of the sequence as the student achieves success.

■ Give general cues with each step: "What should I do first? second? next? now? etc."

■ Encourage the student to look at the pictures in the book as a means of providing a visual sequence.

■ Use a flow chart or mind map (p. 69) to visualize the sequence.

■ Have the student act out the order of events to clarify the sequence.

Difficulty Understanding Inferential Material (LD/SL)

■ Modify general classroom instruction.

   ○ Teach inferential comprehension in a group that is different from the oral reading group.

      🐾 *Some students in the oral reading group might not need instruction in inferential comprehension or might need comprehension instruction on a different level than oral reading.*

   ○ Teach reading comprehension with material that can be read at the independent level and in which all the vocabulary and sight words are understood at the mastery level. Complete ease of reading allows attention to be focused on increasing comprehension skills.

   ○ Divide the reading task into small segments.

   ○ Define abstractions in meaningful terms.

   ○ Relate material to personal experiences.

   ○ Encourage the student to listen to a tape or watch a video on the subject (for example, watching a video from a science series, movie of a famous novel). This provides an overview, or context, in which the inferential material can be understood, memorized and learned. Many neurologically impaired students are "bottom liners"; they cannot learn the parts until they have the "big picture."

■ Teach the student how to understand cause and effect.

   ○ Make sure the student can pick out cause and effect. One thing happens (cause) which makes something else happen (effect). As the student understands simple cause and effect, determine whether the student is also able to understand cause and effect in an inverted order.

- ○ Have the student create cause-and-effect examples.

- ○ Have the student number sentence parts with: (1) for cause and (2) for effect.

- ○ Show the student pictures of cause-and-effect situations. Have the student discuss cause and effect.

- ○ Teach key words indicating cause and effect, for example, "since" and "because."

■ Teach the student how to predict outcomes.

- ○ Have the student look at a visual cue and predict the outcome of an event shown.

- ○ Relate to the student an incident that happened to a peer and ask what probably happened next.

- ○ Ask the student if there is an alternative solution to the negative outcome.

■ Teach the student how to make inferences.

- ○ Have the student generate ideas to explain what might be meant by a statement or action.

- ○ Have the student identify an inference and then apply that example to other situations.

■ Teach the student how to sequence events.

- ○ Have the student or teacher use a mind mapping strategy (p. 69) to sequence events.
- ○ Remind the student to think about the beginning, middle and end of events.

Trouble Comprehending Lengthy Passages (LD/SL)

■ Divide the reading task into small segments.

■ Decrease abstractions.

■ Allow a peer, aide or other adult to read the passages to the students. The student with OCD who experiences a compulsion to read and reread words, sentences, paragraphs or pages will have difficulty reading long selections.

- ○ Suggest that the student use recorded books (p. 73).

- ○ Record the passage on tape for the student.

■ Teach the student an organized strategy for studying literature and textbooks. The following steps are recommended:

- ○ Define vocabulary. Relate the definition to something meaningful in the student's life. Hand out prepared sheets with proper spelling and acceptable definitions.

○ Suggest that the student watch a video, listen to a tape or do a hands-on activity, such as a science experiment, to introduce the subject to be studied.

○ Have the student overview the chapter, story or book before beginning to read.

- Have the student read the title. The title generally reveals the main idea.

- Have the student read the table of contents to obtain an outline of the book. Have the student note how the material is organized and whether it is divided into sections and subsections.

- Have the student read the chapter introduction.

- Have the student read the chapter summary.

○ Encourage the student to work one section at a time.

- Have the student read the section headings and subheadings.

- Have the student look at and discuss all captions and illustrations (maps, charts, graphs, time lines).

- Have the student read the questions at the end of the section as well as any assigned by the teacher. This makes the student aware of the primary stimulus in the chapter.

- Have the student read the section.

- Encourage the student to use a story organizer to list important points in the section (p. 202).

Story Organizer

Characters: **Setting:**

_____   Time: Place:

_____   _____   _____

_____   _____   _____

Problem:

_____

Goal:

_____

Action:

_____

Outcome:

_____

© Dottie Pettes 1993

- Suggest the use of a flow chart or mind map (p. 69) to visualize the information. This provides the same benefits as outlining in a much more visual and nonsequential format.

    🐾 *The problems caused by sequencing in traditional outline form are bypassed by using a mind map.*

- Have the student answer the questions at the end of the section.

O Have the student repeat the above steps for each section.

O Have the student reread the chapter summary.

O Have the student answer all the questions at the end of the chapter or unit and questions assigned by the teacher, looking up answers if necessary.

O Suggest that the parents purchase an additional set of textbooks so key ideas can be underlined or highlighted and notes can be written in the margins. What is underlined or noted can then be easily reread.

O Give the student a written list of the necessary steps for reading a chapter and suggest that the list be placed in the student's "trick" or strategy book (p. 38).

Difficulty Self-Monitoring (LD/SL)

■ Suggest that the student read orally. Reading aloud forces the student to stop, monitor, listen to information about the problem and consider possible solutions.

■ Have the student preview a list of questions that will be asked after reading is completed.

■ Ask the student to note and identify the primary details: who, what, when, where, how and why.

■ When reading silently, have the student highlight details such as names, vocabulary words or definitions. The student might color code main ideas and details.

Written Expression

Written expression requires the simultaneous integration of many cognitive skills, focused and sustained attention, alertness to detail, self-monitoring and efficient fine motor ability. The student must be able to generate, plan, organize and sequence the ideas to be conveyed. While holding the ideas in memory, the student must then be able to shift back and forth between the tasks of selecting specific vocabulary words, spelling the words correctly, utilizing appropriate grammar and recalling capitalization and punctuation rules.

The ADHD/ADD/TS/OCD student has considerable difficulty expressing ideas in writing. The problem usually stems from impaired handwriting skills, inattention, disorganization and/or sequencing problems. If handwriting or spelling have not become automatic skills and the student must actively think about forming and connecting letters or spelling words, the flow of ideas may be disorganized, poorly sequenced or lost. If the student cannot sustain attention to small details and make corrections, there may be spelling, capitalization and punctuation errors despite knowledge of the rules.[44]

---

[44] Levine, M.D. (1987). <u>Developmental Variation and Learning Disorders</u>. Cambridge,MA:Educators Publishing Services, 308-345.

Difficulty Initiating, Planning and Organizing (LD/SL)

- Teach the student how to initiate ideas.

  - Teach the student how to choose ideas for writing from reading materials, movies, discussions, experiences, television and trips.

  - Provide story starters.

- Teach the student how to plan and organize the topic.

  - Teach mind mapping as a prewriting, organizational technique (p. 69). Mind mapping allows ideas to be linked appropriately regardless of the order in which they were generated.

  - Have the student organize thoughts around the key words who, what, when, where, how and why.

  - Encourage the student to place strategies for organizing different kinds of projects in the "trick" book (p. 38).

- Teach the student how to limit the topic.

  - Help the student choose an easily limited topic by using a fill-in-the-blank chart to restrict the amount of information that can be written (pp. 83, 202).

  - Use a mind map (p. 69) or flow chart of the ideas to illustrate excessiveness and the need for topic limitation.

Difficulty Maintaining and Retrieving Ideas (LD/SL)

- Teach, encourage and allow the student to use a computer (pp. 129, 213) with a good word processing program. When using a computer, the student does not have to maintain the sequence of ideas, remember how to handwrite letters and words, spell correctly or recall capitalization and punctuation rules. The computer not only circumvents the student's problems, but also relieves the stress incurred.

- Use a mind map (p. 69) to assist with retrieval and maintenance.

---

44   Marcia D. Rothschild, M.Ed., computer consultant, has provided further information regarding the use of computers, pp. 129, 213.

Impaired Handwriting (LD/OT)

> Have you ever been in a situation where you must go back and fix your mistakes? How about when you cannot sit still and must move some part of your body? Well, that's what it feels like to have OCD and ADHD. Sometimes it gets to the point where no matter how hard you concentrate, you still reactively fix the letters or darken the period. One time in my english class in high school I looked down and saw that my period looked like this:●. I didn't even realize that I had been sitting there and had been darkening the period over and over again. So you see, OCD and ADHD can sometimes be a real pain in the posterior.
>
> Jory, age 20

Sample of Impaired Handwriting of ADHD/OCD Student

The majority of ADHD/ADD/TS students have graphomotor (handwriting) problems. The student with ADHD or ADD often is impulsive and has rapid, unplanned handwriting. When the student is encouraged to finish the work within a specified time frame, both legibility and content are affected. Conversely, when the student tries to write legibly, the process exceeds the allotted time. The TS student may have hand and arm tics which interfere with writing. The OCD student sometimes feels the compulsion to write and rewrite words, count letters or erase until there is a hole in the paper. Because of these problems, assignments and homework are not completed and ideas are not conveyed in writing quickly and effectively—especially on quizzes and tests. All teachers working with the student must understand that the handwriting problems are neurologically based and employ strategies to circumvent this deficit area.

☙ *It is imperative that mastery be assessed by what has been learned rather than by what can be written.*

The following modifications are recommended:

■ Keep handwritten responses to a minimum.

    ○ Reduce the number of problems and answers required on a work sheet, test or homework assignment to a level which accommodates the handwriting deficits and the slowness with which the student works. For example, have the student complete every other question, alternate rows, work selected problems or do half the assignment instead of the whole assignment.

    ○ Permit the student to use the computer.

    ○ Have an adult or peer write what the student dictates.

    ○ If the student works too rapidly, shorter assignments will allow the student time to check the work and increase accuracy.

- Allow the student to demonstrate knowledge in a variety of ways such as creating models, designing posters, making scrapbooks, giving demonstrations or making oral presentations.

- Do not require the student to copy questions or problems before answering them. Always provide the student with prepared or duplicated copies of the board material, class work and questions to be answered. This eliminates the excessive time, frustration and stress produced by copying from the board or the text.

- Do not have the student recopy illegible handwriting. Muscle soreness and fatigue produce stress and cause handwriting to deteriorate.

  ○ Permit the student to use a computer.

  ○ Have an adult or peer write what the student dictates.

- Implement modifications if a student makes errors in math because of misaligned columns or poor handwriting.

  ○ Fold the paper into four or eight sections, placing each problem in a separate section.

  ○ Have the student work on lined paper which has been rotated 90 degrees so the lines become columns.

  ○ Provide grid or graph paper with squares of the appropriate size to allow the student to write one numeral or sign in each box.

- Allow the student to choose either manuscript or cursive writing, depending on which is easier and produces the best results.

- Grade handwriting performance on effort rather than comparing it with the handwriting of students who do not have neurologically based graphomotor problems.

- Permit the student to complete classwork orally rather than in writing. Allow dictation of lessons into a tape recorder or to the teacher or another adult. Ask the student to concentrate on content while the adult does the writing.

- Permit the student to take tests orally. Oral testing is an appropriate means of assessing mastery. Read the questions aloud. Have the student record responses on tape or have an adult record the answers in writing.

- When testing, use a multiple-choice format rather than a short answer or essay format so fewer demands are placed upon handwriting skills.

  ☙ *Fill-in-the-blank questions are difficult for the student with word retrieval problems. The use of a word bank eliminates this problem.*

- Circumvent handwriting problems associated with notetaking. The ADHD/TS student has difficulty writing quickly enough to get the information on paper. The compulsions of the student with OCD may result in the need to write and rewrite, erase and re-erase, cross-out or write every word down.

    ○ Assign a notetaking buddy who is a reliable student and has good handwriting.

    ○ Have a classmate photocopy the notes or use carbon paper while writing.

    ○ Provide the student with a copy of the teacher's notes or lesson plan.

    ○ Give the student an outline listing the main ideas and related subtopics. Provide space for the student to take additional notes.

    ○ Provide the student with a prepared mind map (p. 69).

    ○ Provide a tape recorder with an automatic counter. Have the student tape lectures while also taking notes. When information is missed because of slow handwriting, have the student glance at the counter, jot the number in the notes, leave a space and refocus attention on the lecture. Later the student can listen to the tape at the appropriate place and fill in the missing information.

■ Reduce muscle soreness and fatigue produced by an inappropriate pencil grip.

    ○ Recommend that the student receive services from an occupational therapist (OT) who has been trained specifically to improve alignment, spacing, consistency, slant and formation of letters.

    ○ Suggest that the occupational therapist teach the student how to use a more appropriate pencil grip so handwriting is easier.

    ○ Consult with the occupational therapist about rubber or plastic devices that are available to assist in development of a correct pencil grip and which type would be best for the individual student. Have the student place the rubber grip on the pencil approximately three-quarters of an inch from the point to provide more motor control.

■ Provide direct instruction in computer skills and word processing. The student must be allowed to use a word processor and printer to bypass neurologically based handwriting problems. Using a computer increases attention to task and circumvents impaired graphomotor skills, poor use of space, organizational problems, difficulty recalling capitalization and punctuation rules, incorrect spelling, syntactical errors and many other memory problems.

    🐾 *The computer is the electric wheelchair for the hands of the handicapped ADHD/ADD/TS/OCD student.*

    ○ Modify and de-emphasize keyboarding instruction.

        ■ Do not require motor accuracy and mastery of home key position as prerequisites for use of a word processor since impulsivity and hand tics interfere with accuracy and the ability to hold home key position.

        ■ Eliminate mandatory requirements for timed practice tests and long practice sessions. It is critical that the student view the computer with enthusiasm rather than another boring, difficult chore.

- Schedule short practice periods.

- Assign short tasks or short games which require accurate typing of responses.

- Positively reinforce achievement.

○ Allow the use of a word processor for routine assignments and homework as well as special projects and reports.

○ Allow some responses to be dictated to an adult for transcribing until the student can manage longer sessions at the keyboard. If "hunting and pecking" is too slow and laborious, the student is discouraged from using the computer. Have the student type responses to the first one or two questions and dictate the rest. Then slowly increase the amount of typing required of the student.

■ Grade handwriting ability separately from content.

The following writing examples emphasize the difference in a student's response when an assignment must be handwritten and when an assignment is allowed to be dictated to an adult. Note the difference in the quality and quantity of the writing between the two examples.

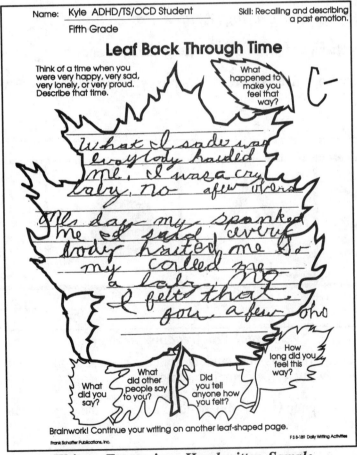

Written Expression, Handwritten Sample

> **Chapter 1**
> **The Missing Medication**
>
> On Saturday, the first of the month, Bess Justice was on her way on a field trip with her mother, Susan. Bess's father, a reporter for the local TV news, was at work that day and the house was empty except for the family dog. Bess's father went to work on that Saturday to train a new camera operator by the name of Cain. During the noon-time newscast Cain became ill and went home early. Also during the day while everyone was gone the dog was heard barking several times.
>
> A neighbor was working in her garden when she noticed the dog barking. The neighbor checked the front and back door of the Justice's house and all seemed safe. She then looked inside the window and saw a shadow of a person walking into the kitchen. She heard a cabinet door slam. She ran home as quickly as she could and called the police. After she called the police she called Mr. Justice at the TV station.
>
> While the neighbor was on the phone to Mr. Justice, Bess and her mother came home. Everything looked fine at the house. Susan then called her husband at work who then told her that he got a call from their neighbor just a few minutes earlier that someone was in the house . . .
>
> Kyle, age 10

Written Expression, Dictated Sample

The complete story of the missing medication appears in the appendix (p. 203).

Difficulty Monitoring and Editing Written Production (LD)

■ Separate the mechanics of writing from the generation and linking of ideas to be written.

■ Teach a visual or cognitive proofreading strategy. Tape the strategy on the student's desk (p. 201).

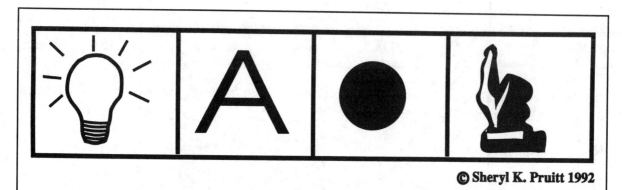

© **Sheryl K. Pruitt 1992**

Visual Proofreading Strategy

○ Light bulb: reminds the student to check to see that a whole idea has been conveyed (written in a complete sentence).

○ Capital A: reminds the student to check that the appropriate letters have been capitalized.

○ Dot: reminds the student to check for appropriate punctuation.

○ Pointing finger: reminds the student to check for appropriate spacing between words. (The width of a finger is usually sufficient.)

○ Cognitive strategy—COPS[45]: Have the student review the composition for:

- ■ (C) Capitalization

- ■ (O) Overall appearance

- ■ (P) Punctuation

- ■ (S) Spelling

☣ *Have the student perform each task separately.*

■ Encourage the student to use a computer word processing program to check spelling, punctuation, syntax and style.

■ Encourage the student to use a personal editor (parent, teacher or peer).

Math Calculation

Difficulty Learning Math Facts (LD/OT)

■ Teach concepts at the concrete level before requiring abstract memory.

■ Input information by combining as many different sensory modalities as possible (verbal, visual, motor, tactile).

■ Allow the use of manipulatives or fingers. Teach the student several different ways to use fingers for calculation.

■ Teach many different strategies for learning facts (pp. 205, 206) such as building on known facts: (if 5 + 5 = 10, then 5 + 6 = 11).

Rote memorization of the math facts is difficult for the ADHD, TS, OCD student. Memorizing abstract, inherently uninteresting math facts requires sustained attention, concentration and sequential memory.

■ Teach the student to visualize math facts with the answers.

■ Use backward chaining (source unknown) to imprint math facts.

---

[45] Schumaker, J.B., Deshler, D.D., Nolan, S., Clark, F.L., Alley, G.R., & Warner, M.M. (1981). Error monitoring: A learning strategy for improving academic performance of LD adolescents, <u>Research Report</u>, <u>32</u>. Lawrence, Kansas: University of Kansas Institute for Research in Learning Disabilities.

Example: If the student is having difficulty learning "7 x 9 = 63," write the problem on a chalkboard, in shaving cream spread on a formica surface or desktop, with a dry erase marker on a white board, with an overhead marker on a transparency or with an erasable marker on a window. Erase the last digit. Have the student rewrite the "3" and say the whole problem. If the student is successful, erase the last two digits. Have the student rewrite the "63" and say the problem. Continue erasing backwards until the student has learned the math fact. Have the student say the problem during each step. Once mastered recheck every week.

■ Have the student use a vertical number line (p. 208).

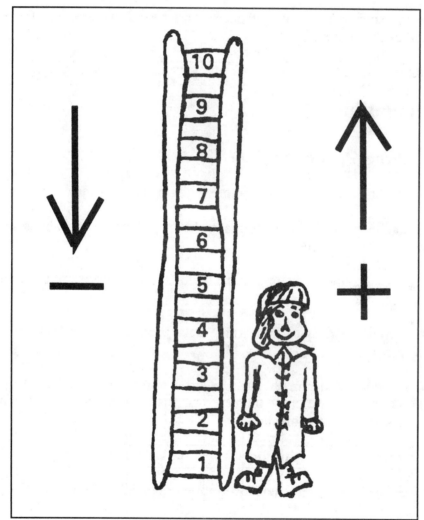

Vertical Number Line

■ Encourage the student to use a math facts chart.

Addition Table

+	0	1	2	3	4	5	6	7	8	9	10	11	12
0	0	1	2	3	4	5	6	7	8	9	10	11	12
1	1	2	3	4	5	6	7	8	9	10	11	12	13
2	2	3	4	5	6	7	8	9	10	11	12	13	14
3	3	4	5	6	7	8	9	10	11	12	13	14	15
4	4	5	6	7	8	9	10	11	12	13	14	15	16
5	5	6	7	8	9	10	11	12	13	14	15	16	17
6	6	7	8	9	10	11	12	13	14	15	16	17	18
7	7	8	9	10	11	12	13	14	15	16	17	18	19
8	8	9	10	11	12	13	14	15	16	17	18	19	20
9	9	10	11	12	13	14	15	16	17	18	19	20	21
10	10	11	12	13	14	15	16	17	18	19	20	21	22
11	11	12	13	14	15	16	17	18	19	20	21	22	23
12	12	13	14	15	16	17	18	19	20	21	22	23	24

Multiplication Table

X	0	1	2	3	4	5	6	7	8	9	10	11	12
0	0	0	0	0	0	0	0	0	0	0	0	0	0
1	0	1	2	3	4	5	6	7	8	9	10	11	12
2	0	2	4	6	8	10	12	14	16	18	20	22	24
3	0	3	6	9	12	15	18	21	24	27	30	33	36
4	0	4	8	12	16	20	24	28	32	36	40	44	48
5	0	5	10	15	20	25	30	35	40	45	50	55	60
6	0	6	12	18	24	30	36	42	48	54	60	66	72
7	0	7	14	21	28	35	42	49	56	63	70	77	84
8	0	8	16	24	32	40	48	56	64	72	80	88	96
9	0	9	18	27	36	45	54	63	72	81	90	99	108
10	0	10	20	30	40	50	60	70	80	90	100	110	120
11	0	11	22	33	44	55	66	77	88	99	110	121	132
12	0	12	24	36	48	60	72	84	96	108	120	132	144

■ Do not drill math facts for speed. Timed tests are highly stress-producing for the student with a neurologically based problem.

■ Do not allow poor mastery of facts to delay or hamper success with math concepts and applications. Encourage and allow the use of calculators. Check to see if the student needs larger keys or larger spaces between the punch keys on the calculator. Allow for calculator errors when finger tics are present.

■ Teach the student how to use cognitive cues to enhance memory (pp. 205, 206).

Example: "Put the big number in your head and the small number on your fingers. Say the number in your head and continue on your fingers until you use them up." Have the student count forward for addition and backward for subtraction.

Trouble Attending to Details (LD/OT)

■ Have the student use a highlighter to mark relevant information.

■ Use a highlighter to color code problems when mixing operations (addition operation sign coded green, subtraction sign coded red).

■ Have the student trace the operational sign with highlighter before working the calculation.

■ Reduce the number of problems so the student has ample time to edit work.

■ Have the student use a cognitive cue card as a visual reminder to check the work.

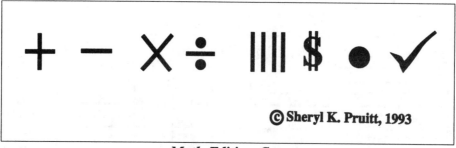

© **Sheryl K. Pruitt, 1993**

Math Editing Cue

The math editing cue is a simple visual reminder of a previously agreed-upon system the student uses to edit math calculations (p. 207).

○ Operational signs: check for correct operation (add, subtract, multiply or divide).

○ Columns: check for alignment of numbers into columns.

○ Dollar sign: check for omission and appropriate placement.

○ Decimal point: review placement and omissions.

○ Check mark: check accuracy with a calculator.

Difficulty Controlling Impulsivity (LD)

■ Use positive reinforcement to reward correct work. Mark only those problems which are correct.

■ Reduce the number of problems to the level at which the student can be successful, and then require accuracy. Use several small groups of problems if more practice is needed.

■ Slow down the approach by having the student trace the operational sign before working each problem.

■ Have the student subvocalize the steps of a problem while working it.

■ Give the student feedback after completing several problems.

Problems Sequencing Calculations (LD/OT)

■ Teach the student how to perform multi-step calculations in the correct sequence.

　○ Have the student use a flow chart to make a "map" of the procedure.

　○ Have the student use color coding to keep track of the steps of the operation.

　　Example:　When calculating a multi-digit multiplication problem requiring regrouping (carrying), use a different color for each digit in the multiplier.

　○ Teach the student how to use a cognitive and visual cue to remember a calculation sequence.

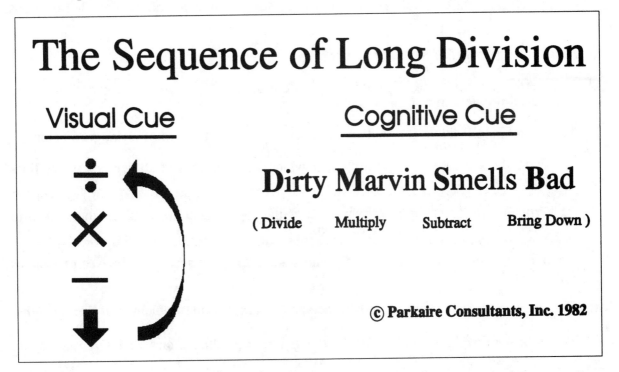

The Sequence of Long Division

Visual Cue　　　　　　　Cognitive Cue

Dirty Marvin Smells Bad

(Divide　　Multiply　　Subtract　　Bring Down)

© **Parkaire Consultants, Inc. 1982**

The cognitive and visual cue "Dirty Marvin Smells Bad" helps the student recall the division sequence "Divide," "Multiply," "Subtract" and "Bring down."

Difficulty Following Directions (LD/SL)

■ Teach the student how to follow directions.

○ Whenever possible, accompany oral instructions with visual stimuli.

○ Teach the student to re-auditorize (repeat to self) oral directions. This strategy helps maintain the verbal information in short-term memory until instructions can be completed.

○ When a complex or lengthy math direction is given, have the student tell the teacher what to do prior to the initiation of the task.

☙ *Avoid using this approach in front of a group.*

○ Divide oral directions into manageable chunks.

Example: State oral directions one step at a time. Say, "Take out your math book. (pause) Turn to page 5. (pause) Do column 1." Avoid saying, "Now take out your math book, turn to page 5 and do column 1."

○ Present verbal directions at a slower rate to ensure the student has time to process all of the information.

○ Create a checklist with visual cues for the student to follow.

○ Check vocabulary words for comprehension before giving math directions.

○ Make frequent comprehension checks to be sure the student understands the directions and can implement them.

Difficulty Aligning Numbers (LD/OT)

■ Reduce the number of problems on a page. Fold the paper into four or eight sections and place each problem in a separate section.

■ Implement modifications if a student makes errors in math because of misaligned columns.

○ Have the student work on lined paper which has been rotated 90 degrees so the lines become columns.

○ Provide grid or graph paper with squares the appropriate size to allow the student to write one numeral or sign in each box.

■ Provide a cognitive cue card to prompt the student to space accurately between problems (pp. 94, 207).

■ Enlarge worksheets and tests to provide adequate space to work problems and line up digits.

☙ *An example of a math worksheet in the appendix (p. 209) shows the effort made by an ADHD student to be neat.*

Problems With Handwriting (LD/OT)

■ Reduce the number of math problems required on the work sheet, test or homework assignment to a level which accommodates the handwriting deficits and the slowness with which the student works. For example, have the student complete every other question or alternate rows, work selected problems or do half the assignment instead of the whole assignment.

   ☙ *Remember, mastery is considered to be nine out of ten problems correct.*

■ Do not require the student to copy the math problems before answering them. This eliminates the excessive time, stress and frustration produced by the copying task. Always provide the student with prepared or duplicated copies of the classwork and board material. Eliminate the need for accurate copying by getting permission to provide a copy of the textbook page or an enlargement of the page.

■ Permit the student to use a computer to assist written production in math.

■ Encourage the student to use a calculator.

Difficulty Monitoring Errors (LD)

■ Provide editing cues in the student's favored sensory or cognitive mode (pp. 94, 207).

■ Provide a personal editor (parent, teacher or peer) to locate errors. A positive way to locate errors is to mark the problems that are correct. Have the student correct those that are not marked.

■ Analyze math error patterns. Teach the student to edit calculations for these errors.

Error Patterns	Remedial Strategies
Copying errors	Provide a worksheet or recopy the text. If copying is necessary: reduce number of problems, encourage use of bookmark to keep place, provide a "window" to show only one problem at a time, teach verbal rehearsal (say the number while copying).

Difficulty lining up and spacing numerals	Use graph paper.
	Turn lined paper sideways.
	Copy problems in a lattice.
	
	      H | T | O
	      2 | 3 | 6
	   – 1 | 2 | 8

Confusing signs	Color code signs. Work all of one operation first, then go on to another operation.
Inaccuracy with facts	Identify error patterns: Which facts were missed? Answers off by one? (Student may be counting.) Wild guessing? Switching operations? Check facts orally (with visual cue such as flash cards). If correct and efficient, check the procedure. If not, teach fact strategies (pp. 205, 206).
Regrouping for addition and multiplication (carrying)	Check understanding of place value and reteach if necessary. Reteach procedure with manipulatives such as place value blocks. When an answer is greater than 9, write the number off to the side and then decide which number to carry: $$\begin{array}{r} 1 \\ 46 \\ + \ 4 \\ \hline 50 \end{array} 10 \qquad \begin{array}{r} 2 \\ 84 \\ \times \ 6 \\ \hline 504 \end{array} 24$$ Instead of "put down the 4 and carry the 2," say, "twenty-four." Write it as you say it, starting with the tens place.
Regrouping for subtraction (borrowing)	Check understanding of place value and reteach if necessary. Play a game with $1, $10 and $100 bills. The student is the banker. You try to withdraw money and the student must make change if you do not have the appropriate denominations. Ex: If you have $356 and want to withdraw $137, student will exchange a $10 bill for ten ones to make it possible. Encourage meaningful self-talk: "Is the big number on top? No, so I have to go next door and borrow a bundle of 10..." Do NOT say, "Can I take 7 away from 6." Students with sequencing problems will reverse the numbers.

Division sequence	Teach a cognitive cue such as:
	
	     Dirty ÷ Does ÷
	     Marvin x McDonalds x
	     Smells – Sell –
	     Bad ↓ Cheese ✓
	                      Burgers ↓ (source unknown)
	The symbols are reminders to: "Divide, multiply, subtract, bring down." OR "Divide, multiply, subtract, check, bring down." Some students will need the cue on a laminated card so they can check off the steps for each problem.

Keeping it all straight in division	Use graph paper. Beginning at the greatest place value, underline until you have a number into which you can divide. Mark the place for the first number in the quotient: $8\overline{\smash)\underline{2\,9}\ 3}$ Say, "8 can't go into 2. It can go into 29. The first digit goes over the 9. The quotient will have two digits." After you find the starting point, the quotient will have one digit over every number in the dividend.

Remedial Strategies for Math Error Patterns

Math Reasoning

Difficulty Handling Abstract Language (LD/SL)

■ Use direct instruction to teach math language.

■ Explain the meaning whenever the student cannot interpret the language.

■ Have a chart available that converts words into symbols.

Trouble Attending to Details (LD/OT)

■ Teach the student to visualize ("Make a movie in your head.") and reconstruct the story when doing word problems.

■ Have the student draw a picture to illustrate a word problem.

■ Role play the problem with the student.

■ Highlight or underline important details in word problems.

Difficulty Sequencing (LD/SL)

■ Provide cognitive cues.

   Example: If a student is having difficulty sequencing place value, use pennies to demonstrate the ones place, dimes to demonstrate the tens place and dollars to demonstrate the hundreds place.

■ Provide sensory cues.

   Example: Using the previous example, ask the student to put together five dollars, eight dimes and six pennies for 586 (use of a visual and tactile cue).

■ Role play the action of the problem.

■ Reconstruct the details—who, what, when, where, how and why. Organize by priority.

   ❦ *Use teacher or peer assistance when necessary.*

Trouble Organizing (LD/SL)

■ Use flow charts to structure procedures.

■ Use a mind map (p. 69) or chart that relates key words to the operation.

Difficulty Remembering Concepts (LD/SL)

■ Provide cognitive cues.

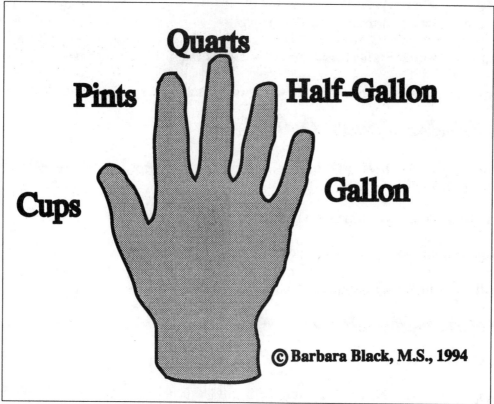

Liquid Measure: The Hand Trick

The thumb represents cups, the pointer finger represents pints, the middle finger represents quarts, the ring finger represents half-gallons and the little finger represents gallons. Starting with the thumb, two of each finger's liquid-measurement unit equals one of the next finger's unit. For example, two cups equals one pint, two pints equals one quart, two quarts equals one half-gallon and two half-gallons equals one gallon. This example brings meaning to an abstract sequential definition by using a cognitive cue linked with a sensory cue.

■ Provide visual, auditory, motor and tactile cues.

    Example: If the student is having difficulty learning the concept of "higher" and "lower" numbers, have two students stand on numbered stairs, starting with zero on the landing. The students can visually observe that the student standing on step 9 is "higher" than the student standing on step 1. Conversely, the student standing on step 1 is "lower" than the student on step 9.

    ☙ *Abstract math terms such as "greater than" and "less than" are more difficult for some neurologically impaired students than concrete terms such as "higher" and "lower".*

■ Use backward chaining (source unknown) to imprint math words when the student must spell correctly for a math test.

Example: If the student is having difficulty learning "Celsius," the teacher writes the word on a chalkboard, in shaving cream spread on a formica surface or desktop, with a dry erase marker on a white board, with an overhead marker on a transparency or with an erasable marker on a window. Erase the last letter. Have the student rewrite the "s" and say "Celsius." If the student is successful, erase the last two letters. Have the student rewrite the "u" and "s" and say the word. Continue erasing backwards until the student has learned the word. Recheck each week thereafter.

🐾 *Knowledge of math concepts is not assessed when spelling errors reduce the test score.*

Problems Tracking (LD/OT)

🐾 *A complete vision examination needs to be performed before interventions are implemented.*

■ Have the student use a finger for assistance.

■ Provide colored plastic overlays in the student's choice of color.

■ Underline or highlight text to assist tracking.

■ Use a guide to isolate the line. For instance, use a ruler or tachistoscope (a rectangle cut out of a piece of paper that allows the student to look only at one line at a time).

Teachers and parents often have difficulty distinguishing how the different disorders affect academic functioning. The chart below provides examples of how the neurological disorders impact learning.

Impact of Neurological Disorders on Learners

	ADHD/ADD	TS	OCD	LD
Learning	Unable to apply learning.	TS symptoms disrupt learning process. Energy to suppress tics preempts learning.	Anxiety or OCD symptoms interfere with learning. Student "stuck."	Information unlearned due to memory impairment.
Memory	Information stored in cognitive file. Lacks organized strategies for storing, accessing information due to forgetfulness, impulsiveness and disorganization.	Pieces of information missing in cognitive file due to TS symptoms interfering with learning by disrupting ability to store information in memory.	Pieces of information missing due to OCD symptoms interfering with learning by disrupting storage process.	Information not stored in cognitive file, or filed incorrectly and cannot be retrieved. Does not know how to label or store information.
Strategies	Does not attend to learn strategies or does not consistently generate strategies.	Understands strategies, able to use strategies except when TS symptoms interfere with ability to use strategies.	Understands strategies except when OCD symptoms interfere with ability to use strategies.	Does not always understand or generate strategies.
Sequencing	Unable to attend or too impulsive to remember to use sequencing.	Able to sequence except when TS symptoms cause impulsivity which interferes with the ability to sequence.	Able to sequence except when OCD symptoms cause cognitive looping.	Difficulty sequencing.
Problem Solving	Unable to remain on-task long enough to problem solve.	Able to problem solve except when TS symptoms interfere with the ability to problem solve.	Able to problem solve except when OCD symptoms interfere with ability to problem solve.	Difficulty problem solving.
Social	Unaware when to use social cognition or when to trust own intuitions.	Social interactions affected by ignorance of others, embarrassment from TS symptoms, teasing, withdrawal.	Social interactions affected by anxiety and OCD symptoms.	Social cognition deficits.

Pitfalls

Homework

Teachers must assign homework that can be completed efficiently and with a minimal amount of stress. They must take into consideration the physical and emotional consequences of having ADHD, ADD, TS and/or OCD and their impact on the ability to focus on and complete homework. All neurologically impaired students' attention and concentration deteriorates as the day progresses. As the end of the school year approaches, the student's ability to complete homework also declines. Teachers must adjust assignments accordingly.

> ☙ *Family stress levels increase during homework time and as the dinner and bedtime hours approach. Homework is often the major cause of family battles and "storms" (p. 21).*

The following recommendations will minimize the stress associated with homework:

■ Insist that the student maintain an assignment book.

   ○ Allow the student to choose the type of assignment sheet or book. The student is less likely to use it if the system feels awkward.

   ○ Have the student design assignment sheets on a computer. List the subjects in the order in which they occur during the day.

   ○ Use the assignment sheet as a communication log with the parents.

      ■ Have the teacher initial that the assignment has been copied correctly.

      ■ Have the parents initial that the assignment has been completed. This prevents unfair accusations if the work itself is misplaced between home and school.

      ■ Use the log to provide an accurate record if weekend privileges are being awarded for completion of work.

      ■ Use the log as a convenient way to send messages between parents and teachers. Accurate communication between the home and the school is crucial.

■ Circumvent the student's disorganization and forgetfulness regarding books and materials.

   ○ Recommend that the parents keep the study area supplied with the necessary materials (paper, pencil, pens, highlighters, scissors, glue, ruler) to reduce the time spent searching for the items.

   ○ Suggest that the parents keep an extra set of books at home. Parents can buy an extra set of books if necessary.

   ○ Provide time throughout the day for the student to organize materials.

○ Allow the student to leave class two to three minutes early at the end of the day. The extra time enables the student to go to the locker to calmly pack the school bag without the distraction of crowds of other students. This helps ensure that the necessary items do go home.

○ Have a classroom teacher, an aide or a resource teacher check the student's school bag to make sure necessary items are included.

○ Color code textbooks, notebooks and folders so each subject is color coordinated. For example, the blue science book goes with the blue notebook and the blue folder. This system makes it easier for the student to find needed materials.

■ Assign work that the student can complete independently.

The neurologically impaired student tends to become discouraged and frustrated when confronted with long assignments and is unable to overcome the inertia caused by feeling overwhelmed. The student may subconsciously forget the assignment to alleviate feelings of discomfort.

○ Check to make sure the student can do the assignment before sending the work home.

○ Do not send unfinished class assignments home. The student who cannot finish classwork at school will not be able to finish it at home because of a decrease in physical and cognitive energy associated with the neurological disorder.

○ Assign homework as a means of practicing previously taught material, not of providing instruction. Find the level at which homework can be completed independently and successfully.

○ Give the student clearly stated, written directions so the parents know what the assignments are and how to provide assistance, if needed.

○ For the first six weeks of school, ask the parents to write down how long it takes the student to complete homework. This allows the teacher to monitor whether the amount of assigned work is realistic.

The student and parents often do not communicate to the teacher that the homework takes an excessive amount of time and causes disruption to the family. Assist the student and family by questioning the effect of homework on the family.

○ Instruct the parents to write a note in the assignment notebook when the student does not know how to complete the assignment.

○ Set aside a time during the school day to provide assistance when the student has difficulty completing homework accurately.

■ Help the parents carefully structure homework time.

○ Suggest that homework be completed before dinner. Often the student and parents are too tired to do it later in the evening.

○ Encourage the parents to allow the student enough time (about 30 minutes) to have a snack, relax and release energy and tics before starting homework, but not enough time to get distracted or involved in another activity which would prevent shifting focus to the homework. It is often difficult for the student to go outside and play with friends and then come in and think about homework. If the student wants more time to play, there must be an agreement to come immediately at the next call, or the privilege will be denied in the future.

■ Teach the parents how to positively reinforce homework initiation and completion.

☙ *Point systems are frequently too abstract and thus are not meaningful to many ADHD/TS students. Use of concrete, meaningful reinforcers increases on-task behavior.*

○ Suggest that the parents give the student two chips (baseball cards, coins, etc.) at the beginning of homework. Each time the student initiates a task or completes work, give the student another chip. Feedback must be immediate and consistent. A reward or privilege should be given at the end of each night in exchange for the chips earned.

○ Instruct the parents to always provide extrinsic rewards rather than expect the student to get adequate reinforcement from an intrinsic feeling of accomplishment. The neurologically impaired student frequently does not internalize intrinsic rewards (praise, smile or nod). Earned chips can be spent on special privileges or rewarding activities. Suggested activities include staying up later than normal bedtime, renting a movie or home entertainment game or having a special occasion with parents or peers.

○ Have the parents make sure the reinforcement is appropriate for the individual student. What is rewarding for one student may not be rewarding for another. Interview the student or observe the student's choice of activities to determine which activities might be used as rewards.

○ Recommend that the parents change rewards frequently. The ADHD/TS student tends to become quickly satiated with a reinforcer.

○ Encourage the parents to accompany the reward with an enthusiastic, clearly stated comment about the student's initiation and attention to task or work completion ("I was impressed with how well you started and stayed on task, and look what happened—you finished all your homework!"). Praise the student, no matter how small the success.

○ Encourage the parents to ignore off-task behavior. Paying attention to off-task behavior increases the likelihood that the student will continue the off-task behavior to get the help needed to complete the work. When the parent's attention is removed, the student typically stops working; therefore, the parent must remain present or provide repeated intervention until the assignment is completed. The simultaneous use of reinforcing the positive and ignoring the negative improves behavior.

■ Teach the student cognitive strategies to assist on-task behavior.

○ Teach the student to verbalize thoughts. Using self-directed speech helps the student focus on the assignment and reduces off-task behavior.

⚻ *Have the parents tape a simple visual cue, such as a picture of the reward, onto the desk or inside the notebook to remind the student to finish an assignment.*

■ When off-task, acting out behavior interferes with the rest of the family, have the parents use the following progression of interventions:

○ Cuing—give the student a previously agreed upon signal to jump-start attention and initiate or increase persistence.

○ Redirection—use the student's own distractibility to switch from off-task to on-task behavior. Refocus the student's attention with a change of physical location or a change of activity.

○ Time-Out (opportunity to regain self-control)—have a prearranged procedure for time-out. There are three types of time-out:

■ Student initiated

⚻ *Reward the student for initiating time-out rather than losing control.*

■ Parent cued

■ Parent directed

○ Natural Consequences

⚻ *If the student does not complete the chores, the chores must be finished before the student can participate in weekend activities.*

⚻ *The school cannot legally give consequences to the student for behaviors associated with the neurological disorder (behaviors associated with impulsivity, hyperactivity and inattention).*

■ Have the student follow the same homework routine every night. Maintain at least a 30-minute study period even when there is no specific assignment.

■ Break homework assignments into small tasks and allow movement between tasks. Movement increases the ability to focus.

■ Structure a study environment that is conducive to work completion.

○ A student usually works best in a quiet environment.

⚻ *Sometimes the student needs to listen to familiar music of his or her choice (rock and roll, country) to block out any noises in the home that are distracting. However, if the privilege is abused (decline in grades, failure to complete homework), the privilege is lost.*

○ Allow the student to choose the location for doing the homework (desk, bed, kitchen table, floor). Explain that if the privilege is abused (decline in grades, failure to complete homework), all work will be completed at a specific desk. After a period of time, permit the student to try again.

○ Allow the student freedom to rotate homework sites.

○ Become aware of the student's sensory preferences that enable the student to focus and concentrate better.

    ■ Sometimes a student can study better with familiar music to mask distracting background noises.

    ■ Sometimes a student prefers soft lighting to bright lighting, or incandescent lighting to fluorescent lighting.

    ■ Sometimes a student prefers a soft chair to a hard chair, or one that rocks or swivels.

    ■ Sometimes a student prefers to walk while reading.

    ■ Sometimes a student prefers rocking to sitting still.

    ■ Sometimes a student needs to eat while studying.

    ■ Sometimes a student prefers a cool room to a warm room.

        ☙ *Recommend that the parents clarify who owns the problem (responsibility) regarding homework and learning style. If the student's grades remain adequate or improve, the student's choice remains appropriate.*

Study Skills

The neurologically impaired student frequently does not use organized and efficient study skills.

■ Encourage the student to subvocalize and rehearse (recite, repeat) when studying new information. After the information has been read, have the student quietly describe it aloud with attention focused on listening to the material again.

    ○ Have the student recite often during a study session, for example after each paragraph or section of a chapter.

    ○ Encourage the student to spend at least as much time reciting as reading.

    ○ Have the student recite while covering or looking away from the material.

    ○ Have the student recite aloud. Encourage the use of inflection to enhance memory.

■ Encourage the student to spend extra time studying the middle sections of study materials, textbook chapters, lectures and presentations. Beginnings and endings are more easily remembered. Middle sections need extra study.

■ Have the student review new information immediately (even if just for five minutes).

    ♣ *Research suggests that most forgetting occurs in the first few minutes after the information is learned. This quick review helps ensure that learning is permanent. It also saves time. Studying the material at a later time requires relearning, not just reviewing.*

■ Have the student role-play or pantomime stories or procedures to strengthen recall of the information.

■ Have the student extract and write down key information to be remembered, such as who, what, when, where, how and why.

■ Have the student do something different each time the material is studied. Reading notes over and over is an ineffective and inefficient means of learning information. A better approach would be to transcribe the notes on a word processor, reorganize, outline or mind map (p. 69) the notes, and then color code the material.

Studying For Tests

A student must be able to remember newly learned information so that the material can be retrieved when taking tests. Frequently, the material learned one day is forgotten on a test.

■ Teach the student how to manage time prior to test taking.

    ♣ *The ADD student typically procrastinates until a day or two prior to the test to begin preparing for the test.*

    ○ Once the test date has been set, have the student determine how much time will be needed to learn and consolidate the material in memory.

    ○ Have the student distribute study periods over several sessions with frequent reviews that reinforce newly learned material rather than having a few long learning sessions that require retention of more information than is possible to learn at one time.

■ Teach the student how to decide what information might be covered.

■ Have the student rephrase main ideas and identify specific details.

■ Have the student review previous tests to determine the type of questions the teacher might ask (multiple-choice, fill-in-the-blank, matching, true-false, short answer, essay).

■ Encourage the student to generate questions that might be asked from the textbook, class notes, cognitive maps and charts.

■ Teach the student how to determine what needs to be memorized and what can be recognized during the test.

■ Teach the student how to select the best strategy for memorizing the material. There are several different strategies for facilitating recall of information (rehearsal, mnemonics, imagery, charts, outlines, diagrams). The technique used should be appropriate for the information to be remembered (p. 79).

🐾 *The student can improve the ability to remember important information by using a strategy to recall the material.*

○ Teach cognitive strategies for associating information to be remembered with other information.

■ Have the student create acronyms by combining the first letters of each word to be learned. For example, an acronym for the names of the Great Lakes—Huron, Ontario, Michigan, Erie, Superior—would be HOMES (source unknown).

■ Have the student use the first letter of each word learned to make a sentence. For example, a sentence to learn E, G, B, D, F, the notes of the treble clef music staff, is "Every Good Boy Does Fine" (source unknown). Have the student emphasize the cadence in the sentence. Encourage the student to create a humorous or personally relevant sentence.

■ Teach the student to associate the information with current knowledge and personal life experiences.

■ Encourage the student to use a strategy to link an abstract concept with a previously learned, meaningful experience because abstractions are more difficult to memorize and retrieve. For example, relating the Shakespearean play *Romeo and Juliet* with Stephen Sondheim's musical *West Side Story* places the play in the vernacular, both culturally and linguistically.

○ Teach the student how to visualize the information to be learned.

■ Have the student create a mental image or a series of pictures about the information. The pictures should be absurd or unusual to enhance recall. Before starting, check to make sure the student can visualize (knows how to make mental pictures).

■ Have the student underline or highlight key words in material for emphasis. Translate the key word into a familiar word that can be easily pictured.

■ Teach the student to draw pictures that illustrate important information to be recalled.

■ If the student must memorize visual material such as diagrams or maps, divide the diagrams into several sections, make meaningful shapes out of the diagrams or color code sections and related items.

○ Encourage the student to use auditory (listening), visual (seeing) and tactile (touching) senses simultaneously. Have the student say aloud, look at and/or write the information to be learned. Multi-sensory input reinforces the material and provides a variety of modalities in which to recall the material.

■ Teach the student how to determine when enough of the information has been mastered. The student can self-test with flash cards or get together with classmates to quiz each other.

Testing

Tests should be used to determine whether the student has mastered learning concepts. The ADHD/ADD/TS/OCD student often has difficulty demonstrating knowledge of information when taking tests. Teachers must make modifications to accommodate the student's special needs.

The following test modifications are recommended:

■ Allow the student to demonstrate mastery by completing a project or giving an oral report rather than taking a traditional test.

■ Allow oral testing. Have aides, volunteers or resource teachers read the questions aloud and write down the answers dictated by the student.

If written tests must be administered:

■ Provide the student sufficient advance notice of tests. A syllabus will give the student ample time to organize and plan for tests, permitting the student to study and prepare at the student's own pace.

■ Specify what information will be covered on the test.

■ Give the student no more than one test each day, as stress aggravates symptoms of neurological disorders. The neurologically impaired student typically experiences considerable test anxiety and cannot sequence information for multiple tests.

■ Waive time limits on nonstandardized tests. Timed tests often penalize the neurologically impaired student and do not accurately assess the amount of knowledge mastered. Note extra time on the test paper.

   ☙ *The ADHD/ADD/TS/OCD student is entitled by the Individuals with Disabilities Education Act, Public Law 94-192, and Section 504 of the Rehabilitation Act to take tests with modified time limits (p. 189). Examinations, including the SAT and the ACT Assessment for college entrance may be administered with modified time limits and given in private (p. 183).*

■ Administer the test in a resource room or another separate room so the student can concentrate on taking the test rather than on suppressing movements or tics. The use of a portable room divider is sometimes appropriate for this purpose.

■ Reduce the number of questions asked on a test.

■ Be sure to assess content, not handwriting, punctuation, syntax or spelling skills.

■ Divide the test into several parts and administer at different times.

■ Write questions in a multiple-choice format rather than in a short-answer or essay format. Fill-in-the-blank questions are difficult for the student who has word retrieval problems. However, this problem is often circumvented by providing a word bank from which to select the answers.

■ When a student has difficulty on multiple-choice tests which require answers to be written out, assign letters to each of the possible answers and allow the student to write the letter of the response, or simply allow the student to circle the answer.

■ Permit the student to write or circle the answers in the test booklet on tests having computer scored answer sheets. Have the teacher or an assistant transfer the responses onto the computer sheet. The student with ADHD and/or TS often has difficulty in filling in the circles on computerized test sheets due to poor fine-motor control and visual attention to detail. The student with OCD may need to compulsively fill in the circles until they are perfect, thus affecting test completion.

Test-Taking Skills

Test-taking skills must be directly taught to the neurologically impaired student. The student does not spontaneously acquire effective strategies for taking tests, tends to become very anxious and forgets what has been learned.

■ Encourage the student to bring all necessary materials, such as pencils, paper, rulers and calculator. Teachers should have extras on hand as well. These extra supplies can be provided by the parents.

■ Allow the student to choose a desk in an area free from distractions and where movements and noises can be released without embarrassment. The student will then be able to concentrate on the test rather than on controlling movement or tics.

■ Have the student review the test before beginning.

  ○ Encourage the student to examine test formats (multiple-choice, matching, true-false, essay).

  ○ Have the student determine the number of points assigned to each question and how much time will be required to answer the question. This will avoid the discovery of an essay question that comprises one-third of the test grade with no time to complete it.

  ○ Have the student read all essay questions and note in the margins ideas that relate to the answers.

  ○ Have the student write outlines for essay questions in the margins if needed.

  ○ Have the student write in the margins information to which mnemonic strategies have been applied.

  ○ Encourage the student to read all the directions carefully and underline all instructional words (define, summarize, compare and contrast). If the student does not understand the directions, the student should ask for clarification.

■ Instruct the student to answer the easiest questions first and mark the more difficult questions for quick location later. After completing the easier questions, have the student answer the more difficult ones.

■ When a student is not sure of an answer, have the student eliminate responses that are clearly not correct and choose from remaining answers.

■ Students who make impulsive errors on multiple choice tests may benefit from covering the answer choices, reading the question and thinking of a response. Then uncover the choices and select the correct response.

■ If the time is expiring, give the student extra time to complete the test, or have the student finish the test later in the day. Suggest that the student outline essay answers to receive partial credit for demonstrating knowledge of the material.

■ Encourage the student to review answers to the questions.

■ Cue the student to check to see that all items have been answered.

■ Have the student review the graded test and determine the reasons for the mistakes. Were the mistakes caused by:

- not studying the appropriate material?
- not using the correct study skills?
- not spending enough time studying?
- not understanding the questions or directions?
- having difficulty with the format of test (fill-in-the-blank, matching, essay)?
- not being able to recall or retrieve the information?
- not asking for help when the material was not understood?
- not paying attention to relevant details?
- making careless mistakes?
- running out of time?
- having to write the answers?
- getting anxious when taking the test?

Long-Term Reports and Projects

The neurologically impaired student needs to learn strategies for completing long-term written reports. An overwhelming assignment can be made more manageable if the student learns to organize and structure the allotted time. The student should use a computer for all long-term reports, term papers and projects. If the student is assigned a long-term project in a content area, allow the student to present the report orally or to impart information through an oral or visual format or construction project, depending on the student's learning style.

Facilitate report writing by teaching the student to use the following steps.

■ Divide the assignment into small, logical, manageable parts and make a time-table for completing each part. For example, have Part I of the assignment due in two days, rather than making the entire project due in three weeks. Schedule only one or two parts for each day. Three weeks to the student is a long time. Being able to handle long periods of time requires organization, sequencing and attention.

■ Photocopy each piece of research material related to the subject, then read and underline or highlight main ideas and important details.

■ Reread the underlined parts and write them on spiral-bound 3" x 5" note cards, putting only one idea or topic on each card.

■ Make a list of important points in the section and assign each one a color. Use a mind map (p. 69) or flow chart to visualize the information. This can be used to create a formal outline if required.

■ Reread the cards and color code them with dots corresponding to the coded subtopics.

■ Remove the cards from the spiral binding and sort them by color. Make decisions concerning where to include information from cards having more than two dots.

■ Read the note cards. Paraphrase the most important information and use it to expand the outline or mind map (p. 69). Eliminate ideas that do not fit.

- Check the outline or map to be sure that the information is balanced appropriately throughout the report.

- Write the first draft of the report on a computer. Print the draft leaving sufficient space between lines to make revisions.

- Review the printout. Proofread a few days after printing. Make sure that the writing makes sense, the ideas are organized in the correct sequence and the vocabulary is appropriate for the student. Use a computerized thesaurus to increase vocabulary level. Elaborate on ideas if necessary. Include additional details if needed and add adjectives and adverbs. Make corrections in spelling, punctuation and grammar.

- Have an adult edit the student's report.

- Transfer corrections from the printout to the computer.

- Print, review and edit the second draft.

- Repeat the revision process until satisfied with the product.

- Print the final report.

School Avoidance and Phobia[46]

School phobia (marked refusal to go to school) is a form of anxiety or panic attack which sometimes is experienced by the TS/OCD student. The student may develop various psychosomatic symptoms, such as headaches and stomachaches. The student may complain that the schoolwork is too difficult or boring, peers are unjustly teasing and criticizing and teachers are too critical and uncaring. An increase in separation anxiety may also occur (the fear of leaving home or leaving the parent).

The following recommendations are suggested when the student refuses to go to school:

- When the student offers psychosomatic complaints, recommend that the parents contact the student's physician to determine whether there is a medical problem.

- Medications such as haloperidol (Haldol™) and pimozide (Orap™) sometimes produce school phobia. Suggest that the parents and student's physician determine whether the school refusal might be a side effect of medication.

- When academic and social problems are reported, examine the validity of the reports. A neuropsychological evaluation might be warranted to determine the cause of the problem.

- Utilize the services of a school counselor, school psychologist, principal and/or clinical psychologist.

- Make sure that the parents understand that school attendance is essential.

    O Encourage the parents to return the student to school.

        - Instruct the parent to avoid engaging in any lengthy or emotional arguments regarding school attendance and to calmly offer matter-of-fact statements indicating that the student will attend school.

---

[46] King, C. (1992). School phobia. Communique. Silver Springs, MD: National Association of School Psychologists.

- Ask the parent who is more able to avoid power struggles to accompany the student to the classroom, notify the teacher that the student has arrived and immediately leave.

- Require the student to attend school one hour a day, then gradually increase the amount of time required at school.

- Permit the student to telephone the parent several times a day, then gradually decrease the number of phone calls allowed.

○ Insist that the student attend school every day.

✋ *If a student is allowed to remain out of school, there will be an increase in the severity of symptoms and level of panic about returning to school.*

■ Project a calm and caring attitude to help the student regain control.

■ Ignore physical complaints (headaches, nausea, stomachaches).

✋ *When adults pay solicitous attention to the student's crying or complaints, the inappropriate behaviors will increase in frequency.*

■ Reinforce the student for school attendance with special privileges, rewards or activities.

○ Have the parents reinforce the student for compliance without arguing and crying.

Sleep and Morning Routines

The neurologically impaired student's deregulated arousal system affects sleep patterns. Some ADHD/TS students do not reach full arousal until late in the evening, while others, although exhausted, have difficulty falling asleep. Waking can then be difficult due to sleep deprivation. Medication side effects may impact arousal.

Recommend to parents the following strategies to facilitate morning routines:

■ Have the student put the homework in the bookbag (p. 44) as soon as it is completed. Place the bookbag in front of the door through which the student leaves in the morning.

○ Help the student purge the bookbag once each week. The bookbag is susceptible to the effects of disorganization.

■ Insist that the student make all decisions about clothes before going to bed. Organizing what to wear is as difficult as organizing a term paper or cleaning up a room.

■ If the student cannot fall asleep, allow the student to read, listen to music or watch television or a favorite video. Listening to white noise or nature sounds is sometimes helpful.

■ If the student is having difficulty waking, purchase two dual alarm clock radios. Place one next to the student's bed and the other across the room.

○ Set one of the alarms on the bedside clock radio to play music of the student's own choice forty-five minutes before it is time to get up. Allow the student to hit the snooze button several times.

○ Set the other alarm on the bedside clock radio to sound an alarm thirty minutes before time to get up. Permit the student to continue to hit the snooze button.

○ Set one alarm on the clock radio across the room to play music on a different station of the student's choice fifteen minutes before it is time to get up. Allow the student to return to the bed.

○ Set the final alarm on the clock radio across the room to sound when it is time to get up. Do not permit the student to return to the bed. Have the student start getting ready for school.

■ Encourage the student to shower after rising. Showering increases arousal and alleviates the stress produced by the dressing and eating routines.

■ Do not allow the student to turn on television in the morning because it interferes with getting dressed and eating breakfast. Music of the student's own choice often reduces the stress produced by having to complete the morning routines.

■ Do not criticize or lecture the student during morning routines. Waking, dressing and leaving for school (a sometimes stressful destination) frequently produce overarousal (p. 20).

■ Prepare breakfast and have all breakfast foods on the table and ready for the student.

○ The younger student must eat breakfast to increase the energy level.

○ Permit the adolescent, who refuses to eat, to miss breakfast. Have available high energy health bars that can be consumed on the bus.

　　🐾 *The OCD student may get "stuck" on a particular food or eating ritual. Drawing attention to the OCD ritual may increase the likelihood of the behavior continuing.*

　　🐾 *The sensory defensive student may have an aversion to certain food textures. Trying to force the student to eat these foods is not worth a "storm" (p. 21) before leaving for school.*

■ If the student misses the bus and must be driven to school, the student loses weekend privileges (staying up late, going to an arcade, playing on the computer, driving the car, going out on Friday night).

Home-School Management

■ Establish daily communication between the teachers and parents. The most important element necessary for the success of the student is positive communication between the home and school.

○ Frequent phone conversations between teachers and parents may be necessary to keep everyone informed regarding new symptoms, changing circumstances and medication adjustments.

■ Use an assignment notebook as a communication log between teachers and parents.

○ Encourage good work and appropriate school behavior by writing notes that compliment the student, rather than contacting the parents only when the student has done something wrong. Comments can be limited on some days to only a few words or a smiley face.

○ Have the teachers initial that homework assignments have been noted correctly and that the homework was received by the teachers.

○ Have the parents initial that assignment has been completed. This prevents unfair accusations if the work itself is misplaced between home and school.

○ Use the log as a means of providing an accurate record if weekend privileges are being awarded for completion of work. A Friday report can determine what rewards a student can earn (watching television, playing arcade games, using the computer, driving, staying up late, receiving an allowance).

○ Use the log as a convenient way to send messages between parents and teachers.

Social Skills

> *Loneliness is:*
>
> *Not having anybody to talk to.*
> *Not having anybody to play with.*
> *Talking to your grandmother and grandfather long distance.*
> *Being in a group where everyone makes fun of you.*
> *Having no friends.*
> *Not being invited to parties.*
> *When people don't want to have anything to do with you.*
> *Kids pointing out and making fun of your mistakes and clumsiness.*
> *That is what loneliness is !!!*
> *PAIN!!!*
>
> Kyle, age 12

The neurologically impaired student often has difficulty acquiring age-appropriate social skills. Failure to successfully develop and maintain relationships results from an inability to:

- express ideas and feelings.
- understand and respond to the ideas and feelings of others.
- evaluate the consequences of behavior before speaking or acting.
- adapt to situations that are unfamiliar and unexpected.
- recognize the effect of behavior on others.
- change behavior to an appropriate response to adjust to the situation.
- generate alternative solutions to problem situations.

Clueless behavior combined with a quick temper, poor impulse control and disruptive behavior in group situations leads to peer rejection. The student is at high risk for losing self-esteem and developing psychological problems secondary to repeated failures in social interactions. Anxiety, withdrawal, isolation and depression are common.

> 🐾 *When designing modifications, remember that the student's cognitive, behavioral, social and emotional age equivalents are approximately 2/3 the student's chronological age.*[47] *For example, a neurologically impaired 12-year old may have a functional age of 8.*

Ensure Availability for Learning Social Skills

■ Recommend that the student's vision and hearing be checked. The student who is visually/hearing impaired cannot process visual/auditory social cues.

---

[47] Barkley, R.A., New ways of looking at ADHD. (Lecture, 1991). Third Annual CH.A.D.D. Conference on Attention Deficit Disorders, Washington, D.C.

- Determine whether medication is at an optimal level and is available when needed in all social settings such as home, school and sports events.

> 🐾 *Clinically, there seems to be an increase in risky behavior for neurologically impaired teenage students who need medication and are unmedicated in unstructured situations (for example, at parties or driving on Saturday night).*

- Recommend that the processing of auditory, visual and tactile modalities be assessed. The student must be able to attend, sequence, organize, process and express that which is seen and heard.

Promote Social Skill Learning in Normal Settings

- Encourage the student to participate in social activities such as scouting, church groups or summer camp to develop social skills and build self-esteem.

- Recommend that the student learn and practice social skills in a socialization group.

> 🐾 *Group therapy is by far the most powerful setting for teaching appropriate social skills. The therapy process must be ongoing, not time limited. Group therapy should be conducted by a trained therapist in combination with an experienced learning specialist who knows how to teach practical strategies for remediating social deficits.*

Teach Social Cognition Skills

Before expecting the neurologically impaired student to exhibit socially acceptable behavior, basic social skills should be taught and practiced to ensure success.

> 🐾 *Sometimes the student has acquired social knowledge, but does not know how to use it.*

Develop Awareness of Feelings in Self

- Streamline the myriad of feeling words and start with four basic words: mad, sad, glad and scared. Teach the student how to use these words to identify and categorize feelings.

- Have the student share past situations in which a particular feeling was experienced. Use these examples to identify the feeling in other situations.

- After the basic feelings are mastered and can be generalized to other situations, gradually increase the student's repertoire of synonyms for the basic feeling words.

Encourage Accurate Perceptions About Self

- Ask the student to think about peers' perceptions of self.

- Ask the student to state whether that image accurately reflects who the student is.

- Ask the student whether his or her image is appealing to classmates.

■ Ask the student to evaluate and tell which personal characteristics feel appropriate and which ones feel inappropriate. Problem-solve with the student to help eliminate inappropriate characteristics.

■ Suggest that the student ask a trusted adult for feedback concerning those behaviors which make the adult feel uncomfortable.

Promote Understanding of Social Interactions

🐾 *The student has difficulty handling unfamiliar, complex social situations because of the large number of cues that must be simultaneously and accurately interpreted. To fully understand the verbal and nonverbal social interactions that are taking place, and the responses demanded, requires comprehension of the social cues.*

■ Use pictures, films and role playing to teach the student how to interpret important social cues and feelings.

■ Have the student predict feelings in hypothetical situations.

■ Have the student discuss feelings experienced in a recent situation.

■ Ask the student to restate the feelings expressed by a classmate during an ongoing situation.

■ Ask the student to state underlying feelings being expressed by a peer by identifying the verbal cues suggesting the feeling (tone of voice, content of the feeling words).

■ Teach recognition and interpretation of the body language of others so the student understands how the peer is feeling about what the student is doing or saying (hand movements, body stance, facial expressions).

■ Have the student find out the feelings of others by asking how they feel.

■ Explain that the student's own feelings are often clues to the feelings of others.

■ Have the student notice feelings about self after being with a friend.

Encourage Understanding of Verbal Exchanges

■ Help the student understand figurative language (slang) used by peers.

■ Have the student ask for clarification when given insufficient or unclear information.

Promote Social Expression

■ Encourage the student to make eye contact during communications.

🐾 *Many neurologically impaired students become overaroused looking into another person's eyes. They cannot listen to someone and make eye contact at the same time.*

○ If the student becomes anxious trying to make eye contact, show the student how to give the appearance of making eye contact by looking at an area surrounding the eyes (forehead, nose).

■ Teach the student how to maintain appropriate prosody (rhythm) and volume when communicating (not speaking too rapidly/too slowly, too loudly/too softly).

○ Provide nonjudgmental corrective feedback (p. 60) on student's performance. Prearranged hand signals for the teacher and the student are helpful.

○ Ask the student to breathe when searching for words, rather than filling the time with additional rapid, irrelevant verbalizations.

○ Teach the student to delay a response when needed ("Let me think a minute.").

■ Teach the student how to use age-appropriate vocabulary.

○ Teach the use of figurative language (slang) used by the peer group.

○ Teach the student to use peer slang only with peers and not with adults.

○ Teach the student the difference between home and school language.

○ Teach the student the appropriate language for treating people with respect.

■ Define respect and why it is important.

■ Teach the student how to thank a peer.

■ Teach the student how to compliment a peer.

■ Teach the student how to show support.

■ Teach the student how to use the feeling words (mad, sad, glad, scared) when communicating.

○ Have the student start a sentence by saying, "I feel _____," or substitute a feeling word for a thinking word.

○ Determine whether the effect of the student is consistent with the feelings stated in the verbalizations. Provide feedback if they are not congruent.

■ Teach the student how to organize communications logically and sequentially.

○ Help the student develop organizational strategies. Begin by having the student decide which information is primary, secondary, etc.

○ Help the student develop organized and sequential time concepts ("first, next" or "first, second, third"). Have the student practice telling a peer about a movie using these time sequencing words.

○ Teach the student to cue the listener when changing time concepts. Have the student use words such as "first" or "next" to organize and sequence information being presented. Have the student practice using these or other cue words to explain the rules of a game or sports activity.

○ Have the student use complete sentences containing pertinent information as opposed to meaningless, disconnected details and fragments of a story or request (who, what, when, where, how and why).

○ Have the student relate a personal story on tape and self-monitor for organization.

○ Use a mind mapping strategy (p. 69).

○ Monitor the student's difficulty with organization and sequencing ("You told me first you _____, but then you said _____.").

■ Teach the student strategies for topic maintenance.

○ Conference with the student privately to establish verbal and visual social cues, such as "I-285" (p. 68) or a hand signal to indicate rambling.

○ Limit the student to responding to the primary stimuli (who, what, when, where, how and why).

○ Make a flow chart or mind map (p. 69) as the student speaks to illustrate inappropriate changes of topic.

○ Model and rehearse appropriate topic maintenance.

■ Teach the student to use clarification strategies when misunderstood.

○ Let the student know that being misunderstood is very common.

○ Explain the importance of accurate self-expression to communicate needs.

○ Suggest that the student use clarifying statements ("I may not have made myself clear. Let me try again.").

○ Have the student reformulate and restate a communication when misunderstood.

○ Encourage the student to ask questions to make sure the other person understands.

■ Teach the student to recognize when it is time to change the topic.

🐾 *A student who frequently perseverates (is "stuck") on a subject may have OCD and be unable to change topics.*

○ Ask the student to stop and note whether the other students have finished talking about one subject and have already moved on to another subject.

○ Use a visual cue to let the student know that the topic has changed.

- ○ Indicate a topic change by verbally stressing the new subject.

- ■ Teach the student how to consider the needs of the listener when communicating.

  - ○ Teach the student how to cue the listener to the topic of discussion.

    - ■ Suggest that the student use words to indicate a change in topic ("The other day I saw a movie.")

    - ■ Have the student state the main idea of a sentence instead of focusing on the details.

  - ○ Teach the student how to clearly communicate wants and needs.

  - ○ Encourage the student to stop and think about the feelings of the listener.

  - ○ Model and rehearse effective responses to the feelings of others.

- ■ Teach the student to follow turn-taking routines.

  - ○ Point out other students in the classroom who demonstrate the appropriate turn-taking behavior. Always define the turn-taking behavior ("I like the way John waited his turn before speaking.").

  - ○ Practice turn-taking in a structured, teacher-directed lesson.

Assist Initiation of Social Interactions

- ■ Teach the student how to approach another student.

  - ○ Teach the student how to recognize the correct timing for approaching another student or entering into a group conversation.

  - ○ Help the student develop appropriate social greetings skills and conversation starters.

  - ○ Teach the student how to identify the other student's response to a greeting and modify the greeting if necessary.

- ■ Teach the student how to choose an appropriate topic of conversation.

  - ○ Ask the student to notice and/or name the topic everyone else is talking about.

  - ○ Teach the student how to find common interests to discuss with peers, such as asking about preferred activities (sports, television, movies, computer games, school).

  - ○ Suggest that the student talk about topics heard at the lunch table.

  - ○ Teach the student how to stop and think about what else might be said about the topic.

Promote Maintenance of Social Relationships

■ Teach the student how to regulate social interactions and not try to develop a friendship too rapidly.

   ○ Discuss the difference between various types of relationships (close friend or parents vs. acquaintance).

   ○ Have the student count the number of times contact is made with a new friend (several times a day, once a day, once a week).

   ○ Have the student determine whether the number of contacts made by the student is similar to the number of reciprocal contacts made by the friend.

   ○ Teach the student how to use self-disclosure appropriately (personal problems are discussed with a close friend or family member, but not with an acquaintance or stranger).

■ Teach the student how and when to give positive feedback and comments.

   ○ Ask the student to praise and make the peer feel good by offering a complementary statement about the other person.

   ○ Ask the student to tell others when they are being helpful, smart or kind.

■ Have the student ask about the other person's feelings.

■ Teach the student how to initiate a feeling comment which relates to the feeling being expressed by a classmate.

■ Suggest that the student listen to a peer without discounting what is being said.

■ Explain the difference between appropriately sharing positive experiences with peers and boasting or bragging.

Develop Strategies for Difficulty Handling Negative/Aggressive Social Interactions

☙ *The student with social skills deficits has a very limited range of behavioral responses available when confronted with problem situations. The student typically becomes aggressive or withdraws. Both responses are ineffective and cause peers to respond negatively. Practicing alternative responses with peers in a therapy group increases the likelihood of their occurrence in a normal social setting.*

■ Teach and promote understanding of the difference between assertive and aggressive language.

■ Help the student talk about what went wrong in a social interaction without blaming others.

■ Have the student apologize for hurting the feelings of the other student.

■ Have the student ask the peer what can be done to restore the relationship so that the friendship can be maintained.

■ Teach the student strategies for decreasing impulsivity.

    ○ Teach the student how to recognize pauses in conversations.

    ○ Teach the student how to inconspicuously place a hand over the mouth when wanting to comment while another person is speaking.

■ Help the student learn how to release anger and aggressive feelings in a socially acceptable manner.

    ○ Teach the student alternative responses to aggression.

        ■ Hold a class meeting. Have the group generate nonaggressive alternatives to real or hypothetical problems that might occur within the social context of the class (fight with words rather than fists, walk away when becoming angry).

        ■ Have the student identify with an adult effective strategies to use in problem situations.

        ■ Teach the student how to use humor to defuse tension. Power struggles with another student cannot be won. The use of humor introduces novelty into the situation and distracts the other student thereby deflecting an impending impasse and helping calm the student.

        ■ Cue the student to use an alternative to aggression when a real problem occurs.

    ○ Provide a safe place to which the student may go to regain control. This area might be supplied with a plastic bat with which to beat a pillow, a heavy cylinder-shaped punching bag and/or other nonbreakable items. The student should be reinforced for using these objects to release anger.

      🐾 *Do not use a light pear-shaped punching bag because it fights back and tends to make the student even angrier.*

    ○ Teach the student how to make a graceful exit. A graceful exit is effected when the student, anticipating or experiencing anger, leaves the room according to a previously agreed upon procedure.

        ■ Privately prearrange a set of options delineating how to exit and where to go. The student often will not be able to ask to leave the room when angry.

        ■ Privately prearrange cues for saving face. These cues may be auditory, visual, motor or tactile or may represent a cognitive frame that has been previously established.

Example: The student agrees that when the teacher notices anger, the student will be given a colored pass to leave the room and perform a particular errand. Allow the student to choose the color of the pass. Choice promotes a positive feeling about using the pass which then enhances the ability to leave gracefully.

🐾 *The student will often save face by muttering and grumbling while exiting. Understand that this is in fact a compliant response. A better exit might be a future expectation and goal.*

■ Teach the student how to avoid entering into a power struggle or adding input to the sensory system. The student must understand that as anger begins to build, further input increases the overstimulation already occurring in the body and leads to an automatic escalation of the event.

■ Reinforce the student for exiting rather than allowing the situation to escalate, even if the exit is less than graceful.

Section III
Computer Use

Computer Use[48]

The Impact of Computers On Productivity and Learning For the ADHD/ADD/TS/OCD Student

For the ADHD/ADD/TS/OCD student, computer technology offers unique opportunities for success in all areas of learning (pp. 88, 213).

This is achieved primarily by enabling the student to 1) bypass some deficit areas and successfully manage others, 2) manage symptoms using technological strategies and 3) participate as a productive member of family, classroom and social groups.

Therefore, access to computers and proficiency in their use are not luxuries for this student, but are actually prerequisites for learning and productivity, and as such fall under the federal mandate of a "free and appropriate education." The following material addresses the impact of computer use on specific problem areas encountered by the ADHD/ADD/TS/OCD student.

Types of Programs Most Often Used in Schools

Remedial/Tutorial

- These programs provide instruction in specific academic skills. They are intended to be assigned by the teacher when a student needs additional instruction to overcome a deficit. They are not intended to replace direct teacher instruction, but are often useful as an extension of teacher instruction or when a different, or less emotionally charged, approach is needed.

- Remedial/tutorial programs are usually designed by educators for use in schools and are generally marketed through distributors of educational materials. The teacher or media specialist will have catalogs from these companies.

Drill and Practice

- These programs may or may not include a tutorial component, but are generally intended to provide practice in a particular skill. They usually require less teacher involvement than remedial/tutorial programs.

- Drill and practice programs tend to be more visually attractive than programs that are strictly remedial/tutorial.

Games

- Games provide a highly motivational approach to enhancement of academic, perceptual and metacognitive skills.

- Games can often provide practice in skills other than those specifically addressed by the program's designer. Examples include curbing impulsivity in games which require waiting and aiming before firing at a target, games which require developing and following a plan of action and arcade style games which call for rapid visual tracking of a ball or other object.

---

[48] All information in this section is provided by Marcia D. Rothschild, M.Ed.

Utility

■ Utility programs are generally designed for use by teachers and other school personnel to maintain records, run grade averages, create worksheets and/or tests and assess student achievement in various areas.

■ Allowing students access to utility software when appropriate provides excellent experience in computer literacy skills, following directions and other important skills.

Productivity

■ Productivity programs, also called applications programs, are the workhorses among computer software packages. Examples include word processing programs, databases, spreadsheets, desktop publishers, calendar creators, graphics libraries, form generators, etc.

■ The ability to produce neat, attractive and informative written material is a prerequisite for success in today's world. Productivity programs are therefore the most important type of software for the ADHD/ADD/TS/OCD student to master since these are the programs which will allow the separation of subject knowledge from mechanics of written language.

 ○ The student can concentrate on the ideas being communicated without worrying about letter formation, spacing and legibility.

 ○ Grammar, syntax, punctuation, spelling and even word usage can each be addressed separately from the expression of ideas with the help of an on-line dictionary, thesaurus, grammar and style checker and spellchecker.

 ○ The teacher can judge the level of the student's knowledge, understanding and ability to synthesize information without being influenced by errors in the mechanics of written language.

Problem Areas Addressed by the Use of Computer Technology With the ADHD/ADD/TS/OCD Student

Arousal, Initiation and Persistence
(motivation and sustained attention)

■ Today's students have grown up with multi-media technology. They are familiar and at ease with it and therefore seldom have to overcome fear of its complexities before putting it to use.

■ Attention is aroused by the appeal of something which the student considers "new" and "modern."

■ The use of computers is particularly appealing to the ADHD/ADD/TS/OCD student because it allows the student to feel an enhanced sense of control. The student is causing things to happen rather than being subject only to control from the outside, which is so often the case with handicapped individuals.

Impulsivity

■ The computer is a tireless producer of immediate feedback and natural consequences. Almost without exception, a given behavior will produce the same response from the machine no matter how often it is repeated.

■ Most computer programs are designed to require confirmation from the user before executing commands which might result in irreversible changes. Furthermore, many newer programs will allow the user to recover material lost through impulsive or unintentional deletions. This is especially important when motor tics are present.

■ Because material written with a word processor can be easily edited and revised, impulsive and/or repetitive actions have less of an impact on the time and effort needed to produce an acceptable result. This relieves some of the stress associated with the production of written work.

Organizational/Study Skills

■ For the student who has difficulty with sequencing, the computer provides an organizational super-structure which guides the student through the various procedures needed to make the system function. In addition, each software program has specific procedural instructions for its installation and use, thus providing excellent practice in sequencing and following directions. It is interesting to note that the ADHD/ADD/TS/OCD student frequently becomes the family or classroom "expert" on loading and managing software.

■ Computer programs such as dictionaries and grammar checkers provide built-in cross-referencing systems which aid in the retrieval of words, rules and ideas.

■ Computer games and puzzles frequently provide practice in logic, reasoning, planning and sequencing skills. By employing task analysis techniques, teachers can pinpoint the specific skills targeted by a given program. Often there are many more skills at work than are listed by the program's designers.

■ Programs such as databases, spreadsheets and even some word processors allow mathematical formulas and other informational data to be entered and memorized by the computer so that only the raw data must be entered by the student. The manipulation of the data is accomplished automatically, thus greatly reducing the frequency of errors in calculation, computer syntax, etc.

■ Outlining programs are available which allow the student to record ideas in whatever order they may occur. Using editing commands, the student can rearrange those ideas, changing the order and level as often as necessary. The program automatically renumbers the entire outline with each change. Some outliners also allow the file to be exported to a word processor so that notations can be expanded directly into full sentences and paragraphs which can then be moved, combined or otherwise edited until the student is satisfied with the work.

Fine Motor Skills

■ It has been established that the majority of individuals with ADHD/ADD have significant difficulty with handwriting skills. The emphasis placed on the quality and appearance of written work during the school years has a major impact on a student's self-esteem. The use of a computer provides a means of circumventing graphomotor (handwriting) problems while expediting written production and producing a visually acceptable result.

■ The use of appropriate computer programs allows for the separation of knowledge and creative expression from the mechanics of written production. This distinction applies not only to lengthy written assignments, but also to repetitive drill and practice assignments such as are found in math and spelling lessons, as well as assignments calling for illustrations and/or graphs, charts or tables.

○ Using a keyboard or a point-and-click device (mouse) involves different muscles than those needed for writing by hand. Fatigue and muscle pain are greatly alleviated or avoided.

○ While computer use does involve sequencing skills, the most intricate demands of fine motor sequencing are alleviated, permitting additional energy to be directed toward the content of the material being written.

○ Computer assistance helps insure accuracy and neatness in measurement and drawing, as well as in written production. Computer graphics, drawing and painting programs and graph generators can enhance the quality of the work while reducing the likelihood of frustration and any behaviors it may cause.

Memory

■ Above all else, the computer is a machine specifically created for the storage, retrieval and manipulation of information. Not only the desktop or laptop computer, but many other electronic devices such as hand-held spellcheckers, phone directories or day planners eliminate the need to remember many things at once and can therefore be invaluable tools for individuals with memory and/or retrieval problems.

■ The correct organizational structure is built into the system so that the user can locate and retrieve information using only a few keystrokes. On-screen help and/or cues are always available to guide the student through the procedural sequence for each task.

■ Changes to information can be made and remade as often as necessary with ease and improved accuracy. Multiple versions can be saved and printed out for easy comparison.

Self-esteem

Productivity and performance at school form the basis of many decisions students make about their own competence and self-worth. The seeds of poor self-esteem are often planted very early in a child's school career and grow into extremely tenacious belief systems if allowed to take root. It is imperative that the ADHD/ADD/TS/OCD student be given every opportunity to succeed on an equal footing with nonhandicapped classmates. Computer technology is an appropriate, available and often essential means of insuring that success.

■ First and foremost, computer technology allows the student to express knowledge and creativity, and allows the teacher to measure the student's conceptual understanding, without the distractions caused by poor punctuation, spelling, sequencing, or graphomotor skills. This separation of ability from disability is crucial to the development of healthy self-esteem.

■ Computer technology is perceived by most students as new and exciting, thereby boosting their motivation to begin tasks and their ability to persist to the task's completion.

- Anxiety is known to exacerbate tics, increase inappropriate behaviors and precipitate withdrawal. The use of a computer alleviates anxiety by:

  ○ Reducing the impact of impulsivity on task completion.

  ○ Providing an organizational superstructure with prompts and cues to assist with the sequencing of keystrokes and commands.

  ○ Reducing the need to rely on inconsistent memory and/or retrieval abilities.

- The use of a computer increases both the volume and the quality of written work, resulting in an informational and visually acceptable product, thus increasing the student's feelings of personal pride.

- Computer literacy developed at an early age will provide the student with the foundation of a marketable skill in the future.

Other Concerns Related to the Use of Computer Technology By ADHD/ADD/TS/OCD Students

There are several issues which arise in almost any discussion of computers and their appropriate use by students and teachers. The following section addresses some of those issues.

Concerns About the Use of Grammar, Style and Spelling Checkers

Many teachers fear they are doing students a disservice by allowing them to use these devices. Teachers worry that students will rely on the machines to the exclusion of learning any spelling, grammar or style rules themselves. Experience has shown that this is not the case. Several facts come to bear:

- Computers do not "read" text in the sense that people do. Computers can only compare one set of electronic impulses to another. A spellchecker searches for strings of letters which do not match any of the strings that have been loaded into its "dictionary." This ability of the computer to flag possible spelling errors first saves time for both the student and the teacher. Second, it focuses the student's attention on the task. Third, and most important, it relieves the student of the need to be concerned with spelling while trying to concentrate on the content of the writing.

- The computer will only flag strings of letters which do not form real words in English (or in whatever language the student is writing). If, for instance, the student omits the "h" from "where," the spellchecker will not recognize this as an error, since "were" is, in fact, a correctly spelled English word. Therefore, the need for careful proofreading by the student is by no means eliminated.

- Once the error has been located, the user is shown a list of words which come close to matching the target word. The student must be able to recognize the correctly spelled word before replacing the misspelled one. The ability of the computer to make this exchange with a single keystroke bypasses impaired memory, sequencing and graphomotor skills, allowing for more success with less anxiety.

■ In addition, if a question arises about the spelling of a word while the student is writing, that word can be checked and the anxiety alleviated, on the spot, without serious interruption of the writing process. Hand-held devices are especially convenient for this purpose since they do not require accessing an entire computer system.

■ Grammar and style checkers flag passages with possible errors and make suggestions based on information selected in advance by the user. These choices include such considerations as writing style (business, technical, literary, etc.), type of audience and which grammar rules to check. Making these selections with the student affords the teacher an excellent opportunity to reinforce grammar and style rules.

■ After the material has been checked, the student must decide which changes to make and which passages to leave alone. Again, the computer has not "read" the material and does not "comprehend" the writer's meaning. The computer will, however, print the rule in question so that the student can review the passage for meaning and make changes if appropriate.

It must be kept in mind that spellcheckers and other electronic writing aids make it possible for the ADHD/ADD/TS/OCD student to communicate effectively in writing. This student's impairment, though often invisible to the untrained eye, is every bit as real and debilitating as the more obvious handicaps of the orthopedically or sensorially impaired. The ADHD/ADD/TS/OCD student is entitled to any necessary modifications to the curriculum and/or delivery model under both the Individuals with Disabilities Education Act (IDEA) and Section 504 of the Civil Rights Act (pp. 189, 237, 239).

Concerns About Typing Skills

■ It is not necessary to learn touch typing in order to use a word processor effectively. What is needed is a solid familiarity with the keyboard so that word processing is indeed less taxing than writing. Some research has shown that children may not be physically ready to learn typing before middle school age. Some students may never develop the dexterity needed for ten-finger typing. This should not be a deterrent to the successful use of a computer for written production.

○ Students often report that they dislike using the computer because they have been restricted from its use until they can type. Learning to type requires practice - not unlike learning to play a musical instrument. Many ADHD/ADD students are unable to maintain the discipline necessary for regular practice, become discouraged and give up on computers entirely. Since the ADHD/ADD/TS/OCD student must develop computer use as a life skill, it is imperative that the student be comfortable with the computer and enjoy using it. Computer literacy instruction should begin as early as possible and encompass a variety of methods for communicating with the machine.

○ Many techniques may be used to teach keyboard familiarization. Games which require some text input from the user provide good practice. There are software programs available which are designed to help students of various ages learn typing and pre-typing skills. However, the best way to learn computer literacy is simply to use a computer as often as possible.

○ Learning to use a word processing program need not be an overwhelming task. It is not necessary for the student to use a high-end, state-of-the-art package. However, even less elaborate programs offer capabilities far beyond the needs of most students. Teach the student only those techniques needed to accomplish the task at hand. Even young children can learn how to make capital letters and how to erase mistakes in the very first writing lesson. Other, more complex, editing procedures can be acquired as they become necessary.

■ Until the student has become familiar with the keyboard and learned a few editing techniques, typing assignments on the computer can be tedious and time consuming. Break the task into manageable segments by sharing the typing with the student. Alternate periods of typing dictated responses with having the student type his/her own responses. Gradually increase the amount of typing required of the student as proficiency improves. Hold the student responsible for the content of assignments, but accept work which has been completed on a computer regardless of who did the actual typing. Remember, be interested in what the student knows, not what can be typed in a reasonable amount of time.

Section IV
Evaluation/Assessment

Evaluation/Assessment

Evaluation

■ Not all students with ADHD, ADD, TS, and/or OCD need to be evaluated. If the student is developing normally, acquiring developmentally appropriate academic skills, functioning adequately in the classroom setting, and initiating and maintaining good peer relationships, assessment is not necessary.

■ If a student is experiencing academic, behavioral or social problems, consult with an Educational Support Team (EST) or Child Study Team (CST) (p. 65). The EST meets on a regular basis to consider the needs of a student having difficulty in the regular classroom. The EST is usually composed of an administrator, one or two classroom teachers, a special education teacher and a school psychologist or a school counselor. EST members brainstorm with the classroom teacher to develop modifications and strategies to help the student circumvent problems and remain in the regular classroom.

■ If those modifications do not help the student make sufficient progress, refer the student for psychoeducational evaluation to determine eligibility for special education services.

🐾 *Parents can also make the referral for assessment.*

■ A full and individual evaluation must be conducted before the student can receive special education services.

   ○ The student has the right to be tested in the language which he/she speaks and understands.

   ○ The student has the right to be tested in such a manner that results are not affected by race or culture.

   ○ The student has the right to be tested by qualified professionals including at least one teacher or specialist who is knowledgeable about the kind of problems the student is thought to have.

   ○ The student has the right to be tested in all areas related to his/her suspected problem.

   ○ The student has the right to be tested through procedures which determine specific areas of educational need, not just an intelligence test.

   ○ The student has the right to have his/her educational program determined on the basis of more than one test. The diagnostic tests administered should cover a broad range of cognitive abilities and not be narrowly focused.

   ○ The assessment should specifically identify not only the student's weaknesses, but also the student's strengths.

■ Once the evaluation is completed, the findings regarding the student's cognitive strengths and weaknesses must be integrated with information obtained from the student's background information (family history, medical history, developmental milestones, temperamental style, school history, and educational environment), direct observations of the student in the classroom and during testing, and the test results. These findings must lead to practical recommendations for class placement, educational modifications, intervention strategies, and appropriate teaching methods and materials.

■ If the parents do not agree with the evaluation provided by the school (the appropriate tests were not given or the school reached the wrong conclusions), the parents have the right to an **independent evaluation** conducted at public expense. An "independent evaluation" means that the student will be tested by a qualified person who is not employed by the school that the student attends.

  ○ The school must inform the parents, upon their request, where independent evaluations are available.

  ○ The school either pays for a private evaluation or arranges for one at no cost to the parents. However, the school has the right to a hearing to show its evaluation was appropriate. If the hearing officer decides that the school's evaluation was appropriate, the parents still have the right to an independent educational evaluation, but not at public expense.

  ○ If the parents have an independent evaluation conducted at their own expense, the results of the evaluation must be considered by the school in any decision regarding the student's education, and may be presented as evidence in a formal hearing.

  ○ If an independent evaluation is requested by the hearing officer as part of the "due process hearing," the evaluation must be at public expense.

  ○ Evaluations conducted at public expense must meet the same criteria (qualifications of the examiner, etc.) as those conducted by the school.

■ The student must receive a complete re-evaluation every three years, or more frequently if necessary or if requested by the parents or the student's teacher.

Assessment Tests

A psychoeducational evaluation includes assessment in the following areas:

Intelligence	Auditory Processing
Executive Functions	Visual Processing
Reasoning and Concept Formation	Tactile Functions
Language Functions	Academic Functions
Memory Functions	Emotional Functioning
Motor Functions	Pre-vocational and Vocational

Intelligence

All students being evaluated for placement in a special education program must be administered an individual intelligence test by a psychologist or psychometrist. The intelligence test **samples** many of those cognitive skills that are needed to learn in school including verbal comprehension and expression, verbal and nonverbal reasoning, concept formation, vocabulary development, numerical reasoning and problem solving ability, auditory and visual immediate memory, visual perception and discrimination, spatial visualization, and visual-motor coordination. Thus, the student's performance on an intelligence test is considered a predictor of academic achievement. An intelligence test does not measure innate intelligence, complex language skills, important memory functions, or academic achievement. An intelligence test does not relate to measures of attention and concentration, organizational skills, the ability to generate and use strategies, or the ability to interact socially with peers.

Tests: Wechsler Intelligence Scale for Children-III (WISC-III)

Wechsler Adult Intelligence Scale-Revised (WAIS-R)

Stanford-Binet Intelligence Scale: Fourth Edition

Executive Functions

Executive functions are those abilities needed for problem solving. Among these are attention and concentration, drive and motivation, mental flexibility, planning and organizational skills, ability to recognize and correct mistakes, ability to respond to feedback cues, and the ability to understand the consequences of behavior.

Tests: Random A's

Trail Making Test

Wisconsin Card Sorting Test

Intermediate Booklet Category Test (ages 9-14)

Booklet Category Test (age 15+)

Reasoning and Concept Formation

Reasoning is the ability to make inferences, draw conclusions, and make judgments. Concept formation is the development of concepts that are ideas based on common characteristics of a group of objects, events or qualities.

Tests: Test of Problem Solving

Test of Nonverbal Intelligence-2

Woodcock-Johnson Psycho-Educational Battery-Revised (Tests of Cognitive Ability)
Analysis and Synthesis
Concept Formation
Verbal Analogies

Language Functions

Speech skills encompass articulation (speech/sound production), voice, and fluency. Language skills include grammar, sentence length and structure, vocabulary and meaning, and auditory processing (auditory discrimination, auditory memory, auditory sequencing, auditory closure).

Expressive Language Functions

Expressive language is the ability to express oneself verbally.

Tests: Wechsler Individual Achievement Test
        Oral Expression

        Expressive One-Word Vocabulary Test-Revised

        Woodcock-Johnson Psycho-Educational Battery-Revised (Tests of Cognitive Ability)
            Picture Vocabulary
            Oral Vocabulary

        Test of Language Development-Primary
            Oral Vocabulary
            Word Articulation

        Test of Language Development-Intermediate
            Sentence Combining
            Word Ordering
            Generals

        Test of Word Finding

        Test of Adolescent/Adult Word Finding

        Clinical Evaluation of Language Functioning-Revised (CELF-R)

        Test of Problem Solving

        Test of Language Competence

        Porch Index of Communicative Abilities in Children (PICAC)

Receptive Language Functions

Receptive language is the ability to understand the spoken word.

Tests: Peabody Picture Vocabulary Test-Revised

        Wechsler Individual Achievement Test
            Listening Comprehension

        Woodcock-Johnson Psycho-Educational Battery-Revised (Tests of Cognitive Ability)
            Listening Comprehension

        Test of Language Development-Primary
            Picture Vocabulary
            Grammatic Understanding
            Grammatic Completion

        Test of Language Development-Intermediate
            Characteristics
            Grammatic Comprehension
        Token Test for Children

Memory Functions

Auditory Memory

Auditory memory is the ability to remember information presented orally.

Tests: Wide Range Assessment of Memory and Learning
            Story Memory
            Memory for Sentences
            Numbers/Letters
            Verbal Learning (repeated over trials)

        Woodcock-Johnson Psycho-Educational Battery-Revised (Tests of Cognitive Ability)
            Memory for Sentences
            Memory for Words
            Numbers Reversed

        Detroit Tests of Learning Aptitude-2
            Memory for Sentences
            Memory for Words
            Oral Directions

        Test of Language Development-Primary
            Sentence Imitation

Auditory Sequential Memory

Auditory sequential memory is the ability to remember a sequence of information presented orally (a series of sounds within a word, a series of words within a sentence, a series of ideas within a story).

Tests: Wide Range Assessment of Memory and Learning
            Story Memory (note whether story repeated in sequence)
            Memory for Sentences
            Numbers/Letters

        Woodcock-Johnson Psycho-Educational Battery-Revised (Tests of Cognitive Ability)
            Memory for Sentences
            Memory for Words
            Numbers Reversed

        Detroit Tests of Learning Aptitude-2
            Memory for Sentences
            Memory for Words

        Test of Language Development-Primary
            Sentence Imitation

Visual Memory

Visual memory is the ability to remember information presented visually.

Tests: Wide Range Assessment of Memory and Learning
                Picture Memory
                Design Memory
                Finger Windows
                Visual Learning (repeated over trials)

           Woodcock-Johnson Psycho-Educational Battery-Revised (Tests of Cognitive Ability)
                Visual Recognition

           Detroit Tests of Learning Aptitude-2
                Design Reproduction

           Bender Visual-Motor Gestalt Test
                Immediate and delayed recall trials

           Rey-Osterrieth Complex Figure Test
                Immediate and delayed recall trials

           Test of Visual-Perceptual Skills
                Visual Memory
                Visual Sequential Memory

Visual Sequential Memory

Visual sequential memory is the ability to remember visual information presented in a sequence.

Tests: Wide Range Assessment of Memory and Learning
                Finger Windows

           Test of Visual-Perceptual Skills
                Visual Sequential Memory

           Illinois Test of Psycholinguistic Abilities
                Visual Sequential Memory (ceiling age 10-0)

Auditory-Visual Associative Memory

Auditory-visual associative memory is the ability to remember verbal and visual information presented simultaneously (sounds associated with letters).

Tests: Wide Range Assessment of Memory and Learning Sound Symbol (repeated over trials)

           Woodcock-Johnson Psycho-Educational Battery-Revised (Tests of Cognitive Ability)
                Memory for Names
                Visual-Auditory Learning

           Goldman-Fristoe-Woodcock Auditory Skills Test (Sound-Symbols)
                Sound-Symbol Association

Motor Functions

Graphomotor Skills

Graphomotor skills are fine motor skills demonstrated when using a pencil. Specific tests and evaluations by a physical therapist or occupational therapist may be necessary for the student who has significant gross motor or fine motor involvement.

Tests: Bender Visual-Motor Gestalt Test

           Beery-Buktenica Developmental Test of Visual-Motor Integration

           Rey-Osterrieth Complex Figure Test

           Woodcock-Johnson Psycho-Educational Test (Tests of Cognitive Ability)
               Handwriting

           Developmental Test of Visual Perception-2
               Eye-Hand Coordination
               Copying

Graphomotor Speed

Graphomotor speed is the speed of motor performance demonstrated when using a pencil.

Tests: Bender Visual-Motor Gestalt Test (timed)

           Detroit Tests of Learning Aptitude
               Motor Speed and Precision

           Woodcock-Johnson Psycho-Educational Battery-Revised (Tests of Cognitive Ability)
               Writing Fluency

           Developmental Test of Visual Perception-2
               Visual-Motor Speed

Auditory Processing

Auditory Discrimination

Auditory discrimination is the ability to differentiate among sounds and words that are similar.

Tests: Goldman-Fristoe-Woodcock Auditory Skills Test (Auditory Discrimination Tests)

           Goldman-Fristoe-Woodcock Auditory Skills Test (Sound-Symbols)
               Sound Mimicry (speech sounds)
               Sound Analysis (speech sounds)

           Woodcock-Johnson Psycho-Educational Battery-Revised (Tests of Cognitive Ability)
               Sound Patterns (musical)

           Test of Language Development-Primary
               Word Discrimination

Auditory Sequential Processing

Auditory sequential processing is the ability to process verbal information in the correct sequence.

Tests: Goldman-Fristoe-Woodcock Auditory Skills Test (Sound-Symbols)
      Sound Recognition
      Sound Blending
      Reading of Symbols
      Spelling of Sounds

      Woodcock-Johnson Psycho-Educational Battery-Revised (Tests of Cognitive Ability)
      Sound Blending

Auditory Figure-Ground

Auditory figure-ground is the ability to discriminate a speaker's voice in the presence of background noise.

Tests: Goldman-Fristoe-Woodcock Auditory Skills Test (Selective Attention)

Auditory Closure

Auditory closure is the ability to understand a word or message when part of the stimulus is missing.

Tests: Woodcock-Johnson Psycho-Educational Battery-Revised (Tests of Cognitive Ability)
      Incomplete Words

Visual Processing

Visual processing is the ability to process what is seen.

Visual Discrimination

Visual discrimination is the ability to differentiate the shapes of letters, numbers, words, pictures or objects.

Tests: Test of Visual-Perceptual Skills
      Visual Discrimination
      Visual-Spatial Relationships

      Developmental Test of Visual Perception-2
      Position in Space

Visual Figure-Ground Discrimination

Visual figure-ground discrimination is the ability to perceive objects as separate from the background.

Tests: Test of Visual-Perceptual Skills
           Visual Figure-Ground
           Visual Form Constancy

          Developmental Test of Visual Perception-2
           Figure-Ground
           Form Constancy

Visual Closure

Visual closure is the ability to discriminate pictures or words with parts missing.

Tests: Test of Visual-Perceptual Skills
           Visual Closure (abstract designs)

          Developmental Test of Visual Perception-2
           Visual Closure

          Woodcock-Johnson Psycho-Educational Battery-Revised (Tests of Cognitive Ability)
           Visual Closure (meaningful objects)

Visual Processing Speed

Visual processing speed is the ability to quickly process visual information.

Tests: Woodcock-Johnson Psycho-Educational Battery-Revised (Tests of Cognitive Ability)
           Visual Matching (numbers)
           Cross Out (abstract designs)

Tactile Functions

Tactile function is the ability to perceive touch.

Tests: Finger Tip Number Writing Test (ages 9 and above)

          Finger Tip Symbol Writing Test (ages 8 and below)

          Tactile Finger Recognition Test

Academic Functions

Diagnostic achievement tests measure the student's present level of academic functioning.

Screening tests measure limited aspects of academic achievement and are used to identify the student who might be experiencing academic difficulty and in need of more comprehensive testing. Diagnostic tests are then used to assess specific deficit areas.

Basic Reading Skills

Basic reading skills include word attack and sequencing skills used to decode unfamiliar words.

Tests: Gray Oral Reading Test-Revised (diagnostic test)
      Passage Score

Kaufman Test of Educational Achievement (diagnostic test)
      Reading Decoding

Peabody Individual Achievement Test-Revised (screening test)
      Reading Recognition

Stanford Diagnostic Reading Tests (diagnostic test)—*timed test*
      Phonetic Analysis
      Structural Analysis

Wechsler Individual Achievement Test (diagnostic test)
      Basic Reading

Wide Range Achievement Test-Revised (screening test)
      Reading

Woodcock-Johnson Psycho-Educational Battery-Revised (Tests of Achievement)
(screening test)
      Letter Word Identification
      Word Attack

Woodcock Reading Mastery Tests-Revised (diagnostic test)
      Word Recognition
      Word Attack

Reading Comprehension

Reading comprehension is the ability to understand the meaning of written language.

Tests: Gray Oral Reading Test-Revised (diagnostic test)
      Comprehension—*measures ability to read a passage and answer questions about the passage*

Kaufman Test of Educational Achievement (diagnostic test)
      Reading Comprehension

Peabody Individual Achievement Test-Revised (screening test)
      Reading Comprehension—*measures ability to read sentences and choose correct stimulus picture*

Stanford Diagnostic Reading Tests (diagnostic test)—*timed test*
      Reading Comprehension—*measures ability to read a passage and answer questions about the passage*

Test of Reading Comprehension (diagnostic test)—*measures ability to read a passage and answer questions about the passage*

Wechsler Individual Achievement Test (diagnostic test)
      Reading Comprehension—*measures ability to read a passage and answer questions about the passage*

Woodcock-Johnson Psycho-Educational Battery-Revised (Tests of Achievement)
(screening test)
      Reading Comprehension—*measures ability to read several sentences and supply a missing word*

Woodcock Reading Mastery Tests-Revised (diagnostic test)
Reading Comprehension—*measures ability to read several sentences and supply a missing word*

Reading Rate

Reading rate is the speed with which reading material is read with comprehension.

Tests: Gray Oral Reading Tests-Revised (diagnostic test)
Passage Score

Stanford Diagnostic Reading Test (diagnostic test)
Reading Rate and Skimming and Scanning

Written Expression

Written expression is the ability to express ideas in writing with appropriate vocabulary, grammar, syntax, spelling, punctuation, and capitalization.

Tests: Test of Written Language-2 (diagnostic test)
Spontaneous Writing—*measures ability to write a passage in response to a stimulus picture*

Wechsler Individual Achievement Test (diagnostic test)
Written Expression—*measures ability to write a passage in response to an orally presented theme*

Woodcock-Johnson Psycho-Educational Battery-Revised (Tests of Achievement) (screening test)
Writing Samples—*measures ability to write a sentence in response to a stimulus picture or as part of a paragraph*

Spelling

Tests: Kaufman Test of Educational Achievement (diagnostic test)
Spelling—*measures ability to spell dictated words*

Peabody Individual Achievement Test-Revised (screening test)
Spelling—*measures ability to choose the correct spelling from among four visually presented words*

Test of Written Spelling (diagnostic test)
Predictable Words—*measures ability to spell phonetically-based words*
Unpredictable Words—*measures ability to spell words that cannot be spelled phonetically and must be memorized*

Test of Written Language-2 (diagnostic test)
Spelling - Contrived Writing—*measures ability to spell words correctly in dictated sentences*
Contextual Spelling - Spontaneous Writing—*measures ability to spell words used in written expression*

Wechsler Individual Achievement Test (diagnostic test)
Spelling—*measures ability to spell dictated words*

Wide Range Achievement Test-Revised (screening test)
　　　Spelling—*measures ability to spell dictated words*

Woodcock-Johnson Psycho-Educational Battery-Revised (Tests of Achievement) (screening test)
　　　Spelling—*measures ability to spell dictated words*

Mechanics of Writing

Tests:　Test of Written Language-2 (diagnostic test)
　　　Style—*measures ability to use punctuation/capitalization rules*
　　　Logical Sentences—*measures ability to correctly rewrite an illogical sentence*
　　　Sentence Combining—*measures ability to write several short sentences into one sentence*

　　Woodcock-Johnson Psycho-Educational Battery-Revised (Tests of Achievement) (screening test)
　　　Dictation—*measures ability to spell correctly, use words appropriately, and use punctuation/capitalization rules*
　　　Proofing—*measures ability to identify spelling, word usage, and punctuation/ capitalization errors in typed sentences*
　　　Punctuation and Capitalization—*measures ability to use punctuation/capitalization rules*
　　　Usage—*measures ability to use words correctly*

Writing Speed

Tests:　Woodcock-Johnson Psycho-Educational Battery-Revised (Tests of Achievement) (screening test)
　　　Writing Fluency—*measures ability to quickly write sentences using three stimulus words within a specified time*

Mathematical Computation

Math computation is the ability to calculate numerical problems.

Tests:　Kaufman Test of Educational Achievement (diagnostic test)
　　　Mathematics Computation
　　KeyMath Diagnostic Arithmetic Test-Revised (diagnostic test)
　　　Addition
　　　Subtraction
　　　Multiplication
　　　Division
　　　Mental Computation
　　Peabody Individual Achievement Test-Revised (screening test)
　　　Mathematics
　　Stanford Diagnostic Arithmetic Tests (diagnostic test)—*timed test*
　　　Computation
　　Wechsler Individual Achievement Test (diagnostic test)
　　　Numerical Operations

Wide Range Achievement Test-Revised (screening test)—*timed test*
Arithmetic
Woodcock-Johnson Psycho-Educational Battery-Revised (Tests of Achievement) (screening test)
Computation

Mathematical Reasoning

Mathematical reasoning is the ability to understand the relationship between mathematical concepts and operations.

Tests: Kaufman Test of Educational Achievement (diagnostic test)
Mathematics Applications
KeyMath Diagnostic Arithmetic Test-Revised (diagnostic test)
Numeration (number concepts)
Rational Numbers (fractions)
Geometry
Measurement
Time and Money
Estimation
Interpreting Data (charts, graphs, maps)
Problem Solving (word problems)
Stanford Diagnostic Arithmetic Tests (diagnostic test)—*timed test*
Number System and Numerations
Applications (word problems)
Wechsler Individual Achievement Test (diagnostic test)
Mathematics Reasoning
Woodcock-Johnson Psycho-Educational Battery-Revised (Tests of Achievement) (screening test)
Applied Problems

Emotional Functioning

Projective or personality tests provide information about a student's coping skills, emotional controls, and inner conflicts. These measures look at the student's attitudes toward himself, family, peers, and school. Projective testing is often necessary to determine whether psychological problems are interfering with the student's ability to learn.

Tests: Sentence Completion Test
House-Tree-Person Drawing Test
Kinetic Family Drawing Test
Rorschach Inkblot Test
Roberts Apperception Test for Children
MMPI- Adolescent

Pre-vocational and Vocational

There are several different categories of vocational assessment:

Vocational Aptitude

Vocational Aptitude tests generally measure skills such as fine eye-hand coordination, manual dexterity, general learning, math computation, and visual perception.

Vocational Interest

Vocational Interest tests measure the student's vocational interests.

Work Samples (simulated task or work sample)

Work Sample tests can be used to assess potential, strengths, limitations, and interests.

Section V
IEP—
Individualized Education Plan

Individualized Education Plan (IEP)[49] _____

If it is determined that the student is handicapped and is in need of special education and related services, an IEP must be developed. An IEP is an individualized education plan which must include a statement of the student's present levels of educational performance, a statement of annual goals and short-term objectives for the student, a statement of the specific special education and related services to be provided, the extent to which the student will be able to participate in regular education programs and the projected dates for beginning the special education and how long it is expected to continue. The plan must also include an objective method of determining, at least annually, whether the student is achieving the short-term objectives that have been set. This IEP must be decided upon in a meeting which includes a representative of the school the student attends (this must be someone who is qualified to provide or supervise special education), the student's teacher, the parents and the student if appropriate. Either the parents or the school may have other individuals participate.

Purpose of the IEP Requirement

■ The IEP provision and regulations in P.L. 94-142 address the IEP meeting(s) and IEP document.

    ○ The IEP meeting(s) is a meeting at which parents and school personnel jointly make decisions about a handicapped student's "program."

    ○ The IEP document is a written record of the decisions reached at the meeting.

■ The overall IEP requirement, comprised of these two parts, has a number of purposes and functions.

    ○ The IEP meeting serves as a communication vehicle between parents and school personnel. It enables them, as equal participants, to jointly decide what the student's needs are, what services will be provided and what the anticipated outcomes may be.

    ○ The IEP itself serves as the focal point for resolving any differences between parents and school—first, through the meeting and, second, through the procedural protections that are available to the parents.

    ○ The IEP sets forth, in writing, a commitment of resources necessary to enable a handicapped student to receive needed special education and related services.

    ○ The IEP is a management tool that is used to insure that each handicapped student is provided special education and related services appropriate to his/her special learning needs.

---

[49]   <u>Final Draft Policy Paper on Individualized Education Programs (IEP)</u> and <u>First Draft Policy Paper on Surrogate Parents</u>. June 4, 1980.

    The information in this section was prepared by Parents Educating Parents (PEP) and presented in "On Public Law 94-142 The Education for All Handicapped Children Act." This information has been edited and supplemented by the present authors. This law is currently called the Individual with Disabilities Education Act (IDEA) (p. 189).

○ The IEP serves as a means for monitoring compliance at the local, state or federal level to determine whether a handicapped student is actually receiving the free appropriate public education agreed to by the parents and the school.

○ The IEP also serves as an evaluation device for use in determining the extent of the student's progress toward meeting the projected outcomes. (Note: The law does not require that teachers or other school personnel be held accountable if a handicapped student does not achieve the goals and objectives set forth in the IEP.)
(PL 94-142 § 300 p. 349)

Information Included on the IEP

Listing of the Student's Current Functioning Ability

■ The IEP should include the following areas stated in terms of abilities, weaknesses and needs. The tests used to determine the student's ability must be named so it can be determined if the tests are appropriate.

○ Developmental skills (if student is at pre-academic level)

○ Academic achievement

○ Auditory and visual processing

○ Language ability (both what the student can express and what the student understands)

○ Motor ability (including muscle and sensory coordination)

○ Self-help skills

○ Social skills

○ Neurological functioning ability

○ Pre-vocational skills

Annual Goals

■ The IEP should contain descriptions of expected educational outcomes by the end of the school year. A statement should be listed for each curriculum area included on the IEP.

Short-Term Instructional Objectives

■ Short-term instructional objectives are the intermediate teaching steps, between the student's current ability and the annual goal which the committee considers attainable within a specified period.

○ Expect about three objectives for each annual goal. Each objective should contain:

■ Statement of the skill to be taught

- The level of skill mastery being worked toward

- Professionals who are responsible for teaching the skill

- When and how the student's progress toward mastery will be reviewed

Related Services

■ Under the regulations for Special Education a variety of services must be made available if needed by the student. These include services such as: Physical Therapy, Occupational Therapy, Speech Therapy, Adaptive Physical Education, Related Vocational Instruction (RVI), special transportation.

   ○ On the IEP, the following information concerning services should appear:

   - Name of special service or material

   - Who will provide the service

   - Objective of the service

   - When it will begin

   - Date of review

   - How many hours per week the service is to be provided

■ If a particular service is needed by your child but is not currently available in the school district, it should still be listed on the IEP. This listing allows the school system to request funds for services from the State Department of Education and to identify their needs accurately.

Participation in Regular Education Program

■ Each student in Special Education should be afforded regular opportunities for contact with typical school students. This contact may take a variety of forms, e.g., participation in regular education classes, physical education, art, vocational education, joint extracurricular activities, peer tutoring, access to cafeteria, etc. Once the type of activity has been determined, the IEP should note when and how often these activities will occur.

IEP Meeting Checklist for Parents

■ Obtain and study all school records, including private assessments, medical records, etc.

   ○ Prior IEPs

   ○ Progress notes, report cards, teachers notes, etc.

■ Make a list of the student's present levels of functioning based on the parent's observations.

   ○ Developmental skills (if pre-academic)

    ○   Academic skills

    ○   Language skills

    ○   Motor skills

    ○   Self-help skills

    ○   Adjustments needed for the student's neurological disorders

    ○   Emotional/behavioral skills

    ○   Pre-vocational and vocational skills

■ List the goals the parents feel the student should have.

■ List related services the student may need.

■ List special education services the student may need.

■ Parents and the school may tape record the meeting.

IEP Tips for Parents

■ An IEP must be developed prior to placement in special education.

■ Remember that parents have equal roles on the IEP team.

■ Be prepared for the meeting.

■ Get anger and frustration out prior to the IEP meeting. Parents may take a friend or advocate with them and if necessary have the friend speak for them.

■ If the parents get upset or angry, ask that the meeting be discontinued until another day.

■ Parents might learn and use assertiveness skills.

■ The IEP should be written at the meeting, not prior to the meeting.

■ Goals should be written in language the parents understand and in a manner which will show progress.

■ All related services should be listed.

■ Insist that services listed in the IEP are based on needs, not availability of services.

■ The IEP should list specific services, not simply learning disabled, emotional and behavior disordered self-contained, etc. Education for the handicapped student is more than academics. Any service the student needs to become independent should be listed.

■ The parents may disagree with the IEP. They do not have to sign. The parents may sign the IEP, but write out an explanation of why they object to certain parts.

■ Parents should receive a copy of the IEP for their records.

■ Parents should ask for a copy of the IEP meeting minutes and should send back a copy of any corrections that should be made.

■ Observe the student's program to insure that the goals are carried out and services listed are provided and monitor the student's progress.

■ Parents may request a review of their child's IEP at any time during the school year.

The following section suggests model goals and objectives that may be copied for personal use to assist in developing an I.E.P.

IEP Annual Goals/Short-Term Objectives

The annual goals and short-term objectives are appropriate for deficits described in the seven areas of learning and areas specific to ADHD/TS/OCD.

Oral Expression

Annual Goal

To improve the ability to use spoken language to communicate.

Short-Term Objectives

1. When given a topic or appropriate stimulus, the student will be able to speak using:

    A. _____ age-appropriate vocabulary
    B. _____ complete sentences
    C. _____ correct grammar
    D. _____ complex and compound sentences
    E. _____ logical sequence
    F. _____ comments that relate to topic being discussed

2. When discussing a topic, the student will be able to:

    A. _____ communicate intent (state purpose)
    B. _____ stay on topic (increase expectations in increments in order to maintain success)
    C. _____ follow turn taking rules
    D. _____ cue the listener to a topic change
    E. _____ use clarifying strategies when misunderstood
    F. _____ return to topic of conversation when cued by teacher

3. When provided a phonetic, associative or multiple-choice cue by the teacher, the student will be able to retrieve words.

Listening Comprehension

Annual Goal

To improve the ability to understand spoken language.

Short-Term Objectives

1. When given a listening task at the _____ grade level, the student will (with teacher cueing) be able to:

    A. _____ answer factual questions
    B. _____ answer inferential questions
    C. _____ express the main idea
    D. _____ express the story sequence
    E. _____ recognize sense and nonsense

F. _____ recognize fact and opinion
G. _____ recognize multiple meanings
H. _____ other _____

2. When given _____ step directions with verbal, visual or cognitive cues, the student will be able to follow directions.

3. When given oral directions, the student will be able to subvocalize the directions.

4. Given teacher assistance, the student will demonstrate understanding of verbal feedback cues (e.g., tone of voice).

Basic Reading Skills

Annual Goal

To improve the student's basic reading skills to the _____ grade level.

Short-Term Objectives

1. When given an unfamiliar word, the student will be able to use appropriate word attack skills to decode:

   A. _____ vowels
   B. _____ consonants
   C. _____ blends
   D. _____ digraphs
   E. _____ diphthongs
   F. _____ multisyllable words
   G. _____ contractions
   H. _____ prefixes
   I. _____ suffixes
   J. _____ root words
   K. _____ plurals
   L. _____ possessives
   M. _____ other _____

2. When given an unfamiliar word, the student will be able to demonstrate the ability to use syllabication skills.

3. When given an unfamiliar word, the student will be able to demonstrate the ability to blend sounds together.

4. When given a passage to read, the student will use appropriate word attack and sight word skills to read:

   A. _____ single words
   B. _____ content materials

5. When given a passage to read, the student will use a finger or marker to track.

6. When given a passage to read, the student will use colored overlays when appropriate.

7. When given material to read, the student will initiate use of earphones or a carrel to block out distractions.

8. When eye tics interfere with reading, the student will (with teacher assistance) request the use of recorded textbooks (p. 73).

9. The student will use a computer at (_____ school, _____ home) to complete routine, repetitive practice tasks otherwise completed with pencil and paper.

10. The student will use a computerized reading series (_____ school, _____ home) when the student is unable to attend to a reading book.

Reading Comprehension

Annual Goal

To improve the student's reading comprehension to the _____ grade level.

Short-Term Objectives

1. When given passages to read at his/her current instructional reading level, the student will be able to answer comprehension questions of the following type:

	Read Orally	Read Silently	Answer Orally	Mind Map*	Answer on Computer
Factual					
Inferential					
Vocabulary					
Sequencing					
Main Idea					

* (mind map p. 69)

2. When given passages to read at the appropriate instructional reading level, the student will be able to use a mind mapping (treeing, webbing) strategy (p. 69) to organize information in the passages.

3. When given passages to read at the appropriate instructional reading level, the student will be able to use pictorial cues to organize information in the passages.

4. When given passages to read at the appropriate instructional reading level, the student will be able to use mnemonics to assist with recall of factual information.

5. When given passages to read at the appropriate instructional reading level, the student will highlight primary details (who, what, when, where, how, why) in the purchased text.

6. When given passages to read at the student's current instructional reading level, the student will use a strategy to initiate use of charts, graphs and tables (pp. 83, 202).

7. When given tasks with written directions, the student will underline, highlight or otherwise mark the key words.

8. When given passages to read, the student will read out loud to improve self-monitoring skills.

Written Expression

Annual Goal

To improve the student's written expression skills in _____ sentences, _____ paragraphs, _____ stories, _____ functional writing to a _____ grade level.

Short-Term Objectives

1. The student will utilize story starters as needed.

2. When given an appropriate stimulus and teacher assistance, the student will use a mind map (treeing, webbing) strategy (p. 69) to generate ideas and limit the topic.

3. When given an appropriate stimulus and teacher assistance, the student will use a printed outline to generate a:

    A. _____ paragraph.
    B. _____ passage.
    C. _____ report.

4. When given an appropriate stimulus and teacher assistance, the student will develop an outline on the computer.

5. When given an appropriate stimulus and visual editing cues, the student will use a computer spellchecker, grammar checker and thesaurus, as appropriate, to edit the computer document.

6. Given a cognitive strategy with a visual cue, the student will edit written work (pp. 90, 201).

7. The student will use an electronic dictionary to edit written assignments.

8. The student will initiate the use of a personal editor (parent, teacher, etc.).

9. The student will initiate use of alternative strategies for notetaking (tape recorder, notetaking buddy, etc.).

10. The student will use a tape recorder to record written assignments in content subjects (social studies, science, literature).

Computer Skills[50]

Annual Goal

The student will use a computer system as an effective tool for learning and productivity.

Short-Term Objectives

1. When given (_____ assistance, _____ minimal assistance, _____ no assistance), the student will:

    A. Turn the computer and needed peripheral equipment on/off.

    B. Handle hardware and software with appropriate care.

    C. Locate and load correct program(s) and file(s).

    D. Make adequate use of:

        ____ cursor, enter, and space keys

        ____ lower case home keys (a, s, d, f, j, k, l, ;)

        ____ lower case extended home keys (g, h, ')

        ____ lower case higher letter keys (q, w, e, r, t, y, u, i, o, p)

        ____ lower case lower letter keys (z, x, c, v, b, n, m)

        ____ upper case extended home keys (A, S, D, F, G, H, J, K, L, :)

        ____ upper case higher letter keys (Q, W, E, R, T, Y, U, I, O, P)

        ____ upper case lower letter keys (Z, X, C, V, B, N, M)

        ____ number keys

        ____ symbol keys

        ____ tab key

        ____ escape key

        ____ mouse

        ____ touch screen

        ____ other pointing device _____

    E. Use a computer at (_____ school, _____ home) to complete routine, repetitive practice tasks otherwise completed with pencil and paper.

---

[50]   Developed by Sheryl K. Pruitt, M.Ed. and Marcia Rothschild, M.Ed.

F. Use a computer at (_____ school, _____ home) to complete written assignments using an age-appropriate word processing program and an on-line:

> ____ editing/revision tool
> ____ spellchecker
> ____ thesaurus
> ____ dictionary
> ____ grammar/style checker

G. Use a computer at (_____ school, _____ home) to retrieve information from an on-line:

> ____ encyclopedia
> ____ atlas
> ____ literary source
> ____ other reference _____

H. Develop keyboarding speed to a level which enables the completion of appropriate assignments in a reasonable amount of time.

Mathematical Calculations

Annual Goal

To improve the student's math calculation skills to the _____ grade level.

Short-Term Objectives

1. The student will use cognitive cues to master math facts (pp. 205, 206).

2. The student will initiate the use of a highlighter to identify operational signs.

3. The student will initiate use of a calculator or math facts chart to solve basic arithmetic problems.

4. When calculating multi-step problems, the student will initiate the use of a cognitive strategy to recall the correct sequence of steps (p. 95).

5. The student will use a cognitive strategy with a visual editing cue to check accuracy of calculations (pp. 94, 207).

6. The student will initiate use of grid, column paper or graph paper to facilitate alignment for accurate calculations.

7. The student will use a computer at (_____ school, _____ home) to complete routine, repetitive practice tasks (math facts, computations) otherwise completed with pencil and paper.

Mathematical Reasoning

Annual Goal

To improve the student's mathematical reasoning skills to the _____ grade level.

Short-Term Objectives

1. When given written word problems, the student will underline or highlight key words which identify the operation to be used.

2. The student will diagram or draw a picture to illustrate a word problem.

3. The student will use a computer at (_____ school, _____ home) to complete routine, repetitive practice tasks (time, money, measurements) otherwise completed with pencil and paper.

Initiation to Task

Annual Goal

To improve the student's initiation to task.

Short-Term Objectives

1. When given an assignment at the appropriate instructional level and a verbal, visual or cognitive cue, the student will initiate work on assignments (p. 50).

2. When given an assignment which the student does not understand, and no more than one teacher intervention, the student will initiate asking questions to clarify the assignment.

3. After an absence, the student will follow a teacher initiated schedule for completing missed assignments.

4. After an absence, the student will ask the teacher about missed assignments, devise a plan for completing the work and report the plan to the teacher.

On-Task Behavior

Annual Goal

To improve the student's on-task behaviors.

Short-Term Objectives

1. With teacher cueing, the student will return to task.

2. When the student displays off-task behavior, the student will, with teacher assistance, verbalize one strategy for getting back on-task.

3. The student will employ a previously learned strategy to return to task.

4. Given teacher assistance, the student will appropriately use prearranged mobility options.

Organization

Annual Goal

To increase organized work habits.

Short-Term Objectives

1. Given teacher assistance, the student will organize and maintain materials in an orderly, sequential manner.

2. The student will utilize strategies to organize and maintain materials in an orderly, sequential manner.

3. Given teacher assistance, the student will design a study schedule.

4. The student will successfully follow a study schedule.

5. The student will initiate obtaining a copy of the class notes from a notetaking buddy or a photocopy of the teacher's lesson plan.

6. Given teacher assistance, the student will devise and maintain an assignment notebook (p.43).

7. Given teacher assistance, the student will write all assignments in the assignment notebook.

8. The student will initiate having the teacher review and sign the assignment notebook.

9. Given a homework assignment and teacher assistance, the student will be able to organize materials needed for homework.

10. Given teacher assistance, the student will identify, prioritize and complete assignments.

11. Given a class or homework assignment and _____ teacher prompts, the student will turn in work.

12. Given teacher assistance, the student will use a home-school communication log to facilitate home-school communication.

13. Given teacher assistance, the student will successfully follow a long-term schedule for tests, projects and reports.

14. Given _____ teacher prompts or pre-established visual cues, the student will appropriately organize the work space.

Social Skills

Annual Goal

The student will be able to demonstrate use of appropriate socialization and coping skills.

Short-Term Objectives

1. The student will physically face the speaker and employ a strategy for appearing to make eye contact.

2. Given teacher assistance, the student will maintain the topic of conversation in social communications.

3. Given teacher assistance, the student will use appropriate language to communicate respect for others.

4. Given teacher assistance, the student will verbalize and use a strategy for maintaining the correct social distance between people.

5. Given teacher assistance, the student will communicate feelings (mad, sad, glad, scared) to others.

6. Given teacher assistance, the student will verbally express the feelings (mad, sad, glad, scared) exhibited by others through their body language.

7. Given teacher assistance, the student will verbally identify and acknowledge the feelings (mad, sad, glad, scared) of others.

8. Given teacher assistance, the student will communicate needs to others.

9. Given teacher assistance, the student will initiate asking how others feel.

10. Given teacher assistance, the student will recognize and identify the expectations of others.

11. Given teacher assistance, the student will correctly identify personal problems.

12. Given teacher assistance, the student will brainstorm alternative solutions to problems.

13. Given teacher assistance, the student will predict the outcome of his/her previous behavior (positive or negative).

14. Given teacher assistance, the student will make positive statements to others.

15. Given teacher assistance, the student will utilize a strategy for accepting and internalizing positive statements about himself/herself.

16. Given teacher assistance, the student will use verbal, visual and cognitive strategies to successfully self-monitor impulse control (p. 50).

17. Given teacher assistance, the student will successfully use a strategy for responding to incidental physical contact.

18. Given teacher assistance, the student will use a strategy for responding appropriately to peer provocation.

19. Given teacher assistance, the student will use previously agreed-upon strategies to avoid escalating negative situations.

20. Given teacher assistance, the student will verbalize feelings instead of engaging in physical aggression.

21. When confronted with an emotionally charged academic situation, the student will leave the setting in a previously agreed-upon manner and go to a previously determined safe place (another classroom, time-out) to vent frustration.

22. When confronted with an emotionally charged social situation, the student will leave the scene in a previously agreed-upon manner and go to a previously determined safe place (another classroom, time-out) to vent frustration.

23. Given teacher assistance, the student will use a previously agreed-upon strategy for responding to correction or failure.

24. Given an emotionally charged situation and teacher cues, the student will use a previously agreed-upon strategy for accepting adult intervention.

25. After control has been regained, the student will, with teacher assistance, assume responsibility for having initiated a conflict.

26. Given teacher assistance, the student will correctly identify the effect of his/her behavior on others.

27. The student will clean up any damage and/or correct any problems that may have resulted from loss of control.

28. Given teacher assistance, the student will verbalize solutions to mend a damaged peer relationship.

Testing Modifications

Individual states typically mandate state wide testing programs. The IEP Committee has the responsibility for addressing the testing program for each handicapped student. The following information should be attached to the IEP:

_____ will take the appropriate:

_____ Criterion Referenced Test; _____ Norm Referenced Test

Name of test:

_____

It is recommended by the Special Education IEP/Placement Committee that this student:

_____ be tested with no modifications.

_____ be tested with the modifications selected below.

_____ not be tested at this time (state reason):

_____

_____

Indicate all modifications recommended for this student.

Scheduling Modifications

Tests should be administered:

_____ at the time of day most beneficial to student (specify):

_____

    ☙ *Late morning is usually best due to slow arousal and decline in attention and physical and mental energy in the afternoon.*

_____ in several sessions of up to _____ minutes with movement opportunities between sessions. (e.g. 20 minutes)

_____ with extended time limits.

Setting Modifications

Tests should be administered:

_____ individually or in a small group.

> 🐾 *Small groups work best for ADHD/TS/OCD student.*

_____ behind a screen.

> 🐾 *This is to release tics and movement without embarrassment.*

_____ in the special education classroom or other school setting, if needed (specify):

_____

_____ by student's special education teacher.

Format and Equipment Modifications

Tests should be administered using:

_____ word banks for fill-in-the blank tests.

_____ placemarkers, graph paper, etc.

_____ a calculator.

_____ noise buffers.

Recording Modifications

The student may:

_____ mark answers in test booklets or on computer.

> 🐾 *Marking computer scorable answer sheets is difficult for these students.*

_____ have answers recorded, recopied or verified by assistant.

Placement

■ The decision to place the student in a specific special education program should be made at the IEP meeting by the parents and a group of professionals capable of interpreting the test results and relating those results to appropriate options.

■ The placement decision should be based on the services that have been determined to be needed by the student rather than on general knowledge of students with similar handicapping conditions.

■ When deciding the best placement for the student, the school must insure that the placement decision is made in such a way that the student's education will be, to the extent appropriate, with students who are not handicapped.

■ Within the school district there must be a variety of placement options and related services available. From these alternatives a placement selection should be as similar to a regular education placement as possible, one in which the student is best able to function and should be near the home.

■ The initial decision for a new placement should include a trial period. That is, any new placement should be for no longer than three months. Following the trial period, a review of the appropriateness of the placement should be made.

■ Any placement or service to be provided must be at public expense. This includes special programs, special materials or equipment, testing, transportation, etc.

■ Should the parents seek a due process hearing because of disagreement with the school system about the student's placement, the student must remain in the current placement until the hearing and appeals are completed. If the student is not attending school and the parents are seeking admission to a public school, then the student must be placed in a public school until the due process and appeals are completed.

Program Areas

The following program areas for special education are listed and defined by the federal government and each state. The following programs are listed as defined in the state of Georgia regulations and procedures and may not apply to other states.

■ **Specific Learning Disabilities**

A specific learning disability is a disorder in one of the basic psychological processes involved in understanding or in using language, spoken or written, that may manifest itself in an impaired ability to listen, think, speak, read, write, spell or do mathematical calculations.

The term includes such conditions as perceptual handicaps, brain injury, minimal brain dysfunction, dyslexia and developmental aphasia. The term does not include students who have learning problems that are primarily the result of visual, hearing or motor handicaps, intellectual disability, emotional disturbance or environmental, cultural or economic disadvantage.

A significant learning deficit must be demonstrated in one or more of the following areas.

○ Oral expression—use of spoken language to communicate ideas (does not include speech disorders).

○ Listening comprehension—ability to understand spoken language at a level that is age-appropriate.

○ Written expression—ability to communicate ideas effectively in writing with appropriate language (as opposed to merely poor spelling or grammatical errors or poor handwriting).

○ Basic reading skills—including use of word attack and sequencing skills in the process of decoding written symbols.

○ Reading comprehension—process of decoding and understanding the meaning of written language.

○ Mathematics calculation—appropriate processing of numerical symbols to derive results, including spatial awareness of symbol placement and choice of sequence algorithms for operations required.

○ Mathematical reasoning—understanding logical relationships between mathematical concepts and operations, including correct sequencing and spatial/symbolic representation.

■ Emotional and Behavioral Disorders

An emotional and behavioral disorder is an emotional disability characterized by the following:

○ An inability to build or maintain satisfactory interpersonal relationships with peers and/or teachers.

○ An inability to learn which cannot be adequately explained by intellectual, sensory or health factors.

○ Consistent or chronic inappropriate type of behavior or feelings under normal conditions.

○ Displayed pervasive mood of unhappiness or depression.

○ Displayed tendency to develop physical symptoms, pains or unreasonable fears associated with personal or school problems.

A student with an emotional/behavorial disorder exhibits one or more of the above emotionally-based characteristics of sufficient duration, frequency and intensity that it interferes significantly with educational performance to the degree that provision of special education services is necessary. The student's difficulty is emotionally based and cannot be adequately explained by intellectual, cultural, sensory or general health factors.

■ **Speech-Language Impairment**

Speech/language impairment programs provide diagnostic (evaluative), therapeutic (habilitative) and consultative services for students handicapped by speech/language disorders. A speech/language disorder is one in which a communication skill differs so significantly in manner or content from that of peers that it calls attention to itself; disrupts communication or affects emotional, social, intellectual or educational growth. Speech/language disorder refers to impairments in the areas of language, articulation, voice and fluency.

A speech/language impairment may range from mild to profound. Individuals may demonstrate any combination of speech/language impairment. The speech/language disorder may be the primary handicapping condition.

   ○ Articulation disorder

   ○ Fluency disorder

   ○ Language disorder

   ○ Voice disorder

■ **Intellectual Disability**

Intellectual disability refers to significantly subaverage general intellectual functioning, existing concurrently with deficits in adaptive behavior that adversely affect educational performance and is manifested during the developmental period. Significantly subaverage general intellectual functioning is defined as approximately 70 IQ or below as measured by a qualified psychological examiner on individually administered, standardized measures of intelligence.

   ○ Mild Intellectual Disability

   ○ Moderate Intellectual Disability

   ○ Severe Intellectual Disability

   ○ Profound Intellectual Disability

■ **Visual Impairment**

Students to be served include those whose visual impairments interfere with functioning in a regular school program or, for preschool-age children, in learning tasks. Examples are students whose visual impairments may result from congenital defects, eye diseases or injuries to the eye. Visual impairment is determined on the basis of a current examination by an ophthalmologist or optometrist.

   ○ Partially sighted

   ○ Legally blind

   ○ Functionally blind

■ **Hearing Impairment**

A hearing impaired student is one who exhibits a hearing loss that interferes with the acquisition or maintenance of auditory skills necessary for the development of speech, language and academic achievement.

○ Hard of hearing

○ Deaf

■ **Deaf-Blind**

Deaf-blind means concomitant hearing and visual impairments, the combination of which causes such severe communication and other developmental and educational problems that students with both impairments cannot be accommodated in special education programs solely for hearing impairments, visual impairments or severe disabilities.

■ **Orthopedic Impairment**

Orthopedically impaired refers to students whose orthopedic impairments affect their educational performance to a degree that they cannot be educated in regular classes of the public schools on a full-time basis, without the provision of special education services.

■ **Significant Development Delay (ages three through five)**

The state board defines preschool children with disabilities as those three through five-year-old children who meet categorical eligibility, significant developmental delay eligibility or qualify for services by deferred diagnosis.

■ **Autism**

Autism is a developmental disability, generally evident before age three, that adversely affects a student's educational performance and significantly affects developmental rates and sequences, verbal and non-verbal communication and social interaction and participation. Other characteristics often associated with autism are unusual responses to sensory experiences, engagement in repetitive activities and stereotyped movements and resistance to environmental change or change in daily routines.

■ **Traumatic Brain Injury**

Traumatic brain injury is an acquired injury to the brain caused by an external physical force, resulting in total or partial functional disability or psychosocial impairment, or both, that adversely affects the student's educational performance. The term applies to open or closed head injuries resulting in impairments which are immediate or delayed in one or more areas, e.g., cognition, language, memory, attention, reasoning, abstract thinking, judgment, problem solving, sensory, perceptual and motor abilities, psychosocial behavior, physical functions, speech and information processing. These injuries may intensify pre-existing problems in these areas as well. Resulting impairments may be temporary or permanent in nature. The term does not apply to brain injuries that are congenital or degenerative in nature, brain injuries induced by birth trauma or those resulting from internal occurrences such as stroke, tumor or aneurysm.

■ **Other Health Impairment**

○ *Definition*

Other health impairment (OHI) refers to students whose chronic or acute health problems result in limited strength, vitality or alertness and adversely affect their educational performance to the degree that the student requires special education. Examples may include, but are not limited to, AIDS, tuberculosis, asthma, diabetes, heart condition, seizure disorder, leukemia, nephritis, sickle cell anemia, lead poisoning, Attention Deficit Disorder and Tourette syndrome.

🐾 *OCD is also considered a chronic health problem.*

The other health impaired student exhibits a medically diagnosed physical condition of a permanent, temporary or intermittent nature that causes reduced efficiency in school participation and performance. Limitations on the student due to health impairment may take the form of extended absences, inability to attend a full academic schedule and/or inability to attend to tasks for the same length of time as peers of the same age and grade expectancy level and requires the provision of specialized instructional services and modifications in order to participate in the school program.

○ *Eligibility and Placement*

Every effort should be made to adapt the regular classroom environment to meet the needs of students with health impairments.

Any student with impaired health who, after appropriate intervention(s) in the regular classroom, is thought to need consideration for special education services shall be referred by the student support team to the local special education program and afforded all rights under due process. Documentation must be provided through the student support team's report that alternative strategies and modifications were attempted, but proved inappropriate to meet the student's educational needs.

In cases where the student support team is bypassed due to the nature and severity of the health impairment, this decision shall be clearly documented.

In cases of students with infectious diseases, decisions on environmental restrictions shall be made through a team process, involving a student's parent(s)/guardian(s) and personal physician, school officials and public health personnel. These decisions shall be reviewed annually or more frequently if removal of the student from the school environment has been implemented.

Evaluation for eligibility shall include:

■ A current medical evaluation from a licensed physician. This evaluation shall confirm the following:

   • Diagnosis/prognosis of the student's health impairment.

   • Information about medications, special health care procedures, special diet or activity restrictions.

The evaluation report used for initial eligibility shall be current within one year and subsequent reports for reevaluation shall be obtained at least every three years.

This report should be updated more frequently than yearly if warranted by the prognosis of the specific health impairment.

■ A comprehensive developmental or educational assessment that documents the adverse effects of the health impairment on the student's educational progress. Assessments should document a deficit in pre-academic, academic, social/behavioral, communication or motor development resulting from the health impairment.

○ *Delivery of Services*

The educational needs of some students with health impairments may be met through placement in a regular education program with modifications and support services that are not considered special education.

A student meeting eligibility criteria as other health impaired and needing special education services on a resource or self-contained basis may receive those services through one of the following programs, based on documentation of the needs described below through assessment and the development of the student's IEP.

■ *Orthopedic Impairment* — based on impairments in orthopedic functioning which limit abilities to participate in the academic setting in terms of ambulation, posture and/or body use, as determined by an evaluation of motor development.

■ *Specific Learning Disabilities* — based on observed, documented deficits in basic learning behavior(s) not related to below average cognitive functioning that are demonstrated by a discrepancy between actual achievement and expected performance. These deficits could include problems in attending, discrimination/perception, sensory integration, organization, sequencing, short-term memory, long-term memory and/or conceptualization/reasoning.

■ *Emotional and Behavioral Disorders* — based on observed, documented emotional difficulties manifested within the school environment related to peer or teacher relationships, inappropriate behaviors or mood demonstrations or manifestation of physical symptoms or fears.

■ *Mild Intellectual Disability* — based on subaverage general intellectual functioning as measured by appropriate psychological evaluations, existing concurrently with deficits in adaptive behavior which adversely affect educational performance.

Students with health impairments functioning with moderate, severe or profound intellectual disabilities should receive services through the programs for which they are eligible. Likewise, other students with health impairments who demonstrate primary disabilities in the areas of hearing or vision impairments or severe emotional and behavioral disorders should receive services through those programs as eligible.

Special education services should be provided to other health impaired students on a short-term, long-term or intermittent basis, in classroom and/or hospital/homebound settings, depending on individual needs documented in the IEP.

The final placement decision, including delivery model and personnel to provide services, shall be clearly documented in minutes or other student records. Adapted physical education and/or related services should be provided as necessary.

○ *Additional Information*

Both regular and special education programs should be adapted when appropriate to meet the unique needs of students with health impairments. Adaptations may include the following:

- A shortened school day/week

- Provision of special equipment

- Remedial education programs

- Individual consultation

- Use of assistive technology

When ADHD/ADD/TS/OCD alone are not recognized placement categories under IDEA and state special education regulations, they may be handicapping conditions under Section 504, thereby entitling the student to special services, either in regular education or special education. During the process of amending IDEA in 1990, Congress debated an amendment to establish Attention Deficit Disorder (ADD) as a new eligibility category, but decided against it. However, Congress instructed the federal Department of Education to accept comments from the public concerning the issue. The Department received more than 2000 written statements. In an attempt to clarify the requirements for serving students with ADD, a memorandum was jointly issued on September 16, 1991, by the Department of Education's Office of Special Education and Rehabilitative Services (the division that oversees IDEA), the Office for Civil Rights (the division that oversees Section 504) and the Office of Elementary and Secondary Education. A copy of that memorandum is included in the appendix (p. 237).

Section VI
Modifications for College Admissions Testing

Modifications for College Admissions Testing

Scholastic Aptitude Tests[51]

The College Entrance Examination Board (CEEB) provides special testing arrangements and modifications for students with disabilities in order to minimize the effects of disabilities on test performance. Nonstandard testing arrangements are available for the PSAT/NMSQT and SAT Program Tests (SAT I Reasoning Test and SAT II Subject Tests). The following information is presented in the "SAT Services for Students with Disabilities, Brochure of Supplemental Information."

Eligibility

■ To be eligible for special testing arrangements, the student must have:

○ a disability that necessitates special test accommodations,

○ documentation on file at school (IEP, 504 plan, or evaluation by a qualified professional that states a diagnosis and need for accommodations), and

○ accommodations for classroom tests and/or standardized tests provided by the school.

Exceptions. A student with a documented disability who does not receive accommodations in school may be eligible for special accommodations on the PSAT/NMSQT or an SAT Program Test. To request such an exception, the test coordinator or appropriate school official may send (1) a letter explaining why the student needs special testing accommodations *and* (2) an evaluation and recommendation from a qualified professional (a person licensed or certified to diagnose the student's disability). A panel of qualified professionals will review the request.

Testing Modifications

■ The designation "Nonstandard Administration" is written on the score report to reflect special arrangements.

■ The result of a four-year research project by the College Board, Educational Testing Service, and the Graduate Record Examinations (GRE) indicated that test scores were comparable measures of cognitive abilities of both handicapped and non-handicapped test takers and that admission decisions were related to test scores and prior grades in much the same manner for handicapped and non-handicapped applicants.[52]

> ❧ *It is recommended by the authors that the ADHD/ADD/TS/OCD student take the PSAT/NMSQT in both the tenth and eleventh grades and take the SAT I one or two years prior to submitting the college entrance application. This will help the student*

---

[51] The following information has been provided by Educational Testing Services (ETS).

[52] Wilingham et.al., <u>Testing handicapped people</u>. Needham Heights, MA: Allyn and Bacon.

become familiar with the test format and thereby reduce test anxiety. The student should take the test at least two times, once under standard administrative conditions and once with needed modifications. The scores are cumulative and all are reported.

■ Plan A (Special Accommodations) SAT I and SAT II

Plan A is available to students with documented hearing, learning, physical, and/or visual disabilities and permits special test editions, special answer sheets, extended testing time, testing aids (reader, recorder, abacus, calculator and typewriter) and flexible test dates.

○ *Test Format*

The SAT I is available in five editions: regular type, large type, braille, cassette and script. Subject Tests are available in regular type, large type and braille. Responses may be recorded on machine-scannable or large block answer sheets. The students may use a reader or a person to record the answers.

○ *Test Administration*

■ The SAT I may be administered with extended time. Each section of the test must be completed the day it is started. It is not necessary to use all the allotted time.

■ Extended time is also available for Subject Tests. Subject Tests may be administered over three consecutive days. Each Subject Test must be completed the day it is started.

■ The SAT II: Writing Test must be taken at a national test center. Extended time is available.

■ The tests may be taken in a separate room.

■ Aids include a reader, recorder, abacus or typewriter.

■ Tests are administered in the student's high school.

■ Plan B (SAT I Extended Time Only)

Plan B is available to students with documented learning disabilities and provides no accommodation except additional testing time for the SAT I. Under Plan B, students are allowed one and one-half hours of additional testing time (a total of four and one-half hours). No aids are permitted.

■ Requirements vary from year to year. Further information can be obtained from:

SAT Services for Students with Disabilities
P.O. Box 6226
Princeton, NJ 08541-6226
(609) 771-7137
(609) 822-4118

ACT Assessment[53]

The ACT Assessment also provides special arrangements and modifications for students with disabilities. The following summarizes information found in the form "Request for ACT Assessment Special Testing."

Eligibility

- To be eligible, a student must have a current documented disability diagnosed or reconfirmed within the last three years.

- An Individual Education Plan or 504 plan on file at the school within the last three years can serve as confirmation of a handicapping condition.

- The application asks for information about the diagnosis, the requested ACT accommodations and the current accommodations allowed for classroom and standardized tests.

Testing Modifications

Test Format

- The formats available are regular-type, large-type, braille, reader's script, audio cassette with regular copy and audio cassette with raised line/braille tables and illustrations.

Test Administration

- Tests are normally administered at the student's high school. Supervisor qualifications are listed in the "Request for ACT Assessment Special Testing."

- Extended time is available if the need is supported by the documentation. The extension allowed varies according to disability and test format. If extended time is approved, each of the four tests may be administered on a different day. Each test must, however, be completed on the day it is started.

- Students with documented motor or visual disabilities may have assistance marking the responses.

- A calculator may be used if the school allows the same modification.

- Requirements and procedures may vary from year to year. Further information and a copy of the current "Request for ACT Assessment Special Testing" should be obtained from:

Special Testing - 61
Act Universal Testing
P.O. Box 4028
Iowa City, IA 52243-4028
Ph. (319) 337-1332
Fax (319) 337-1285

---

[53]   The following information has been provided by ACT.

Section VII
Federal Laws
Pertaining to Handicapped Students

Federal Laws Pertaining to Handicapped Students[54]

Individuals with Disabilities Education Act (IDEA)

The Individuals with Disabilities Education Act (IDEA), U.S. Public Law 94-142 Part B requires a free appropriate public education in the least restrictive environment for all handicapped children from pre-school through high school.

Key Provisions of the Law

Identification. The state and local education agencies must actively seek out and identify children who have special education needs (Child Find).

Evaluation. The child must be evaluated appropriately prior to placement. All methods used for testing and evaluation must be racially and culturally non-discriminatory and must be in the primary language or "mode of communication" of the child. No one test may be the determining factor for placement.

Individualized Education Plan (IEP). An IEP must be prepared for each child based on each child's individual educational needs.

Parents. The parents are equal participants in the decision-making process and students may be participants in their IEP development.

Related Services. Related services must be provided on an individualized basis to assist the child to benefit from special education.

Least Restrictive Environment. The child must be educated to the maximum extent appropriate with children who are non-handicapped. The child must be educated in more restrictive (different) settings only when less restrictive alternatives are not appropriate.

Private School. When the child is placed in a private school by state or local education agencies in order to receive an appropriate education, this must be done at no cost to the parents; private school programs must meet standards set by law.

Pre-school. The law encourages the establishment of pre-school programs by creating a special incentive grant for ages 0-5 years.

Due Process. Due process rights of the parents and the child must be guaranteed by states and localities, including the right to notification, a hearing and appeal procedures.

Advisory Board. Each state must set up an advisory board which includes handicapped individuals, teachers and parents of handicapped children.

---

[54] The information in this section was prepared by Parents Educating Parents (PEP) and presented in "On Public Law 94-142 The Education for All Handicapped Children Act." This information has been edited and supplemented by the present authors.

Funds. P.L. 94-142 provides flow through funds to supplement state and local program efforts. Funds may be withheld for non-compliance.

Records. Parents have access to their child's educational records and can request that they be amended.

Rights as Parents of a Handicapped Student

The Individuals with Disabilities Education Act includes numerous rights to which the parents are entitled. These rights were summarized by PEP in the following terms:

Notice. Before the student is tested or placed in a special educational program, parents have the right to be notified of what the school plans to do.

Consent. Parents must give consent before special tests are conducted and before the student is placed in a special educational program.

Evaluation. Parents have the right to a full evaluation of the student's individual educational needs.

Records. Parents have the right to know what records are kept on the student and a right to see them.

Confidentiality of Information. With the exception of certain individuals (school officials, for example, and teachers with legitimate educational interests), no one may see the student's record unless the parent has given written permission.

Least Restrictive Environment. Parents have the right to have the student educated with non-handicapped children to the maximum extent appropriate.

Hearings. If at any point along the way, the parents do not agree with the way the school is dealing with the student, they have the right to request a hearing. This means that the parents may seek a formal review if they and the school cannot reach an agreement concerning identification, evaluation or educational placement of the student.

Rehabilitation Act of 1973 (Public Law 93-112)

This law was created to insure affirmative action in employment and non-discrimination because of a handicapping condition and was amended in 1974, 1978 and 1984. It is usually referred to by specific sections which address different issues:

Section 501 - Employment of Handicapped Individuals

Section 502 - Architectural and Transportation Board Compliance

Section 503 - Employment under Federal Contracts

Section 504 - Non-discrimination under Federal Grants (Civil Rights Act)

Federal Grants (Section 504)

This section reads as follows: "No otherwise qualified handicapped individual... shall solely by reason of his handicap; be excluded from participation in, be denied the benefits of or be subjected to discrimination under any program or activity receiving federal assistance."

Major Differences in P.L. 94-142 and Section 504

Enforcement. As an education statute, enforcement of P.L. 94-142 is administered by the Office of Special Education of the U.S. Department of Education and each state department of education that subscribes to P.L. 94-142. Because Section 504 is a civil rights statute, enforcement is the responsibility of the Office for Civil Rights of the U.S. Department of Education.

Federal Funding. P.L. 94-142 provides federal funding in the form of grants to assist in education of handicapped children and to assist in monitoring these programs. Section 504, as a civil rights law, is concerned with a broader range of issues, including employment discrimination, education at all levels and accessibility. Section 504 does not furnish federal funds for implementation of its requirements. However, because Section 504 covers recipients of federal funds and P.L. 94-142 subscribers are recipients of federal funds, all recipients of P.L. 94-142 funds are required to meet the mandates of Section 504.

Definition of Handicap. Section 504 deals with a very broad definition of handicapped persons which includes both actual and perceived handicaps, as well as some conditions that are not normally considered to be handicapping conditions (in educational terms). This definition includes persons who may be amputees, temporarily handicapped, wheelchair-bound or have cancer or other serious physical diseases yet do not need special education services. In contrast, the definition of a "handicapped child" in P.L. 94-142 is much more specific and focuses on educational and medical conditions that have been appropriately identified and evaluated.

Age Requirements. One of the specific criteria of Section 504 is that services be provided to handicapped persons to "whom the state is required to provide a 'free appropriate education' under Section 612 of the Education of the Handicapped Act." P.L. 94-142 is more specific than Section 504 in that it specifies the ages when services must be provided. It requires that states provide education to all handicapped students between three and twenty-one. On the other hand, P.L. 94-142 provides certain flexibility to the state in meeting those specific requirements. State law or practice or any court order takes precedence regarding the provision of services to three to five and eighteen to twenty-one year old students.

Family Educational Rights and Privacy Act of 1976 (FERPA)

The Family Educational Rights and Privacy Act of 1976 is also known as the Buckley Amendment.

FERPA provides for confidentiality of all school records and ensures parents and eligible students (18 years or older) the right to review and inspect any educational records or copies of the records that pertain to the student. Sections of the Buckley Amendment were incorporated into P.L. 94-142 and guarantee the right to examine and review all records that relate to identification, education and placement. School personnel must provide appropriate interpretations of the records so that the parents clearly understand what is contained in the records.

The law allows parents the right to challenge and amend any educational record that they consider inaccurate, misleading or in violation of the privacy or rights of the student. If the school decides not to amend the record as requested, the school informs the parents of their right to a hearing. If it is determined at a hearing that the record is inaccurate, misleading or violates the rights of the student, the school must amend the record. If, however, it is decided that the record is accurate, parents have the right to add a written statement to the record expressing their objections.

The Buckley Amendment also allows parents and eligible students the right to release the student's records to a third party. Before the school can reveal any information contained in the records, the parents must provide written consent indicating the specific educational records to be disclosed, the purpose of the disclosure and the name of the person to whom the records are to be released.

The Educational Rights and Privacy Act Office in Washington, DC, enforces the rights granted in the Buckley Amendment.

Section VIII
Appendices

Appendix A:
Educational Strategies and Work Samples

Shark Theory of Arousal
Hand Drawing

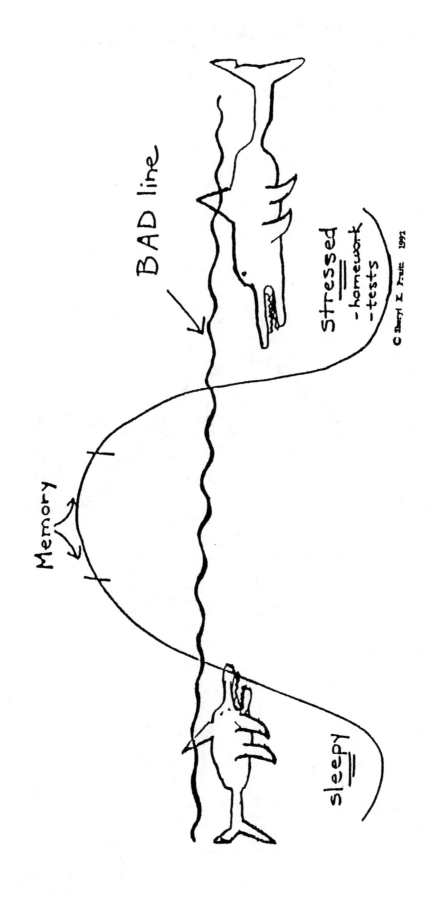

BAD line

Memory

Stressed
- homework
- tests

sleepy

© Sheryl K. Pruitt 1992

Sharks drawn by Michael, age 8
and Michael, age 12
© 1991 Sheryl K. Pruitt, M.Ed.

Shark Theory of Arousal
Computer Drawing

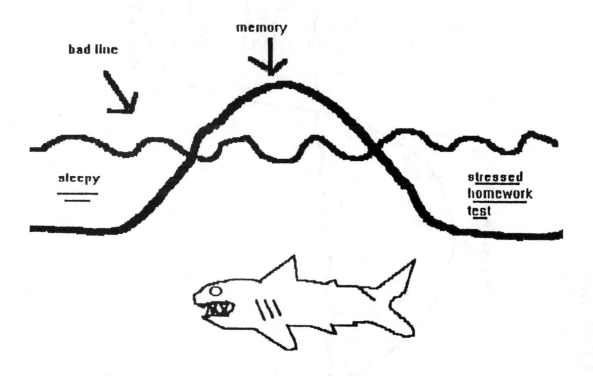

bad line

memory

sleepy

stressed
homework
test

Drawing by Daniel, age 14
© 1992 Sheryl K. Pruitt, M.Ed.

The Story of Mother Vowel

"The Story of Mother Vowel" was developed by Sheryl K. Pruitt and Vickie Rhinehart, Parkaire Consultants, Inc., 1988. The student quickly learns the story and enjoys retelling it. The meaningful story assists the student with the retrieval of the abstract sounds of the short (baby) vowels. As the student reads, the teacher cues with the appropriate hand signal from "The Story of Mother Vowel." Hand signals also allow the student to demonstrate that the student knows the vowel sound, but needs additional time to retrieve and produce the sound.

Mother Vowel and her five babies live on a farm. The babies' names are "a," "e," "i," "o," and "u." The babies are too young to talk and only make sounds. Poor mother vowel does not always know what they want.

One day Baby "a" was hungry and saw the apple tree. Pointing to the apple tree with her arm raised up in the air, Baby "a" began to shout, "Aaaaaaaaaaaaaaa!" as in the beginning sound of "apple." Mother Vowel was thrilled to know that Baby "a" would raise her hand and shout, "Aaaaaaaaaaaaaaa!" each time she wanted an apple. [A mirror is helpful to allow the student to see the mouth pull way back when making the (short) baby "aaaa" sound.]

   Hand signal: Raise hand and wave as if trying to reach an apple.

Baby "e" loved scrambled eggs. Mother Vowel scrambled a dozen eggs. She put them on the dining room table when all of a sudden the phone rang in the kitchen. While Mother Vowel was talking on the phone, Baby "e" climbed up onto the table and ate all twelve of the eggs. When Mother Vowel returned from the kitchen, Baby "e" was holding his hands on his stomach saying, "Eeeeeeeeeeeeeh!" as in the beginning sound of egg. Boy! Did his stomach ache! If anyone tried to serve Baby "e" eggs, he would hold his stomach and say, "Eeeeeeeeeeeeeh!"

   Hand signal: Hold stomach with both hands and lean over as if stomach aches.

Baby "i" was holding onto the fence at the pig sty looking at the pigs. All of a sudden he slipped and fell head first into the pig sty. He was covered from head to toe in mud. He ran straight to Mother Vowel and said, "Iiiiiiiiiiiicky, iiiiiiiiiiicky, iiiiiiiiiiicky!" while shaking the pig's mud off his hands. As he said, "Icky!" the skin on his nose wrinkled up. (The teacher needs to make a wrinkled nose and have the student feel the wrinkles on the nose of both the student and the teacher.) Whenever Baby "i" saw the pigs, he would shake his hands and say, "Icky, icky, icky!"

   Hand signal: Shake hands with fingers down as if shaking off mud.

Mother Vowel called all the babies to come see the new animal that they were going to raise on the farm. Baby "o" crawled out and could not believe her eyes. She looked up, and looked up, and looked up, and saw the biggest bird she had ever seen in her whole life. There was an ostrich! She was so surprised at the size of this bird that as she looked up, her head went further and further back, and all she could say was, "Aaahhhhhhhhhhhhh!" From that day on, every time she saw the ostrich she would pull her head back and say, "Aaahhhhhhhhhh!"

   Head signal: Slowly pull head back all the way as if looking up at an ostrich.

There is always one mischievous one in every crowd. Baby "u" crawled into Mother Vowel's closet, saw her sewing kit and pulled out her scissors. He then spotted her new umbrella and began cutting it up. In walked Mother Vowel looking for her umbrella and saw what Baby "u" was doing. She shook her finger at him and said, "UH! UH! UH!" From then on, every time it rained and Mother Vowel got out her umbrella, Baby "u" shook his finger and said, "UH! UH! UH!"

> Hand signal: Shake finger as if saying, "Naughty, naughty!"

After the consonant and vowel sounds are mastered, the student is ready to read simple words and sentences written with a color cuing system. The vowels are red to attract attention, the consonants are black, the blends are green. Once the student is ready for the word families, they are written in blue.

Abstract rules are very difficult for students with neurological impairments to learn. The fewer and the more meaningful the better. The first phonetic rule is: when the baby vowels start walking they need to hold both of their parents' (consonants) hands. The baby is not old enough to go out walking by himself. One vowel out walking with a consonant (parent) on either side equals the short, "baby" name. The second rule is: as the baby learns to walk better, he can let go of one of his parents and knows his name, so the vowel becomes long, "more grown-up." The vowel is able to go out walking with vowel friends when he knows his grown-up letter name and has learned good manners. For example, if two vowels are walking together, only the first one speaks in order to be polite and not talk at the same time as his friend.

Some consonants like to come over frequently and play on the farm. Three are close cousins of the Vowel family, "y", "w", and "r." Cousin "y" never could decide if he was a consonant or a vowel. He even bought two hats, one black (consonant) and one red (vowel). He wears his black hat at the beginning of words or syllables. At other times he wears his red hat and pretends he is a grown-up vowel, such as in "by," or a second vowel walking after "a," such as in "day."

Cousin "w" is a scamp! He likes to make all the rules go crazy. He pretends he is a vowel when he follows "o" around and makes her say her grown-up name, such as in "snow." Then suddenly he pinches her and makes her say "ow!" "W" can then become sympathetic to "o" and get with his friend "a" and make her feel better by saying, "Awwwwwwwwwwww!"

Cousin "r" likes to play tiger games. He chases "e," "i," and "u" all over, growling, "rrrrrrrrrrrrrhh!" such as in "her," "dirt" and "hurt."

> Hand Signal: Cue students to bend pointer finger to make a tiger's claw while making a growling sound, "rrrrrrrrrrrrrhhh!"

As the vowels get older romance blooms! Cousin "r" falls in love with "a." "R" always acts grown-up when he follows "a" and says his grown-up name, as in "car." "R" can say his baby name, "rrrrrrrrrrrrhhh," OR his grown-up sound "R."

Visual Proofreading Strategies

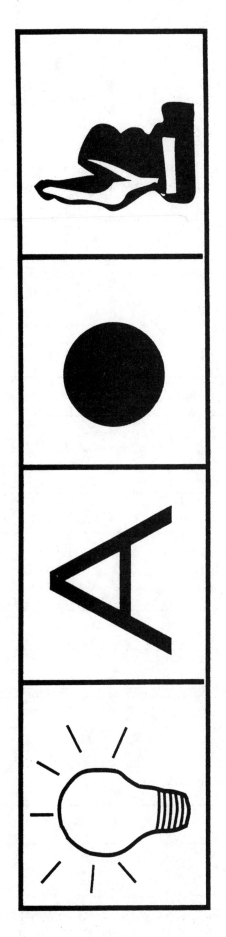

© Sheryl K. Pruitt 1992

Story Organizer _____

Name:_____ **Date:**_____

Characters: **Setting:**

_____   Time: Place:

_____   _____   _____

_____   _____   _____

_____

Problem:

_____

_____

Goal:

_____

_____

Action:

_____

_____

_____

_____

Outcome:

_____

_____

©Dottie Pettis, 1993

The Missing Medication

This story was written by Kyle, an OCD/TS/ADHD student, when allowed to use the computer to compose his story for a class assignment. Kyle's attempt to complete the assignment on the provided form in pencil appears on page 90.

Chapter 1
The Missing Medication

On Saturday, the first of the month, Bess Justice was on her way on a field trip with her mother, Susan. Bess's father, a reporter for the local TV news, was at work that day and the house was empty except for the family dog. Bess's father went to work on that Saturday to train a new camera operator by the name of Cain. During the noontime newscast Cain became ill and went home early. Also during the day while everyone was gone the dog was heard barking several times.

A neighbor was working in her garden when she noticed the dog barking. The neighbor checked the front and back door of the Justice's house and all seemed safe. She then looked inside the window and saw a shadow of a person walking into the kitchen. She heard a cabinet door slam. She ran home as quickly as she could and called the police. After she called the police she called Mr. Justice at the TV station.

While the neighbor was on the phone to Mr. Justice, Bess and her mother came home. Everything looked fine at the house. Susan then called her husband at work who then told her that he got a call from their neighbor just a few minutes earlier that someone was in the house and she should get out of the house immediately. Mr. Justice said that he was trying to leave but he had trouble finding his keys. He then told Susan that he found his keys and would meet her and the police at the neighbor's house.

Mr. Justice, Susan and Bess along with the police searched the house. The only thing missing was Bess's medicine for her Tourette syndrome.

Chapter 2
Meeting Detective Pruitt

As they finished the search of the house looking for anything else that might have been stolen, Detective Pruitt introduced herself to the Justice family and told Bess that she would help find her medication.

Detective Pruitt told Bess that the burglar might have thought that the pills were drugs that would make him high; obviously he was wrong.

Bess then called her friends with Tourette syndrome to come over to meet Detective Pruitt. Eric, Michael, Jon, Patrick, Elizabeth and Casey all came over to meet Detective Pruitt. Detective Pruitt told the children to look for clues, like finger prints, something the burglar might have left behind or a strange car in the neighborhood earlier in the day.

Detective Pruitt called Dr. Dornbush to ask her what would happen if someone took the medication for Tourette syndrome. Dr. Dornbush told Detective Pruitt that if someone took too much of the medicine that person's heart might quit beating and they could die. If they took just a little bit the person would probably get sleepy.

Detective Pruitt finished her search of the house and told the kids to start their search for clues.

Chapter 3
Searching For Clues

Bess knew that her dog only barked at strangers. So, she told Detective Pruitt that the thief must be a stranger, not from her neighborhood. Mr. Justice also told Detective Pruitt that his keys were misplaced earlier in the day.

While the kids were searching for clues the police were checking the fingerprints they had found to their computer records. Michael then came running in to tell Detective Pruitt that one of the other neighbors had seen a strange blue car with a white stripe down the middle earlier in the day. Mr. Justice then said that the new camera operator at the TV station had a car like that and his name was Cain and he said he was sick and left earlier in the day.

Detective Pruitt decided to set a trap. She had Mr. Justice call Cain and invite him over to the house.

Chapter 4
Mystery Solved - Case Closed

Cain arrived at the Justice's house within the hour. The minute he got there the dog began barking and would not stop even though Bess tried to get him to quit.

When Cain came in the kids noticed that he was yawning and yawning. Cain was surprised to see Detective Pruitt at the Justice's house. When he did see her he ran to his car only to find that the kids had put Bess's dog in his car. He was so scared that he ran back into the house and Detective Pruitt captured him. When Detective Pruitt searched Cain she found a key that would open the front door of the Justice's house. Cain admitted that he had stolen the drugs and returned the container with the remaining medicine.

The kids then explained what Tourette syndrome was to Cain and that the medicine they take is a helpful drug not a bad drug and if he took too much it could have made his heart stop and he could have died.

Addition Fact Strategies

Present these strategies to the students in the order listed below.

To Add:	Strategy:
0	The answer is the other number.
1	Go up one. If not automatic: Practice with manipulatives. Practice rote counting. Play games to drill "What number comes after ____?"
2	Go up two. Start counting audibly - for 5+2, think "5" and say, "6...7." Or, use 2 dots to count up: 5+2. Gradually fade auditory and visual cues.
10	Put a "1" in front of the other number. Do examples and have students discover the pattern. Use visual cues and then fade.
9	Add 10 and go down one. Demonstrate with manipulatives so students see why it works. Start by writing the number you get when 10 is added; gradually fade visual cue.
the doubles: 9+9=18 8+8=16 7+7=14 6+6=12 5+5=10	First, be sure students can count by 2's efficiently. Use manipulatives to demonstrate the relationship between these facts. Write this set of facts as shown, with 9+9 at the top. Help students to visualize the facts in order. When students have learned one fact, use it to help them remember the next one. Ex: "If 5+5=10, what is 6+6?" Use similar principles for 3+3 and 4+4.
the doubles plus one: 3+4= 7 4+5= 9 5+6=11 6+7=13 7+8=15 8+9=17	Be sure "the doubles" are automatic before going on to this strategy. Use manipulatives to demonstrate. Ex: "You know 5+5=10. Let's add one more. 5+6 must be 11." Use the cue, "Which one of the doubles is it next to?" Teach the student to verbalize, "That's easy! I know 6+6=12, so 6+7 must be 13." Even after students begin to get the answer automatically, have them tell you their thinking process. It reduces impulsivity and teaches self-checking.
ways to make 10: 10+0=10 9+1=10 8+2=10 7+3=10 6+4=10 5+5=10	These combinations are very important! Knowing them automatically will help with subtraction, adding columns, making change and more. Drill using fingers, abacus, games with number pairs which add up to 10, etc. Be sure to include practice with one missing addend: 9+__=10.
5+7 5+8	To solve 5+7, think, "5+5=10 and 2 more is 12." To solve 5+8, think, "5+5=10 and 3 more is 13."

3+5
3+6
3+8
4+7
	When students have mastered the above strategies, only a few facts remain.
	Help students come up with strategies that work best for them.
	   Ex: for 6+8, think of 6+6 and go up 2;
	      for 4+7, think of 3+7 and go up 1.
	
	Compiled by Donna Cherry, 1993

Multiplication Facts Strategies _____

Present these strategies to the students in the order listed below.
*Master one strategy before going on to another.
*Remind students to cue themselves, "What's my strategy?" before giving an answer.

To X by:	Strategy:
0	The answer is always 0.
1	The answer is the other number.
2	Double the other number. See addition strategies for doubles. This method is more efficient than counting by 2's and prepares students for the 4's strategy below.
5	Look at the clock. For example, when the big hand is on the 6, it is 30 minutes after, so 5x6=30. Pointing to numerals on the classroom clock, ask students, "If the big hand is on the __, it is how many minutes after?" Drill the 3, 6, 9 and 12 first. Then work on the numbers in between. Later, practice using a quickly drawn clock. Finally, encourage students to visualize the clock and solve multiplication problems.
9	Finger trick. Palms down, assign a number to each finger from 1-10 (left to right). For 9x4, bend down finger number 4. There will be 3 fingers to the left of the bent finger, and 6 fingers to the right, so the answer is 36. Try other examples. Practice until students can solve automatically - without counting fingers. (source unknown)
10	Write the other number and put a zero after it. Later, fade the visual cue.
11	Write the number twice. If students have been exposed to 2 digit multiplication, show them why this works.

Drill the above strategies until the student uses them efficiently before going on to the more difficult strategies below. There are only 15 more facts to master!

3	Count by 3's. Begin with manipulatives - count objects in groups of threes. Then, count on fingers by 3's. Palms down, assign a number to each finger from 1-10 (left to right). As students count, have them wiggle the appropriate finger. Help them associate each finger with the corresponding multiplication problem. Ex: For 3x8, the student will wiggle the 8th finger and say, "24."
4 4x4=16 4x6=24 4x7=28 4x8=32	Double the other number. Then double again. Ex: 4x7 is the same as saying: 7+7=14, and then 14+14=28. Since students have already mastered the doubles, the first step is easy. Most students will need to write down the second step until more automatic. Gradually fade the visual cues.
6x4=24 6x6=36 6x8=48	Say in rhythm. Notice that students now have 2 strategies for 6x4 (see 4's trick).
7x8=56	Think of the two numbers before 7 and 8. Say, "5 . . . 6 . . . 7 . . . 8." The 5 and 6 give you the answer (56).
8x8=64	Starting with 8, count backwards by 2's: 6, 4 - the answer is 64 or *8x8 fell on the floor, when it got up it was 64. (*Leslie Seeley)
That leaves: 7x6=42 7x7=49	Help students invent a strategy for these. Or, practice with backward chaining: Write problem and answer on dry erase board in color of student's choice. Student says the whole problem (ie: 7x7=49). Teacher erases the last numeral. Student replaces the numeral and says the whole problem again. Repeat the procedure, with the teacher erasing the last two, then three, then four characters, etc. Continue until the student can say and write the problem without prompts. If a student makes an error at any point, begin again. Note: Try backward chaining with erasable markers on windows. Or, try using shaving cream on a table. (source unknown)

Compiled by Donna Cherry and Sheryl Pruitt, 1993

Math Editing Cue

© Sheryl K. Pruitt, 1993

Math Ladder

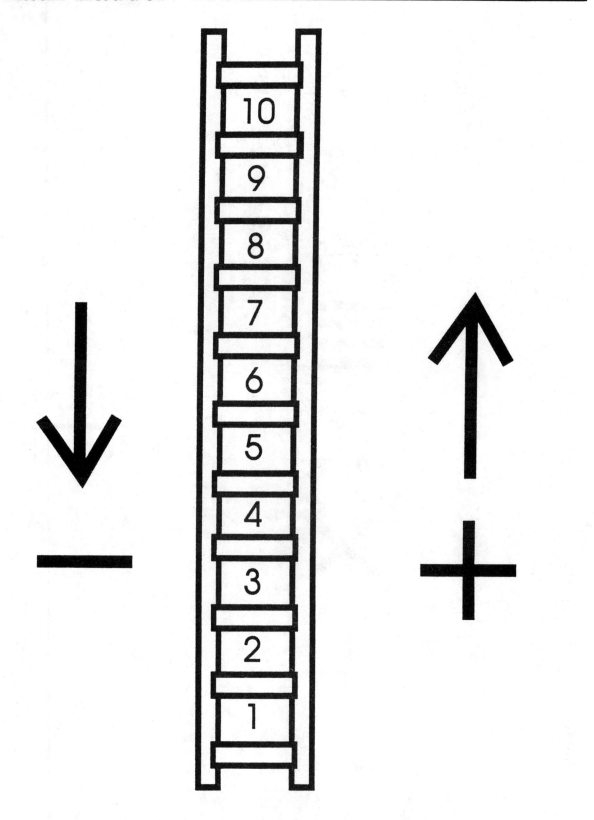

Math Worksheet _____

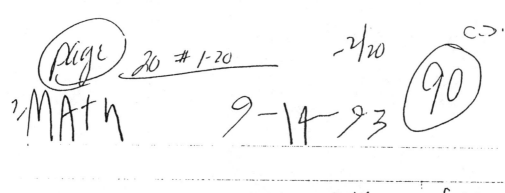

Page 20 # 1-20   -2/20

MATH   9-14-93   (90)

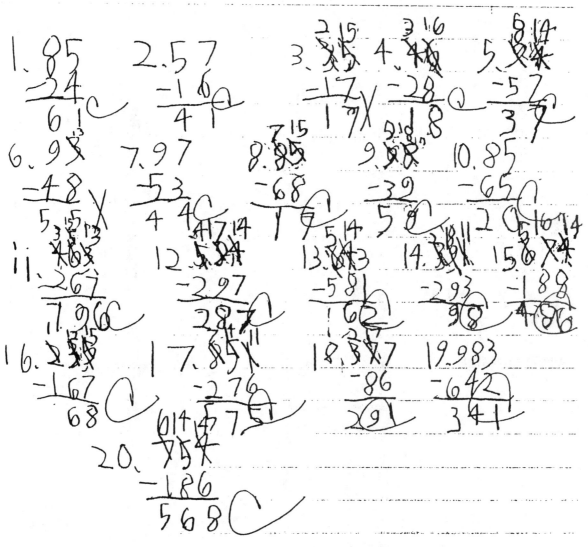

1. 85   2. 57   3. $\cancel{85}$ 4. $\cancel{46}$ 5. $\cancel{84}$
   -34   -16   -17   -28   -57
   61   41   17   18   37

6. $\cancel{96}$ 7. 97   8. $\cancel{85}$ 9. $\cancel{68}$ 10. 85
   -48   -53   -68   -39   -65
   58   44   19   58   20

11. $\cancel{863}$ 12. $\cancel{584}$ 13. $\cancel{843}$ 14. $\cancel{861}$ 15. $\cancel{874}$
    -267   -297   -58   -293   -188
    196   287   162   98   486

16. $\cancel{835}$ 17. $\cancel{853}$ 18. $\cancel{877}$ 19. 983
    -167   -276   -86   -642
    68   77   91   341

20. $\cancel{854}$
    -186
    568

Appendix B:
Computer Software

Computer Software _____

The information in this section was researched and compiled by Marcia D. Rothschild, M.Ed., October, 1994.

The software packages in the following list are suggested as appropriate to address a variety of specific personal, perceptual and academic needs. This list is not intended to be exhaustive, since excellent programs are being published every day. Rather, the purpose is to provide a starting point for selecting high quality, easily obtainable software that will help students achieve success both in academic and extra-curricular endeavors.

The prices listed here are estimates based on surveys of shelf prices in software stores and on selected catalog prices. Actual prices may vary. If a program is available in both floppy disk and CD-ROM formats, the CD-ROM price, which is usually slightly higher, is given.

Always check the system requirements listed on any software package being considered to be sure the program will run on your system. (If your system does not include a sound card, this addition is highly recommended in order to gain the most benefit from many of these programs.) Most of the programs listed here are designed for use on IBM compatible computers (PCs), although some are also available for Mackintosh systems. Titles available only for Mac are so noted. Many promising CD-ROM programs are rapidly appearing on the market. Educational programs often use music, sound effects and speech to enhance learning. Because of its large storage capacity, CD-ROM technology allows access to entire reference libraries and also supports more elaborate use of graphics and sound. If your system does not include a sound card, CD-ROM drive and speakers, you might seriously consider these additions. CD-ROM software will often, **but not always**, run on both Mac and IBM type systems. Programs published on CD-ROM may also be available in floppy disk format. Check your catalog or ask at your software store. On the following pages, the notation following the price indicates the format(s) available for each title.

When selecting software for ADHD/ADD/TS/OCD students, carefully consider each student's preferences, interests, abilities and symptoms. A package that has been successful with one student may not fit the style or needs of another even though both students may have the same academic requirement. For example, some simulation games provide excellent practice in thinking and problem solving but are too open-ended for some students with OCD. These students often cannot stop playing a game unless it comes to a recognizable end. A program which requires rapid, precise cursor moves would not be appropriate for a TS student experiencing motor tics of the hand or fingers. An ADHD/ADD student may not be successful with a program which requires too many correct answers before allowing access to the reward activity.

The following list is alphabetical within sections according to the general skill area being addressed. Each entry concludes with either a list of the specific skills primarily involved or a description of the program, whichever is most appropriate for that entry.

Note: Prices subject to change.

_____

Readiness

Busytown (Richard Scarry)
Publisher: Computer Curriculum Corporation
Price/Format: $42.00; Floppy Disk/CD-ROM
Grade Levels: Pre-K - 1
Skills: Critical thinking, decision-making, interpersonal skills, vocabulary, eye-hand coordination

Early Games
Publisher: Springboard
Price/Format: $35.00; Floppy Disk
Grade Levels: Pre-K - 1
Skills: Visual perception, readiness level letter and number skills, keyboard awareness

Early Math
Publisher: Sierra On-Line, Inc. (Bright Star)
Price/Format: $35.00; Floppy Disk/CD-ROM
Grade Levels: Pre-K - 2
Skills: Counting, number recognition, addition, subtraction, shape recognition, position in space

Learn the Alphabet
Publisher: Top Class
Price/Format: $15.00; Floppy Disk
Grade Levels: K - 1
Skills: Letter recognition, alphabetical order, letter-sound correspondence, auditory and visual discrimination

McGee Series (Three titles now packaged together)
Publisher: Lawrence Publications
Price/Format: $35.00; Floppy Disk
Grade Levels: Pre-K - K
Skills: Combination pack of three McGee programs—NO reading required—excellent for language stimulation, visual tracking, visual memory, cause/effect

Millie's Math House
Publisher: Edmark Corporation
Price/Format: $50.00; Floppy Disk
Grade Levels: Pre-K - K
Skills: Counting, sequencing, number recognition, shape recognition

Putt-Putt Goes to the Moon
Publisher: Humongous Entertainment
Price/Format: $50.00; Floppy Disk/CD-ROM
Grade Levels: Pre-K - 1
Skills: Interpersonal skills, computer literacy

Putt-Putt's Fun Pack
Publisher: Humongous Entertainment
Price/Format: $45.00; Floppy Disk/CD-ROM
Grade Levels: Pre-K - 1
Skills: Visual discrimination, visual memory, sequencing, letter recognition, letter-sound correspondence, thinking skills

Reader Rabbit: Ready for Letters
Publisher: The Learning Company
Price/Format: $40.00; Floppy Disk
Grade Levels: K - 1
Skills: Visual form constancy, visual memory, language, skills—shape matching, comparative words, prepositions

Reading/Language Arts

Ace Reporter: Main Idea and Details
Publisher: Mindplay
Price/Format: $35.00; Floppy Disk
Grade Levels: 2 - 6
Skills: Main idea, details, organizational skills, critical thinking

Bailey's Book House
Publisher: Edmark Corporation
Price/Format: $50.00; Floppy Disk/CD-ROM
Grade Levels: Pre-K - 2
Skills: Letter recognition, word recognition, vocabulary, auditory discrimination, visual discrimination, rhyming, memory

Computer Scrabble
Publisher: Electronic Arts
Price/Format: $40.00; Floppy Disk
Grade Levels: 4 and up
Skills: Vocabulary and spelling. Program includes spellcheck.

Electric Reading Land
Publisher: DCTrue
Price/Format: $33.00; Floppy Disk
Grade Levels: K - 3
Skills: Letter recognition, letter-sound correspondence, auditory attention, auditory discrimination, visual discrimination, phonics, rhyming, sequencing

Fun School: Learning With Freddy Frog
Publisher: Europress Software
Price/Format: $20.00; Floppy Disk
Grade Levels: 1 - 5
Skills: Alphabetical order, antonyms, word recognition. (See also Math and Keyboarding.)

Logic Master
Publisher:	Unicorn
Price/Format:	$35.00; Floppy Disk
Grade Levels:	5 - 12
Skills:	Analogies, logic, thinking--uses words and numbers

Mickey's Crossword Puzzle Maker
Publisher:	Disney Software
Price/Format:	$21.00; Floppy Disk
Grade Levels:	1 - 5
Skills:	Vocabulary, spelling, attention to detail, sequencing

Phonics Pinball
Publisher:	Southwest EdPsych (available through Special Times Catalog)
Price/Format:	$35.00; Floppy Disk
Grade Levels:	1 - 4
Skills:	Letter/sound correspondence, word recognition, phonics, auditory and visual discrimination

Phonics Plus
Publisher:	Stone & Associates
Price/Format:	$28.00; Floppy Disk
Grade Levels:	1 - 3
Skills:	Letter/sound correspondence, word recognition, phonics

Phraze Maze: Grammar Through Phrases
Publisher:	Word Associates
Price/Format:	$45.00; Floppy Disk
Grade Levels:	7 - 12
Skills:	Common parts of speech plus verbals and appositives

Read 'n Roll
Publisher:	Davidson & Associates
Price/Format:	$33.00; Floppy Disk
Grade Levels:	3 - 7
Skills:	Visual tracking, reading comprehension—main idea, details, sequence, inference

Reader Rabbit 1
Publisher:	The Learning Company
Price/Format:	$35.00; Floppy Disk
Grade Levels:	K - 2
Skills:	Letter/sound correspondence, word recognition, consonant/vowel substitution, phonics

Reader Rabbit 2
Publisher:	The Learning Company
Price/Format:	$35.00; Floppy Disk
Grade Levels:	1 - 3
Skills:	Visual memory, compound words, ABC order, rhyming, antonyms

Reading Adventures in Oz
Publisher:	Davidson and Associates
Price/Format:	$35.00; Floppy Disk
Grade Levels:	K - 2
Skills:	General reading comprehension, listening comprehension, letter-sound correspondence, vocabulary, sight words, rhyming, motor planning

Reading and Thinking: Levels III and IV
Publisher:	Intellectual
Price/Format:	$55.00 each; Floppy Disk
Grade Levels:	6 - 8 and 9 - 12
Skills:	Drawing conclusions, deductive and inductive reasoning, convergent and divergent thinking, inferential comprehension

Rusty and Rosie Read With Me: Volume II
Publisher:	Waterford Institute
Price/Format:	$50.00; Floppy Disk
Grade Levels:	Pre-K - 2
Skills:	Letter recognition, letter-sound correspondence, decoding, phonics, rhyming, vocabulary

Sound It Out Land
Publisher:	Conexus
Price/Format:	$40.00; CD-ROM
Grade Levels:	K - 2
Skills:	Auditory attention, auditory discrimination, letter-sound correspondence, phonics, decoding, word recognition, visual tracking

Sound It Out Land 2
Publisher:	Conexus
Price/Format:	$33.00; CD-ROM
Grade Levels:	K - 2
Skills:	Auditory attention, auditory discrimination, letter-sound correspondence, phonics, decoding, sight words

Stickybear Spellgrabber
Publisher:	Weekly Reader
Price/Format:	$35.00; Floppy Disk
Grade Levels:	2 - 4
Description:	Visual spelling drill

Stickybear's Reading Room (Mac only)
Publisher:	Weekly Reader Software
Price/Format:	$60.00; Floppy Disk
Grade Levels:	K - 2
Skills:	Letter/sound correspondence, word recognition, auditory skills, phonics

Super Solvers: Midnight Rescue

Publisher:	The Learning Company
Price/Format:	$35.00; Floppy Disk
Grade Levels:	3 - 5
Skills:	Detail, inferential comprehension, drawing conclusions, deductive reasoning

Super Solvers: Spellbound

Publisher:	The Learning Company
Price/Format:	$33.00; Floppy Disk/CD-ROM
Grade Levels:	2 - 5
Description:	Visually based spelling practice (can use any words desired)

The New Kid on the Block

Publisher:	Broderbund
Price/Format:	$42.00; CD-ROM
Grade Levels:	4 - 8
Skills:	Auditory attention, figurative language, listening comprehension, literature, rhyming

Think Analogy Puzzles, Grades 7 - 12

Publisher:	Critical Thinking Press & Software
Price/Format:	$55.00; Floppy Disk
Grade Levels:	7 - 12 (also available for grades 4 - 7)
Skills:	Part to whole, classification, vocabulary, thinking

Ticket to London (also available for Paris, Spain, Washington, DC)

Publisher:	Blue Lion Software
Price/Format:	$55.00 each; Floppy Disk
Grade Levels:	7 - 12
Skills:	Organization, reasoning, general reading comprehension

Toward Better Reading Skills, Levels E & F

Publisher:	IBM
Price/Format:	$40.00; Floppy Disk
Grade Levels:	7 - 8
Skills:	Figurative language, perceiving emotions, multiple meanings, dictionary skills, vocabulary

Word Attack 3

Publisher:	Davidson and Associates
Price/Format:	$35.00; Floppy Disk
Grade Levels:	5 and up
Skills:	Vocabulary, word recognition, spelling (pronounces words with sound card; allows user to input word lists; prints lists, tests, flash cards)

Word City

Publisher:	Magic Quest
Price/Format:	$33.00; Floppy Disk
Grade Levels:	3 - 8
Skills:	Alphabetical order, spelling, context clues, general reading comprehension, parts of speech, affixes, vocabulary, reading rate

Word Hunt
  Publisher: Computer Easy
  Price/Format: $15.00; Floppy Disk
  Grade Levels: 4 - 12
  Skills: Visual tracking, spelling (involves generating as many words as possible from letters presented in a grid)

Word Munchers
  Publisher: MECC
  Price/Format: $20.00; Floppy Disk
  Grade Levels: 1 - 4
  Skills: Auditory discrimination, phonics (vowel sounds only)

Word Rescue
  Publisher: Shareware Testing Laboratories
  Price/Format: $6.00; Floppy Disk
  Grade Levels: K - 3
  Skills: Word recognition, sight words, decoding, eye-hand coordination, motor planning

Written Language

(See also "Productivity/Test Preparation")

Blackout! A Capitalization Game
  Publisher: (Not Given)
  Price/Format: $50.00; Floppy Disk
  Grade Levels: 3 - 8
  Skills: Capitalization

Big Book Maker: Tall Tales and American Folk Heroes
  Publisher: Pelican
  Price/Format: $50.00; Floppy Disk
  Grade Levels: K - 8
  Description: Story starters. Includes graphics to stimulate written language.

Grammar Baseball (Level A)
  Publisher: Gamco
  Price/Format: $50.00; Floppy Disk
  Grade Levels: 3 - 6
  Description: Drill and practice in correct grammar usage

Grammar Examiner (Within Jr. High Combination Package)
  Publisher: Britannica
  Price/Format: $20.00; Floppy Disk
  Grade Levels: 4 - 12
  Skills: Punctuation, capitalization, word usage

Monsters and Make-Believe
Publisher:	Toucan
Price/Format:	$50.00; Floppy Disk
Grade Levels:	3 - 8
Description:	Story starters.Create whimsical monsters from selection of body parts, then write accompanying stories.

Punctuation Baseball (Level A)
Publisher:	Gamco
Price/Format:	$50.00; Floppy Disk
Grade Levels:	3 - 6
Description:	Drill and practice in punctuation

Super Scoops I and II
Publisher:	Queue
Price/Format:	$45.00; Floppy Disk
Grade Levels:	5 - 12
Skills:	Organization, gathering information, story writing

That's My Story
Publisher:	Mindscape
Price/Format:	$60.00; Floppy Disk
Grade Levels:	2 - 12
Description:	Story starters. Uses low reading level, simple usage,flexibility and structure.

Reader Rabbit 3
Publisher:	The Learning Company
Price:	$35.00; Floppy Disk
Grades:	2 - 5
Description:	Drill and practice program to improve skills in sentence construction, parts of speech, and sequencing

Math

Advanced Math Shop
Publisher:	Scholastic
Price/Format:	$18.00; Floppy Disk
Grade Levels:	7 and up
Skills:	Algebra, fractions, decimals, square roots, consumer problems

Alge-blaster Plus
Publisher:	Davidson and Associates
Price/Format:	$35.00; Floppy Disk
Grade Levels:	7 and up
Skills:	Positive and negative numbers, monomials, polynomials, factoring, graphing

Algebra Word Problems I - VII
   Publisher: Microcomputer Workshops
   Price/Format: $40.00 each (Complete set, $250) ; Floppy Disk
   Grade Levels: 7 and up
   Description: Each package deals with a particular type of word problem such as motion, age, percent mixture, etc.

Bake and Taste
   Publisher: Mindplay
   Price/Format: $35.00; Floppy Disk
   Grade Levels: 2 - 5
   Skills: Following directions, fractions, measurement

Calendar Skills
   Publisher: Hartley
   Price/Format: $50.00; Floppy Disk
   Grade Levels: 1 - 3
   Skills: Calendar facts, abbreviations, sequencing

Clock
   Publisher: Hartley
   Price/Format: $50.00; Floppy Disk
   Grade Levels: 1 - 4
   Skills: Telling time using analog and digital clocks

Delta Drawing Today
   Publisher: Power Industries
   Price/Format: $55.00; Floppy Disk
   Grade Levels: K - 8
   Skills: Basic math, geometry, estimation, symmetry, creative thinking, problem solving

Fun School: Learning Adventures with Freddy Frog
   Publisher: Europress Software
   Price/Format: $20.00; Floppy Disk
   Grade Levels: 1 - 5
   Skills: Math facts in addition, subtraction, multiplication, division, and money skills

Kids Math (Mac only)
   Publisher: Great Wave
   Price/Format: $35.00; Floppy Disk
   Grade Levels: Pre-K - 3
   Skills: Early math concepts and skills

Market Place
   Publisher: Summit Educational Software
   Price/Format: $15.00; Floppy Disk
   Grade Levels: 2 - 8
   Skills: Cause and effect, consumer problems, decision making, estimation, money, computation

Math Ace
Publisher:	Magic Quest
Price/Format:	$33.00; Floppy Disk
Grade Levels:	4 and up
Skills:	Consumer problems, whole numbers, decimals, fractions, percents, place value, estimation, math language

Math Blaster Mystery
Publisher:	Davidson and Associates
Price/Format:	$33.00; Floppy Disk
Grade Levels:	4 and up
Skills:	Consumer problems, critical thinking, deductive and inductive reasoning, whole numbers, decimals, percents

Math Blaster Plus
Publisher:	Davidson and Associates
Price/Format:	$30.00; Floppy Disk
Grade Levels:	1 - 6
Skills:	Number facts in addition, subtraction, multiplication, and division

Math Mind Games
Publisher:	Diversified Educational Ent.
Price/Format:	$40.00; Floppy Disk
Grade Levels:	6 - 8
Skills:	Computation, measurement, money, word problems

Math Rescue
Publisher:	Titanium Seal (Shareware, may have several publishers.)
Price:	$6.00; Floppy Disk
Grade Levels:	1 - 5
Skills:	Addition and subtraction facts, motor planning, visual tracking, sequencing. (Additional levels through multiplication and division available through product registration.)

Math Shop
Publisher:	Scholastic
Price/Format:	$18.00; Floppy Disk
Grade Levels:	3 - 8
Skills:	Computation, whole numbers, fractions, percents, consumer problems

Math Shop Spotlight
Publisher:	Scholastic
Price/Format:	$18.00; Floppy Disk
Grade Levels:	4 and up
Skills:	Fractions, decimals, percents, measurement, consumer problems

Math Treks
Publisher:	Earthquest
Price/Format:	$60.00; Floppy Disk
Grade Levels:	3 - 12
Skills:	Basic math, algebra, geometry, fractions, exponents

Math Zone
   Publisher: Millikin
   Price/Format: $35.00; Floppy Disk
   Grade Levels: K - 3
   Skills: Visual and auditory presentation, number recognition, place value, addition and subtraction to three digits with regrouping

Mental Math Games
   Publisher: Broderbund/Waterford
   Price/Format: $60.00; Floppy Disk
   Grade Levels: K - 6
   Skills: Addition, subtraction, multiplication, division facts

New Math Rabbit
   Publisher: The Learning Company
   Price/Format: $35.00; Floppy Disk
   Grade Levels: K - 3
   Skills: Visual memory, motor planning, number recognition, counting, beginning addition and subtraction

Number Maze
   Publisher: Great Wave
   Price/Format: $60.00; Floppy Disk
   Grade Levels: K - 6
   Skills: Counting, early math concepts, computation, problem solving

Number Munchers
   Publisher: MECC
   Price/Format: $20.00; Floppy Disk
   Grade Levels: 2 - 8+
   Skills: Visual tracking, math facts in all four operations, thinking skills, motor planning

Operation Neptune
   Publisher: The Learning Company
   Price/Format: $60.00; Floppy Disk/CD-ROM
   Grade Levels: 5 - 9
   Skills: Whole numbers, fractions, decimals, percents, measurement, motor planning, eye-hand coordination

Stickybear Math 1
   Publisher: Weekly Reader/Optimum Resource
   Price/Format: $28.00; Floppy Disk
   Grade Levels: 1 - 3
   Skills: Visual presentation, addition and subtraction

Stickybear Math 2
   Publisher: Weekly Reader/Optimum Resource
   Price/Format: $28.00; Floppy Disk
   Grade Levels: 3 - 5
   Skills: Visual presentation, multiplication and division

Stickybear's Math Town (Mac only)
    Publisher: Weekly Reader/Optimum Resource
    Price/Format: $42.00; Floppy Disk
    Grade Levels: K - 5
    Skills: Addition, subtraction, multiplication, division (presented in English and Spanish)

Super Solvers Outnumbered
    Publisher: The Learning Company
    Price/Format: $50.00; Floppy Disk
    Grade Levels: 3 - 5
    Skills: Visual tracking, math facts, word problems

Treasure Math Storm
    Publisher: The Learning Company
    Price/Format: $40.00; Floppy Disk
    Grade Levels: 2 - 4
    Skills: Math facts, telling time, money, motor planning, memory

What's My Angle
    Publisher: Davidson and Associates
    Price/Format: $33.00; Floppy Disk
    Grade Levels: 8 and up
    Skills: Geometry, measurement, part-to-whole relationships, visual discrimination, sequencing

Science

3-D Body Adventure
    Publisher: Knowledge Adventure
    Price/Format: $50.00; CD-ROM
    Grade Levels: 5 and up
    Skills: Anatomy, visual discrimination, research skills, vocabulary

Body Transparent (Within Jr. High Combination Package)
    Publisher: Britannica
    Price/Format: $20.00; Floppy Disk
    Grade Levels: 5 - 8
    Skills: Visual discrimination, visual memory, anatomy, physiology

Bugs! An Insect Adventure
    Publisher: Knowledge Adventure
    Price/Format: $50.00; CD-ROM
    Grade Levels: All
    Skills: Reading comprehension, organization, memory, sequencing, research skills

Dinosaur Adventure
    Publisher: Knowledge Adventure
    Price/Format: $50.00; Floppy Disk/CD-ROM
    Grade Levels: 4 and up
    Skills: Reading comprehension, organization, memory, sequencing, research skills

Dyno-Quest
   Publisher: Mindplay
   Price/Format: $50.00; Floppy Disk
   Grade Levels: 3 - 7
   Skills: Vocabulary, organizational skills, sequencing, cause and effect, visual memory

Mystery Matter
   Publisher: MECC
   Price/Format: $70.00; Floppy Disk
   Grade Levels: 3 - 6
   Skills: Scientific method, attention to detail, organizational skills, vocabulary, drawing conclusions

Mystery Objects
   Publisher: MECC
   Price/Format: $70.00; Floppy Disk
   Grade Levels: 2 - 4
   Skills: Scientific method, organizational skills, attention to detail, drawing conclusions

Our Body Mind Games
   Publisher: Diversified Educational Ent.
   Price/Format: $40.00; Floppy Disk
   Grade Levels: 4 - 10
   Skills: Body structure, systems, nutrition, health

Prehistoria
   Publisher: Grolier
   Price/Format: $49.00; CD-ROM
   Grade Levels: 4 and up
   Skills: Biology, thinking skills, details, research skills, history, vocabulary

Science Adventure
   Publisher: Knowledge Adventure
   Price/Format: $55.00; Floppy Disk
   Grade Levels: 4 and up
   Skills: General science, chemistry, biology, physics, geography, sequencing, research skills

SimAnt
   Publisher: Maxis/Davidson
   Price/Format: $45.00; Floppy Disk
   Grade Levels: 6 and up
   Skills: Cause and effect, critical thinking, decision making, drawing conclusions, observation skills

Space Adventure

Publisher:	Knowledge Adventure
Price/Format:	$55.00; Floppy Disk
Grade Levels:	4 and up
Skills:	Reading comprehension, astronomy, memory, research skills, sequencing, organization

Treasure Cove

Publisher:	The Learning Company
Price/Format:	$40.00; Floppy Disk
Grade Levels:	2 - 4
Skills:	Factual information about the ocean environment, deductive reasoning, organizational skills, memory, sequencing

Weather Flight

Publisher:	Excellent Software Corporation
Price/Format:	$60.00; Floppy Disk
Grade Levels:	2 - 6
Skills:	Vocabulary, factual information, visual memory, measurement

Wood Car Rally

Publisher:	MECC
Price/Format:	$70.00; Floppy Disk
Grade Levels:	3 - 8
Skills:	Simple machines, physics, organizational skills, cause and effect

Zoo Keeper

Publisher:	Davidson and Associates
Price/Format:	$36.00; Floppy Disk
Grade Levels:	1 - 5
Skills:	Problem solving, organizational skills, cause and effect, factual information

Social Studies

All About America

Publisher:	Unicorn
Price/Format:	$35.00; Floppy Disk
Grade Levels:	1 - 6
Skills:	History, geography, map skills, reading comprehension

Knowledge Adventure

Publisher:	Knowledge Adventure, Inc.
Price/Format:	$55.00; Floppy Disk
Grade Levels:	5 and up
Skills:	Factual information, reading comprehension, research skills, memory, organization, drawing conclusions

Maps 'N' Facts
Publisher: Broderbund
Price/Format: $45.00; Floppy Disk
Grade Levels: 5 and up
Skills: Map skills, directionality, geography, research skills, factual information, data interpretation

Nigel's World: Adventures in World Geography
Publisher: Lawrence Publications
Price/Format: $28.00; Floppy Disk
Grade Levels: 2 - 5
Skills: Geography, organization, reading comprehension, auditory discrimination, auditory memory

Stickybear Town Builder
Publisher: Weekly Reader/Optimum Resource
Price/Format: $40.00; Floppy Disk
Grade Levels: K - 3
Skills: Map skills, problem solving, directionality, organizational skills

The Oregon Trail
Publisher: MECC
Price/Format: $48.00; Floppy Disk/CD-ROM
Grade Levels: 5 and up
Skills: History, reading comprehension, deductive reasoning, organization, decision making, map skills

Timeliner
Publisher: Tom Snyder Productions
Price/Format: $60.00; Floppy Disk
Grade Levels: K - 12
Skills: Organizational skills, sequencing, time measurement. (Creates time lines. May be used with any subject. Allows grouping by days, weeks, years.)

Time Riders in American History
Publisher: The Learning Company
Price/Format: $50.00; Floppy Disk
Grade Levels: 5 - 9
Skills: History, reading comprehension, deductive reasoning, organization

Where in ????? is Carmen Sandiego?
Publisher: Broderbund
Price/Format: $60.00; Floppy Disk/CD-ROM
Grade Levels: 5 - 12
Skills: Visual organization, thinking skills, civilization, history, map skills

World Mystery Series: America's Neighbors Mystery
Publisher: International Educations
Price/Format: $20.00; Floppy Disk
Grade Levels: 6 - 12
Skills: Geography, factual information, organization, thinking, problem solving

World Mystery Series: European Mystery
Publisher:	International Educations
Price/Format:	$20.00; Floppy Disk
Grade Levels:	6 - 12
Skills:	Geography, factual information, organization, thinking, problem solving

World Mystery Series: Middle Eastern Mystery
Publisher:	International Educations
Price/Format:	$20.00; Floppy Disk
Grade Levels:	6 - 12
Skills:	Geography, factual information, organization, thinking, problem solving

Productivity/Test Preparation

American Heritage Dictionary
Publisher:	WordStar International
Price/Format:	$60.00; Floppy Disk
Grade Levels:	6 and up
Description:	General use dictionary, provides definitions, also finds word when given partial spelling or definition

Compton's Interactive Encyclopedia
Publisher:	Compton's New Media
Price/Format:	$300.00; CD-ROM
Grade Levels:	1 and up
Description:	Includes dictionary and thesaurus. Designed to be understood by children as young as six years.

Grammatik 5
Publisher:	Reference Software
Price/Format:	$70.00; Floppy Disk
Grade Levels:	6 and up
Description:	Grammar and style checker, includes spell-checker

Grolier Multimedia Encyclopedia
Publisher:	Grolier Electronic Publishing, Inc.
Price/Format:	$250.00; CD-ROM
Grade Levels:	2 and up
Description:	General encyclopedia, allows cross-referencing and searching

Kid Pix 2
Publisher:	Broderbund
Price/Format:	$38.00; Floppy Disk
Grade Levels:	All
Description:	Children's drawing and painting program, includes Kid Pix Companion

Kid Works 2

Publisher:	Davidson and Associates
Price/Format:	$36.00; Floppy Disk/CD-ROM
Grade Levels:	Pre-K - 3
Description:	Children's writing and drawing program, includes spelling assistance, reads compositions back to the child

MacMillan Dictionary for Children

Publisher:	MacMillan New Media
Price/Format:	$30.00; CD-ROM
Grade Levels:	1 - 3
Description:	Beginning dictionary pronounces words, includes several word games

Microsoft Encarta

Publisher:	Microsoft Corporation
Price/Format:	$200.00; CD-ROM
Grade Levels:	4 and up
Description:	General encyclopedia, excellent use of multimedia functions

PFS: Write

Publisher:	Spinnaker
Price/Format:	$50.00; Floppy Disk
Grade Levels:	5 and up
Description:	Word processor with some desk-top publishing capability—includes outliner, spell-checker, thesaurus, grammar checker, and clip art

Picture Wizard

Publisher:	Computer Support Corporation
Price/Format:	$55.00; Floppy Disk
Grade Levels:	All
Description:	Scaled down desktop publisher. Includes hundreds of pictures, several choices of type styles, ability to size objects as desired. Wonderful for making games, report covers, signs, etc.

Princeton Review SAT Computer Diagnostic

Publisher:	The Princeton Review
Price/Format:	$20.00; Floppy Disk
Grade Levels:	9 - 12
Description:	Diagnostic practice test for the new SAT-I

Print Shop Deluxe

Publisher:	Broderbund
Price/Format:	$55.00; Floppy Disk
Grade Levels:	3 and up
Description:	Creativity package for greeting cards, banners, calendars, etc.

Random House Webster's School & Office Dictionary
Publisher:	WordPerfect Main Street
Price/Format:	$27.00; CD-ROM
Grade Levels:	5 and up
Description:	Dictionary works within most word processors, allows search by word, partial word, or definition

Right Writer, version 6.0
Publisher:	Que Software
Price/Format:	$55.00; Floppy Disk
Grade Levels:	5 and up
Description:	Grammar and style checker, includes spell-checker

The Student Writing Center for Windows
Publisher:	The Learning Company
Price/Format:	$50.00; Floppy Disk/CD-ROM
Grade Levels:	K - 9
Description:	Simplified, but complete, word processor including multiple fonts, graphics, spell-checker, thesaurus, bibliography maker and grammar and style tips

The Writing Center (Mac only)
Publisher:	The Learning Company
Price/Format:	$55.00; Floppy Disk/CD-ROM
Grade Levels:	K - 5
Description:	Writing tool for elementary students—includes pictures, spell-checker, thesaurus

Your Personal Trainer for the SAT
Publisher:	Davidson & Associates
Price/Format:	$60.00; CD-ROM
Grade Levels:	9 - 12
Description:	Testing skills and content preparation for new SAT-I, organizational skills, self-monitoring

Perception/Thinking/Organization/Problem Solving

Ancient Empires
Publisher:	The Learning Company
Price/Format:	$33.00; Floppy Disk
Grade Levels:	5 and up
Skills:	Motor planning, motor sequencing, visual tracking, organization, thinking skills

Doodle-mation
Publisher:	Screen Magic
Price/Format:	$30.00; Floppy Disk
Grade Levels:	All
Skills:	Creativity, eye-hand coordination, form constancy, position in space, shape recognition, visual discrimination, visual tracking

Lemmings
Publisher:	Psygnosis
Price/Format:	$32.00; Floppy Disk
Grade Levels:	5 and up
Skills:	Motor planning, motor sequencing, visual tracking, organization, thinking skills

Lenny's Music Toons
Publisher:	Paramount Interactive
Price/Format:	$42.00; CD-ROM
Grade Levels:	3 and up
Skills:	Auditory attention, auditory discrimination, auditory memory, auditory sequencing, organizational skills, computer literacy

Mickey's Jigsaw Puzzles
Publisher:	Disney Software
Price/Format:	$21.00; Floppy Disk
Grade Levels:	K - 4
Skills:	Visual perception, motor planning, motor control—delightful program using sound and animation

Microsoft Entertainment Packs for Windows (#'s 1-4)
Publisher:	Microsoft
Price/Format:	$35.00; Floppy Disk
Grade Levels:	3 and up
Skills:	Visual discrimination, visual tracking, motor planning, motor sequencing, thinking

Mind Games
Publisher:	ComputerEasy
Price/Format:	$12.00; Floppy Disk
Grade Levels:	5 and up
Skills:	Thinking, logic and organizational skills

Mosaic Magic
Publisher:	Kinder Magic
Price/Format:	$21.00; Floppy Disk
Grade Levels:	K - 2
Skills:	Visual perception, position in space, problem solving

School House
Publisher:	Maverick Software
Price/Format:	$15.00; Floppy Disk
Grade Levels:	4 - 12
Skills:	Sequencing, thinking, factual information, ABC order, self-monitoring

Shanghai II: Dragon's Eye
Publisher:	Activision
Price/Format:	$35.00; Floppy Disk
Grade Levels:	4 and up
Skills:	Visual discrimination, motor planning, visual sequencing

Super Munchers
Publisher:	MECC
Price/Format:	$35.00; Floppy Disk
Grade Levels:	3 and up
Skills:	Visual tracking, inferential comprehension, deductive reasoning, logic, motor planning, motor sequencing

Super Tetris
Publisher:	Spectrum Holobyte
Price/Format:	$35.00; Floppy Disk
Grade Levels:	4 and up
Skills:	Visual discrimination, visual tracking, motor planning, motor sequencing

Symantic Game Pack for Windows
Publisher:	Symantic
Price/Format:	$35.00; Floppy Disk
Grade Levels:	3 and up
Skills:	Visual discrimination, visual tracking, motor planning, motor sequencing, thinking, memory

Tesserae
Publisher:	Gametek
Price/Format:	$18.00; Floppy Disk
Grade Levels:	6 and up
Skills:	Thinking, cause and effect, predicting outcomes, visual perception

The Market Place
Publisher:	Summit Educational Software
Price/Format:	$15.00; Floppy Disk
Grade Levels:	3 - 12
Skills:	Estimation, cause and effect, reasoning.

Tristan (Solid State Pinball)
Publisher:	Amtex
Price/Format:	$49.00; Floppy Disk
Grade Levels:	All
Skills:	Visual tracking, eye-hand coordination, sequencing, motor planning

Keyboarding

Kid Keys
Publisher:	Davidson and Associates
Price/Format:	$25.00; Floppy Disk
Grade Levels:	Pre-K - 2
Skills:	Visual sequencing, motor planning, motor memory, typing, auditory discrimination, auditory memory, letter recognition

Kid's Typing

Publisher:	Sierra On-Line, Inc. (Bright Star)
Price/Format:	$33.00; Floppy Disk/CD-ROM
Grade Levels:	3 - 8
Skills:	Visual sequencing, motor planning, motor memory, typing, auditory attention, auditory memory

Mario Teaches Typing

Publisher:	Interplay
Price/Format:	$30.00; Floppy Disk
Grade Levels:	4 - 12
Skills:	Visual sequencing, motor planning, motor memory, typing

Stickybear Typing

Publisher:	Weekly Reader/Optimum Resource
Price/Format:	$35.00; Floppy Disk
Grade Levels:	2 - 6
Skills:	Visual sequencing, motor planning, motor memory, typing

Typing Tutor 6

Publisher:	Simon and Schuster
Price/Format:	$30.00; Floppy Disk
Grade Levels:	5 and up
Skills:	Visual sequencing, motor planning, motor memory, typing

Publishers and Sources Of Software Useful in Education

The Big Five

Broderbund Software
PO Box 12947
San Rafael, CA 94913
800/521-6263

Learning Company
6493 Kaiser Drive
Fremont, CA 94555
800/852-2255

Davidson and Associates
3135 Kashiwa Street
Torrance, CA 90505
800/545-7677

MECC
660 Summit Drive
Minneapolis, MN 55430
800/685-6322

Weekly Reader Software
Optimum Resource
10 Station Place
Norfolk, CT 06058
800/327-1473

Other Publishers of Educational Software

Britannica Software
Bright Star
DLM
Hartley
Lawrence Publications
Millikin

Mindplay
Scholastic
Stone and Associates
Tom Snyder Productions
Unicorn Software

Publishers of Teacher Utility and/or Productivity Software

MECC   **Microsoft Corporation**   **Spinnaker**

Catalogs of Educational Software

Educational Resources
1550 Executive Drive
Elgin, IL 60123
800/624-2926

Educational Software Institute
4213 South 94th Street
Omaha, NE 68127
800/955-5570

Special Times
Cambridge Development Laboratory, Inc.
86 West Street
Waltham, MA 02154
800/637-0047

Appendix C:
Legal Documents

OFFICE FOR CIVIL RIGHTS
U.S. DEPARTMENT OF EDUCATION

The Office for Civil Rights (OCR) enforces four federal statutes that prohibit discrimination in programs and activities receiving federal financial assistance from the Department of Education (ED). Discrimination on the basis of race, color, and national origin is prohibited by Title VI of the Civil Rights Act of 1964; sex discrimination is prohibited by Title IX of the Education Amendments of 1972; discrimination on the basis of handicap is prohibited by Section 504 of the Rehabilitation Act of 1973; and age discrimination is prohibited by the Age Discrimination Act of 1975. OCR also assists other departmental offices in ensuring that federal assistance administered by those offices is consistent with federal civil rights laws.

OCR has authority to enforce these laws in all programs and activities that receive funds from ED. These include programs and activities operated by institutions and agencies, such as state education agencies, elementary and secondary schools, colleges and universities, vocational schools, vocational rehabilitation agencies, libraries, and museums.

OCR investigates complaints filed by individuals, or their representatives, who believe that they have been discriminated against because of race, color, national origin, sex, handicap, or age. It also initiates compliance reviews of recipient institutions and agencies, and monitors the progress in eliminating discriminatory practices of institutions and agencies that are implementing plans negotiated by OCR. OCR attempts to resolve compliance problems through negotiation. However, if unable to do so, OCR initiates the actions necessary to enforce the law.

OCR also offers technical assistance to help recipients voluntarily comply with civil rights laws and to inform citizens of their rights under these laws. As part of its technical assistance activities, OCR distributes information and materials and provides consultations on the requirements of the civil rights laws under its authority.

OCR maintains a headquarters office in Washington, D.C., and ten regional offices. The addresses and phone numbers of the regional offices are listed on the following page. For more information about the civil rights laws enforced by OCR, how to file a complaint, or how to obtain technical assistance, contact the OCR regional office that serves your state or territory.

U.S. DEPARTMENT OF EDUCATION
OFFICE FOR CIVIL RIGHTS
REGIONAL CIVIL RIGHTS OFFICES

REGION I

CONNECTICUT, MAINE MASSACHUSETTS, NEW HAMPSHIRE, RHODE ISLAND, VERMONT

Office for Civil Rights, Region I
U.S. Department of Education
John W. McCormack POCH
Room 222, 01-0061
Boston, Massachusetts 02109-4557
(617) 223-9662; TDD (617) 223-9695

REGION II

NEW JERSEY, NEW YORK, PUERTO RICO, VIRGIN ISLANDS

Office for Civil Rights, Region II
U.S. Department of Education
26 Federal Plaza, 33rd Floor
Room 33-130, 01-1010
New York, New York 10278-0082
(212) 264-4633; TDD (212) 264-9464

REGION III

DELAWARE, DISTRICT OF COLUMBIA, MARYLAND, PENNSYLVANIA, VIRGINIA WEST VIRGINIA

Office for Civil Rights, Region III
U.S. Department of Education
3535 Market Street
Room 6300, 03-2010
Philadelphia, Pennsylvania 19104-3326
(215) 596-6772; TDD (215) 596-6794

REGION IV

ALABAMA, FLORIDA, GEORGIA, KENTUCKY MISSISSIPPI, NORTH CAROLINA SOUTH CAROLINA, TENNESSEE

Office for Civil Rights, Region IV
U.S. Department of Education
P.O. Box 2048, 04-3010
Atlanta, Georgia 30301-2048
(404) 331-2954; TDD (404) 331-7816

REGION V

ILLINOIS, INDIANA, MINNESOTA MICHIGAN, OHIO, WISCONSIN

Office for Civil Rights, Region V
U.S. Department of Education
401 South State Street
Room 700C, 05-4010
Chicago, Illinois 60605-1202
(213) 886-3456; TDD (312) 353-2541

REGION VI

ARKANSAS, LOUISIANA, NEW MEXICO, OKLAHOMA, TEXAS

Office for Civil Rights, Region VI
U.S. Department of Education
1200 Main Tower Building
Suite 2260, 06-5010
Dallas, Texas 75202-9998
(214) 767-3959; TDD (214) 767-3639

REGION VII

IOWA, KANSAS, MISSOURI, NEBRASKA

Office for Civil Rights, Region VII
U.S. Department of Education
10220 N. Executive Hill Blvd.
8th Floor, 07-6010
Kansas City, Missouri 64153-1367
(816) 891-8026; TDD (816) 374-6461

REGION VIII

COLORADO, MONTANA, NORTH DAKOTA SOUTH DAKOTA, UTAH, WYOMING

Office for Civil Rights, Region VIII
U.S. Department of Education
Federal Building
1244 Speer Blvd., Suite 310, 08-7010
Denver, Colorado 80204-3582
(303) 844-5695; TDD (303) 844-3417

REGION IX

ARIZONA, CALIFORNIA, HAWAII, NEVADA, GUAM, TRUST TERRITORY OF THE PACIFIC ISLANDS, AMERICAN SAMOA

Office for Civil Rights, Region IX
U.S. Department of Education
Old Federal Building, 09-8010
50 United Nations Plaza, Room 239
San Francisco, California 94102-4102
(415) 556-7000; TDD (415) 556-6806

REGION X

ALASKA, IDAHO, OREGON, WASHINGTON

Office for Civil Rights, Region X
U.S. Department of Education
915 Second Avenue
Room 3310-10-9010
Seattle, Washington 98174-1099
(206) 553-6811; TDD (206) 553-4542

*U.S. Government Printing Office: 1991

UNITED STATES DEPARTMENT OF EDUCATION
OFFICE OF SPECIAL EDUCATION AND REHABILITATIVE SERVICES

THE ASSISTANT SECRETARY

<u>MEMORANDUM</u>

DATE: SEPT 16, 1991

TO: Chief State School Officers

FROM: Robert R. Davila
             Assistant Secretary
             Office of Special Education and Rehabilitative Services

             Michael L. Williams
             Assistant Secretary
             Office for Civil Rights

             John T. MacDonald
             Assistant Secretary
             Office of Elementary and Secondary Education

SUBJECT: Clarification of Policy to Address the Needs of Children with Attention Deficit
             Disorders within General and/or Special Education.

I. <u>Introduction</u>

There is a growing awareness in the education community that attention deficit disorder (ADD) and attention deficit hyperactive disorder (ADHD) can result in significant learning problems for children with those conditions.[55] While estimates of the prevalence of ADD vary widely, we believe that three to five percent of school-aged children may have significant educational problems related to this disorder. Because ADD has broad implications for education as a whole, the Department believes it should clarify State and local responsibility under Federal law for addressing the needs of children with ADD in the schools. Ensuring that these students are able to reach their fullest potential is an inherent part of the National education goals and AMERICA 2000. The national goals, and the strategy for achieving them, are based on the assumptions that: (1) all children can learn and benefit from their education; and (2) the educational community must work to improve the learning opportunities for all children.

This memorandum clarifies the circumstances under which children with ADD are eligible for special education services under Part B of the Individuals with Disabilities Education Act (Part B), as well as the Part B requirements for evaluation of such children's unique educational needs. This memorandum will also clarify the responsibility of State and local educational agencies (SEAs and LEAs) to provide special education and related services to eligible children with ADD under Part B. Finally, this memorandum clarifies the responsibilities of LEAs to provide regular

---

[55]   While we recognize that the disorders ADD and ADHD vary, the term ADD is being used to encompass children with both disorders.

Page 2 - Chief State School Officers

or special education and related aids and services to those children with ADD who are not eligible under Part B, but who fall within the definition of "handicapped person" under Section 504 of the Rehabilitation Act of 1973. Because of the overall educational responsibility to provide services for these children, it is important that general and special education coordinate their efforts.

II. Eligibility for Special Education and Related Services Under Part B

Last year during the reauthorization of the Education of the Handicapped Act (now the Individuals with Disabilities Education Act), Congress gave serious consideration to including ADD in the definition of "children with disabilities" in the statute. The Department took the position that ADD does not need to be added as a separate disability category in the statutory definition since children with ADD who require special education and related services can meet the eligibility criteria for services under Part B. This continues to be the Department's position.

No change with respect to ADD was made by Congress in the statutory definition of "children with disabilities;" however, language was included in Section 102(a) of the Education of the Handicapped Act Amendments of 1990 that required the Secretary to issue a Notice of Inquiry (NOI) soliciting public comment on special education for children with ADD under Part B. In response to the NOI (published November 29, 1990 in the Federal Register), the Department received over 2000 written comments, which have been transmitted to the Congress. Our review of these written comments indicates that there is confusion in the field regarding the extent to which children with ADD may be served in special education programs conducted under Part B.

A. Description of Part B

Part B requires SEAs and LEAs to make a free appropriate public education (FAPE) available to all eligible children with disabilities and to ensure that the rights and protections of Part B are extended to those children and their parents. 20 U.S.C. 1412(2); 34 CFR §§300.121 and 300.2. Under Part B, FAPE, among other elements, includes the provision of special education and related services, at no cost to parents, in conformity with an individualized education program (IEP). 34 CFR §300.4.

In order to be eligible under Part B, a child must be evaluated in accordance with 34 CFR §§300.530-300.534 as having one or more specified physical or mental impairments, and must be found to require special education and related services by reason of one or more of these impairments.[56] 20 U.S.C. 1401(a)(1); 34 CFR §300.5. SEAs and LEAs must ensure that children with ADD who are determined eligible for services under Part B receive special education and related services designed to meet their unique needs, including special education and related services needs arising from the ADD. A full continuum of placement alternatives, including the regular classroom, must be available for providing special education and related services required in the IEP.

---

[56]   The Part B regulations define 11 specified disabilities. 34 CFR §300.5(b)(I)-(II). The Education of the Handicapped Act Amendments of 1990 amended the Individuals with Disabilities Education Act [formerly the Education of the Handicapped Act) to specify that autism and traumatic brain injury are separate disability categories. See section 602(a)(1) of the Act, to be codified at 20 U.S.C. 1401(a)(1).

Page 3 - Chief State School Officers

B. Eligibility for Part B Services Under the "Other Health Impaired" Category

The list of chronic or acute health problems included within the definition of "other health impaired" in the Part B regulations is not exhaustive. The term "other health impaired" includes chronic or acute impairments that result in limited alertness, which adversely affects educational performance. Thus, children with ADD should be classified as eligible for services under the "other health impaired" category in instances where the ADD is a chronic or acute health problem that results in limited alertness, which adversely affects educational performance. In other words, children with ADD, where the ADD is a chronic or acute health problem resulting in limited alertness, may be considered disabled under Part B solely on the basis of this disorder within the "other health impaired" category in situations where special education and related services are needed because of the ADD.

C. Eligibility for Part B Services Under Other Disability Categories

Children with ADD are also eligible for services under Part B if the children satisfy the criteria applicable to other disability categories. For example, children with ADD are also eligible for services under the "specific learning disability" category of Part B if they meet the criteria stated in §§300.5(b)(9) and 300.541 or under the "seriously emotionally disturbed" category of Part B if they meet the criteria stated in §300.5(b)(8).

III. Evaluations Under Part B

A. Requirements

SEAs and LEAs have an affirmative obligation to evaluate a child who is suspected of having a disability to determine the child's need for special education and related services. Under Part B, SEAs and LEAs are required to have procedures for locating, identifying and evaluating all children who have a disability or are suspected of having a disability and are in need of special education and related services. 34 CFR §§300.128 and 300.220. This responsibility, known as "child find," is applicable to all children from birth through 21, regardless of the severity of their disability.

Consistent with this responsibility and the obligation to make FAPE available to all "eligible children with disabilities" SEAs and LEAs must ensure that evaluations of children who are suspected of needing special education and related services are conducted without undue delay. 20 U.S.C. 1412(2). Because of its responsibility resulting from the FAPE and child find requirements of Part B, an LEA may not refuse to evaluate the possible need for special education and related services of a child with a prior medical diagnosis of ADD solely by reason of that medical diagnosis. However, a medical diagnosis of ADD alone is not sufficient to render a child eligible for services under Part B.

Under Part B, before any action is taken with respect to the initial placement of a child with a disability in a program providing special education and related services, "a full and individual evaluation of the child's educational needs must be conducted in accordance with requirements of §300.532." 34 CFR §300.531. Section 300.532(a) requires that a child's evaluation must be conducted by a multidisciplinary team, including at least one teacher or other specialist with knowledge in the area of suspected disability.

Page 4 - Chief State School Officers

B. Disagreements Over Evaluations

Any proposal or refusal of an agency to initiate or change the identification, evaluation, or educational placement of the child, or the provision of FAPE to the child is subject to the written prior notice requirements of 34 CFR §§300.504-300.505.[57] If a parent disagrees with the LEA's refusal to evaluate a child or the LEA's evaluation and determination that a child does not have a disability for which the child is eligible for services under Part B, the parent may request a due process hearing pursuant to 34 CFR §§300.506-300.513 of the Part B regulations.

IV. Obligations Under Section 504 of SEAs and LEAs to Children with ADD Found Not To Require Special Education and Related Services under Part B

Even if a child with ADD is found not to be eligible for services under Part B, the requirements of Section 504 of the Rehabilitation Act of 1973 (Section 504) and its implementing regulation at 34 CFR Part 104 may be applicable. Section 504 prohibits discrimination on the basis of handicap by recipients of Federal funds. Since Section 504 is a civil rights law, rather than a funding law, its requirements are framed in different terms than those of Part B. While the Section 504 regulation was written with an eye to consistency with Part B, it is more general, and there are some differences arising from the differing natures of the two laws. For instance, the protection of Section 504 extend to some children who do not fall within the disability categories specified in Part B.

A. Definition

Section 504 requires every recipient that operates a public elementary or secondary education program to address the needs of children who are considered "handicapped persons" under Section 504 as adequately as the needs of nonhandicapped persons are met. "Handicapped person" is defined in the Section 504 regulation as any person who has a physical or mental impairment which substantially limits a major life activity (e.g., learning). 34 CFR §104.3(j). Thus, depending on the severity of their condition, children with ADD "may" fit within that definition.

B. Programs and Services Under Section 504

Under Section 504, an LEA must provide a free appropriate public education to each qualified handicapped child. A free appropriate public education, under Section 504, consists of regular or special education and related aids and services that are designed to meet the individual student's needs and based on adherence to the regulatory requirements on educational setting, evaluation, placement, and procedural safeguards. 34 CFR §§104.33, 104.34, 104.35, and 104.36. A student may be handicapped within the meaning of Section 504, and therefore entitled to regular or special education and related aids and services under the Section 504 regulation, even though the student may not be eligible for special education and related services under Part B.

---

[57] Section 300.505 of the Part B regulations sets out the elements that must be contained in the prior written notice to parents: (1) a full explanation of all of the procedural safeguards available to the parents under Subpart E; (2) a description of the action proposed or refused by the agency, an explanation of why the agency proposes or refuses to take the action, and a description of any options the agency considered and the reasons why those options were rejected; (3) a description of each evaluation procedure, test, record, or report the agency uses as a basis for the proposal or refusal; and (4) A description of any other factors which are relevant to the agency's proposal or refusal. 34 CFR §300.505(a)(1)-(4).

Page 5 - Chief State School Officers

Under Section 504, if parents believe that their child is handicapped by ADD, the LEA must evaluate the child to determine whether he or she is handicapped as defined by Section 504. If an LEA determines that a child is not handicapped under Section 504, the parent has the right to contest that determination. If the child is determined to be handicapped under Section 504, the LEA must take an individualized determination of the child's educational needs for regular or special education or related aids and services. 34 CFR §104.35. For children determined to be handicapped under Section 504, implementation of an individualized education program developed in accordance with Part B, although not required, is one means of meeting the free appropriate public education requirements of Section 504.[58] The child's education must be provided in the regular education classroom unless it is demonstrated that education in the regular environment with the use of supplementary aids and services cannot be achieved satisfactorily. 34 CFR §104.34.

Should it be determined that the child with ADD is handicapped for purposes of Section 504 and needs only adjustments in the regular classroom, rather than special education, those adjustments are required by Section 504. A range of strategies is available to meet the educational needs of children with ADD.

Regular classroom teachers are important in identifying the appropriate educational adaptions and interventions for many children with ADD.

SEAs and LEAs should take the necessary steps to promote coordination between special and regular education programs. Steps also should be taken to train regular education teachers and other personnel to develop their awareness about ADD and its manifestations and the adaptations that can be implemented in regular education programs to address the instructional needs of these children. Examples of adaptations in regular education programs could include the following:

> providing a structured learning environment; repeating and simplifying instructions about in-class and homework assignments; supplementing verbal instructions with visual instructions; using behavioral management techniques; adjusting class schedules; modifying test delivery; using tape recorders, computer-aided instruction, and other audio-visual equipment; selecting modified textbooks or workbooks; and tailoring homework assignments.

Other provisions range from consultation to special resources and may include reducing class size; use of one-on-one tutorials; classroom aides and note takers; involvement of a "services coordinator" to oversee implementation of special programs and services, and possible modification of nonacademic times such as lunchroom, recess, and physical education. Through the use of appropriate adaptations and interventions in regular classes, many of which may be required by Section 504, the Department believes that LEAs will be able to effectively address the instructional needs of many children with ADD.

C. Procedural Safeguards Under Section 504

Procedural safeguards under the Section 504 regulation are stated more generally than in Part B. The Section 504 regulation requires the LEA to make available a system of procedural safeguards

---

[58] Many LEAs use the same process for determining the needs of students under Section 504 that they use for implementing Part B.

Page 6 - Chief State School officers

that permits parents to challenge actions regarding the identification, evaluation, or educational placement of their handicapped child whom they believe needs special education or related services. 34 CFR §104.36. The Section 504 regulation requires that the system of procedural safeguards include notice, an opportunity for the parents or guardian to examine relevant records, an impartial hearing with opportunity for participation by the parents or guardian and representation by counsel, and a review procedure. Compliance with procedural safeguards of Part B is one means of fulfilling the Section 504 requirement[59]. However, in an impartial due process hearing raising issues under the Section 504 regulation, the impartial hearing officer must make a determination based upon that regulation.

V. Conclusion

Congress and the Department have recognized the need to provide information and assistance to teachers, administrators, parents and other interested persons regarding the identification, evaluation, and instructional needs of children with ADD. The Department has formed a work group to explore strategies across principal offices to address this issue. The work group also plans to identify some ways that the Department can work with the education associations to cooperatively consider the programs and services needed by children with ADD across special and regular education.

In fiscal year 1991, Congress appropriated funds for the Department to synthesize and disseminate current knowledge related to ADD. Four centers will be established in fall, 1991 to analyze and synthesize the current research literature on ADD relating to identification, assessment, and interventions. Research syntheses will be prepared in formats suitable for educators, parents and researchers. Existing clearinghouses and networks as well as Federal, State and local organizations will be utilized to disseminate these research syntheses to parents, educators and administrators, and other interested persons.

In addition, the Federal Resource center will work with SEAs and the six regional resource centers authorized under the Individuals with Disabilities Education Act to identify effective identification and assessment procedures, as well as intervention strategies being implemented across the country for children with ADD. A document describing current practice will be developed and disseminated to parents, educators and administrators, and other interested persons through the regional resource centers network, as well as by parent training centers, other parent and consumer organizations and professional organizations. Also, the Office for Civil Rights' ten regional offices stand ready to provide technical assistance to parents and educators.

It is our hope that the above information will be of assistance to your state as you plan for the needs of children with ADD who require special education and related services under Part B, as well as for the needs of the broader group of children with ADD who do not qualify for special education and related services under Part B, but for whom special education or adaptations in regular education programs are needed. If you have any questions, please contact Jean Peelen, office for Civil Rights; (Phone: 202/732-1635), Judy Schrag, Office of Special Education Programs; (Phone: 2022/732-1007); or Dan Bonnes, Office of Elementary and Secondary Education (Phone: 202/401-0984).

---

[59]   Again, many LEAs and some SEAs are conserving time and resources by using the same due process procedures for resolving disputes under both laws.

Georgia Department of Education
Office of the State Superintendent of Schools
Twin Towers East
Atlanta, Georgia 30334-5001

Werner Rogers
State Superintendent of Schools

November 14, 1991

MEMORANDUM

TO: System Superintendents
           Special Education Directors

FROM: Werner Rogers

SUBJECT: Information Regarding Attention Deficit
           Disorder and Recent U.S. Department of
           Education Memorandum

Enclosed is a memorandum from the U.S. Department of Education clarifying the requirements for serving students with Attention Deficit Disorder (ADD). A summary of significant and relevant points of this clarification, which you may find helpful to review prior to reading the entire memo, is attached.

We hope this information will be useful to you and your staff. If you have questions, please contact either Dr. Joan A. Jordan or Ms. Donna Blaeser at 404-656-2425.

PW:bgw
Enclosures
cc: Distribution A & B
    RESA Directors
    School Curriculum Directors
    GLRS Directors
    Psychoeducational Directors
    School Psychologists
    Section 504 Coordinators

INFORMATION REGARDING ADD AND RECENT U.S. DEPARTMENT OF EDUCATION MEMORANDUM

- What is new, generally, is the re-emphasis on the obligation to educate ADD students, <u>if eligible</u> for services through the framework of Section 504 of the Rehabilitation Act of 1973 <u>or</u> under the Education of the Handicapped Act, now re-named the Individuals with Disabilities Education Act (IDEA). Local school systems have a responsibility to evaluate any student suspected of having a disability as defined under IDEA or Section 504 of the Rehabilitation Act of 1973.

- What is familiar is the emphasis on serving attention deficit disordered students in the least restrictive setting possible. In fact, the prevailing option is that, with appropriate modifications, most ADD students can be served in the regular classroom.

- A number of other conditions can resemble ADD; therefore, our most prudent approach is to deal with symptoms first with appropriate modifications in the regular classroom. Should these fail to remedy the problem adequately the student support team (SST) should address the case.

- The SST is an interdisciplinary group that addresses the needs of students having problems in school. The SST should develop an educational plan that includes appropriate accommodations, curricula recommendations and instructional strategies and/or alternatives for the student. If those strategies and/or accommodations are not considered sufficient, the SST should refer the student to special education for evaluation and determination of eligibility for one of the special education categories. Students with obvious and severe disabilities that prevent them from succeeding in the regular classroom may be exempted from the SST process, referred directly to special education and documented accordingly.

- A student with ADD may be eligible for special education services in any one of the existing categories: specific learning disabilities, emotional/behavior disorders, intellectual disability, hearing impaired, visually impaired, orthopedically impaired or other health impaired. The student must meet the eligibility criteria for the disability area and is <u>not automatically eligible because of a medical diagnosis of ADD or any other existing condition.</u>

- Be aware that the news media, unfortunately, may have given incomplete coverage of this federal clarification. As a result, some parents were given the impression that their ADD child automatically qualifies for special education without regard for demonstrated need or prior interventions. This is not the case.

- The memo states that if the ADD adversely affects the student's alertness and the student's ability to benefit from instruction in the regular classroom, the student may be comprehensively evaluated and considered for eligibility in the other health impaired category by the individual education program/placement committee. This language is included in the other health impaired (OHI) category of <u>Georgia's Special Education Regulations and Procedures.</u> Eligibility criteria are clearly spelled out in the OHI category as it is with all other areas of special education. <u>Eligibility criteria have not changed. Students with ADD may be served in any special education category as long as existing eligibility criteria are met as indicated above.</u>

- Local school systems (LSS) have a responsibility to provide services to all identified and eligible students with disabilities under IDEA. LSS also have a responsibility to identify and serve students with handicaps under Section 504; many times this means making needed adjustments in the regular classroom to meet the student's needs. The SST may be the process by which plans are made to accommodate the needs of students not eligible under IDEA, but who are eligible under 504 as students with disabilities and special learning needs that require alternative instructional strategies or special accommodations (aids/materials). Examples of adaptations in regular education programs are included on page seven in the U. S. Department of Education memo. Please note that necessary steps should be made to promote coordination between special education and regular education programs. Steps should also be taken to train regular education teachers and other personnel to develop their awareness about ADD and its manifestations and the adaptations that can be implemented in regular education programs to address the instructional needs of these students.

- In summary, emerging state and local responsibilities under federal law require careful identification, evaluation and services as necessary and appropriate to address the needs of students with ADD in the schools. In Georgia, an important resource available to begin addressing these needs is the student support team with involvement, as necessary, of school psychologists, special education teachers, counselors, principals, lead teachers, etc.

Appendix D:
Reading Lists

Reading List (by subject and title) ————————

Attention Deficit Disorder

Advice to Parents on Attention-Deficit Hyperactivity Disorder
　　Larry Silver, M.D.
　　American Psychiatric Press, Inc., 1992

All Kinds of Minds: A Young Student's Book about Learning Abilities and Learning Disorders
　　Mel Levine, M.D.
　　Educators Publishing Service, Inc., 1993

Attention Deficit Disorder and the Law: A Guide for Advocates
　　Peter S. Latham, J.D. and Patricia H. Latham, J.D.
　　JKL Communications, 1992

Attention Deficit Hyperactivity Disorder: A Handbook for Diagnosis and Treatment
　　Russell A. Barkley, Ph.D.
　　Guilford Press, 1990

CH.A.A.D. Educators Manual
　　Mary Cahill Fowler
　　Caset Associates, 1992

Driven to Distraction
　　Edward M. Hallowell, M.D. and John J. Ratey, M.D.
　　Pantheon Books, a Division of Random House, Inc., 1994

The Hyperactive Child, Adolescent, and Adult: Attention Deficit Disorder Through the Lifespan
　　Paul Wender, M.D.
　　Oxford Press, 1987

Keeping A Head in School: A Student's Book About Learning Abilities and Learning Disorders
　　Mel Levine, M.D.
　　Educators Publishing Service, Inc., 1987

Maybe You Know My Kid: A Parent's Guide to Identifying, Understanding and Helping Your Child with Attention-Deficit Hyperactivity Disorder
　　Mary Cahill Fowler
　　Birch Lane Press, 1990

Practitioner's Guide to Managing Attention Disorder in Children
　　Sam Goldstein, Ph.D., and Michael Goldstein, M.D.
　　John Wiley and Sons, 1990

You Mean I'm Not Lazy, Crazy, or Stupid?
　　Kate Kelly
　　Partners Book Distributing, Tyrel Jamie Publishing, 1993

Your Hyperactive Child: A Parent's Guide to Coping with Attention Deficit Disorder
> Barbara Ingersoll, Ph.D.
> Doubleday, 1988

Tourette Syndrome

Adam and the Magic Marble
> A. Buehrens and C. Buehrens
> Hope Press, 1991

Children With Tourette Syndrome: A Parent's Guide
> Edited by Tracy Haerle
> Woodbine House, 1992

Don't Think About Monkeys-Extraordinary Stories by People with Tourette Syndrome
> Adam Ward Seligman and John S. Hilkevich
> Hope Press, 1992

Echolalia - An Adult's Story of Tourette Syndrome
> Adam Ward Seligman
> Hope Press, 1992

Handbook of Tourette's Syndrome and Related Tic and Behavioral Disorders
> Edited by Roger Kurlan
> Marcel Dekker, Inc., 1993

Hi, I'm Adam
> Adam Buehrens
> Hope Press, 1991

RYAN - A Mother's Story of Her Hyperactive-Tourette Syndrome Child
> Susan Hughes
> Hope Press, 1990

Toughing Out Tourette's
> Baton Rouge TS Support Group
> Baton Rouge, Louisiana, 1989

Tourette Syndrome: Genetics, Neurobiology, and Treatment Advances in Neurology, Volume 58
> Thomas N. Chase, Arnold J. Friedhoff and Donald J. Cohen
> Raven Press, 1992

Tourette's Syndrome and Tic Disorders: Clinical Understanding and Treatment
> Donald J. Cohen, Ruth D. Bruun and James F. Leckman
> John Wiley and Sons, 1988

Tourette Syndrome and Human Behavior
> David E. Comings, M.D.
> Hope Press, 1990

Obsessive-Compulsive Disorder

The Boy Who Couldn't Stop Washing: The Experience and Treatment of Obsessive Compulsive Disorder
 Judith Rapoport, M.D.
 Plume Books, 1990

Getting Control: Overcoming Your Obsessions and Compulsions
 L. Baer
 Little, Brown and Company, 1991

Learning to Live with OCD
 B. L. VanNoppen, M. T. Pato and S. Rasmussen
 OC Foundation, 1993

Obsessive Compulsive Disorder: A Guide
 J. H. Greist
 Obsessive Compulsive Information Center, Dean Foundation for Health, Research and Education, 1992

Obsessive Compulsive Disorder in Children and Adolescents: A Guide
 H. F. Johnston
 Child Psychopharmacology Information Center, University of Wisconsin, 1993

Obsessive Compulsive Disorders: Theory and Management
 M. A. Jenike, L. Baer and N. E. Minichiello
 PSG Publishing Co., 1989

Polly's Magic Games
 C. Foster
 Dilligaf Publishing, 1994

Stop Obsessing: How To Overcome Your Obsessions and Compulsions
 Edward Foa, Ph.D. and Rick Wilson, Ph.D.
 Reid Bantam Books, 1991

When Once Is Not Enough
 Gail Steketee, Ph.D. and Kevin White, M.D.
 New Harbinger Publications, 1990

Supplemental List

Helping the Child Who Doesn't Fit In Decipher the Hidden Dimensions of Social Rejection
 Stephen Nowicki, Jr., Ph.D. and Marshall P. Duke, Ph.D.
 Peachtree Publishers, LTD., 1992

The Misunderstood Child
 Larry B. Silver
 McGraw-Hill, 1984

Negotiating the Special Education Maze: A Guide for Parents and Teachers
Winifred Anderson, Stephen Chitwood, and Deidre Hayden
Woodbine House, 1989

No One to Play With: The Social Side of Learning Disabilities
Betty B. Osman
Random House, 1982

The Special Education Handbook
Kenneth Shore
Teachers College Press, 1986

Teacher and Child: A Book for Parents and Teachers
Haim G. Ginott, Ph.D.
Collier Books, 1993

For the Professional

Assessment of Children, Third Edition
Jerome M. Sattler
Jerome M. Sattler Publisher, 1988

Developmental Variation and Learning Disorders
Mel Levine, M.D.
Educators Publishing Service, Inc., 1987

Diagnosing Learning Disorders: A Neuropsychological Framework
Bruce Pennington
Guilford Press, 1991

Intelligence Testing with the WISC-R
Alan S. Kaufman
John Wiley and Sons, 1979

Neuropsychology of Learning Disabilities: Essentials of Subtype Analysis
Byron P. Rourke, Editor
Guilford Press, 1988

Reading List (by author)

Anderson, W., Chitwood, S., and Hayden, D.
Negotiating the Special Education Maze: A Guide for Parents and Teachers
Woodbine House, 1989.

Baer, L.
Getting Control: Overcoming Your Obsessions and Compulsions
Little, Brown and Company, 1991

Barkley, Russell A., Ph.D.
Attention Deficit Hyperactivity Disorder: A Handbook for Diagnosis and Treatment
Guilford Press, 1990

Baton Rouge TS Support Group
Toughing Out Tourette's
Baton Rouge, Louisiana, 1989

Buehrens, Adam
Hi, I'm Adam
Hope Press, 1991

Buehrens, A. and Buehrens, C.
Adam and the Magic Marble
Hope Press, 1991

Chase, T. N., Friedhoff, A. J. and Cohen, D. J.
Tourette's Syndrome: Genetics, Neurobiology, and Treatment Advances in Neurology, Volume 58
Raven Press, 1992

Cohen, D. J., Bruun, B. D. and Leckmen, J. F.
Tourette's Syndrome and Tic Disorders: Clinical Understanding and Treatment
John Wiley and Sons, 1988

Comings, David E., M.D.
Tourette Syndrome and Human Behavior
Hope Press, 1990

Fowler, Mary Cahill
CH.A.A.D. Educators Manual
Casset Associates, 1992

Fowler, Mary Cahill
Maybe You Know My Kid: A Parent's Guide to Identifying, Understanding and Helping Your Child with Attention-Deficit Hyperactivity Disorder
Birch Lane Press, 1990

Foa, Edward, Ph.D. and Wilson, Rick, Ph.D.
Stop Obsessing: How to Overcome Your Obsessions and Compulsions
Reid Bantam Books, 1991

Foster, C.
Polly's Magic Games
Dilligaf Publishing, 1994

Ginott, Haim G., Ph.D.
Teacher and Child: A Book for Parents and Teachers
Collier Books, 1993

Goldstein, Sam, Ph.D. and Goldstein, Michael, M.D.
Practitioner's Guide to Managing Attention Deficit Disorder in Children
John Wiley and Sons, 1990

Greist, J. H.
Obsessive Compulsive Disorder: A Guide
Obsessive Compulsive Information Center, Dean Foundation for Health,
Research, and Education, 1992

Haerle, Tracy, Ed.
Children With Tourette Syndrome: A Parent's Guide
Woodbine House, 1992

Hallowell, Edward M., M.D. and Ratey, John J., M.D.
Driven to Distraction
Pantheon Books, a Division of Random House, Inc., 1994

Hughes, Susan
RYAN - A Mother's Story of Her Hyperactive - Tourette Syndrome Child
Hope Press, 1990

Ingersoll, Barbara, Ph.D.
**Your Hyperactive Child: A Parent's Guide to Coping with Attention
Deficit Disorder**
Doubleday, 1988

Jenike, M. A., Baer, L. and Minichiello, N. E.
Obsessive Compulsive Disorders: Theory and Management
PSG Publishing Co., 1989

Johnston, H.F.
Obsessive Compulsive Disorder in Children and Adolescents: A Guide
Child Psychopharmacology Information Center, University of Wisconsin, 1993

Kaufman, Alan S.
Intelligence Testing with the WISC-R
Alan S. Kaufman
John Wiley and Sons, 1979

Kelly, Kate
You Mean I'm Not Lazy, Crazy, or Stupid?
Partners Book Distributing, Tyrel Jamie Publishing, 1993

Kurlan, Roger, Ed.
Handbook of Tourette's Syndrome and Related Tic and Behavioral Disorders
Marcell Dekker, Inc., 1993

Latham, Peter S., J.D. and Latham, Patricia H. J.D.
Attention Deficit Disorder and the Law: A Guide for Advocates
JKL Communications, 1992

Levine, Mel, M.D.
**All Kinds of Minds: A Young Student's Book About Learning Abilities
and Learning Disorders**
Educators Publishing Service, Inc., 1993

Levine, Mel, M.D.
Developmental Variation and Learning Disorders
Educators Publishing Services, inc. 1987

Levine, Mel, M.D.
**Keeping A Head in School: A Student's Book About Learning Abilities
and Learning Disorders**
Educators Publishing Service, Inc., 1987

Nowicki, Stephen, Jr., Ph.D. and Duke, Marshall, P., Ph.D.
**Helping the Child Who Doesn't Fit In Decipher the Hidden Dimensions
of Social Rejection**
Peachtree Publishers, LTD., 1992

Osman, Betsy, B.
No One to Play With: The Social Side of Learning Disabilities
Random House, 1982

Pennington, Bruce
Diagnosing Learning Disorders: A Neuropsychological Framework
Guilford Press, 1991

Rapoport, Judith, M.D.
**The Boy Who Couldn't Stop Washing: The Experience and Treatment
of Obsessive Compulsive Disorder**
Plume Books, 1990

Rourke, Byron, P., Ed.
**Neuropsychology of Learning Disabilities
Essentials of Subtype Analysis**
Guilford Press, 1988

Sattler, Jerome M.
Assessment of Children, Third Edition
Jerome J. Sattler Publisher, 1988.

Seligman, Adam Ward
Echolalia - An Adult's Story of Tourette Syndrome
Hope Press, 1992

Seligman, Adam, W. and Hilkevich, John S.
**Don't Thing About Monkeys - Extraordinary Stories by People with
Tourette Syndrome**
Hope Press, 1992.

Shore, Kenneth
The Special Education Handbook
Teacher College Press, 1986.

Silver, Larry, M.D.
Advice to Parents on Attention-Deficit Hyperactivity Disorder
American Psychiatric Press, Inc., 1992

Silver, Larry, M.D.
The Misunderstood Child
McGraw-Hill, 1984

Steketee, Gail, Ph.D. and White, Kevin, M.D.
When Once is Not Enough
New Harbinger Publications, 1990

Van Noppen, B.L., Pato, M.T. and Rasmussen, S.
Learning to Live With OCD
OC Foundation, 1993

Wender, Paul, M.D.
**The Hyperactive Child, Adolescent, and Adult: Attention Deficit
Disorder Through the Lifespan**
Oxford Press, 1987

Appendix E:
Organizations

Organizations

Children and Adults with Attention Deficit Disorders (CH.A.A.D.)
National Office
499 N.W. 70th Avenue, Suite 308
Plantation, Florida 33317
(305) 587-3700

Children and Adults with Attention Deficit Disorders (CH.A.A.D.)
North Atlanta Chapter
P.O. Box 467607
Atlanta, Georgia 30346
(770) 381-8687

Learning Disabilities Association of America
4165 Library Road
Pittsburgh, Pennsylvania 15234
(412) 341-1515

Learning Disability Association (L.D.A.)
State of Georgia
P.O. Box 965505
Marietta, Georgia 30066
(770) 514-8088

Obsessive-Compulsive Foundation, Inc.
P.O. Box 70
Millford, Connecticut 06460-0070
(203) 878-5669
(203) 874-2826 Fax
(203) 874-3843 Info-line

Obsessive-Compulsive Information Center
Dean Foundation for Health, Research and Education
8000 Excelsior Drive, Suite 302
Madison, Wisconsin 53717-1914
(608) 836-8070

Office for Civil Rights
U.S. Department of Education
400 Maryland Avenue, S.W.
Washington, D.C. 20202-4135
(202) 401-3020

Orton Dyslexia Society
8600 La Salle Road
Baltimore, Maryland 21204-6020
(301) 296-0232

Parents Educating Parents
Sponsored by the:
Association for Retarded Citizens
College Park, Georgia 30337
(404) 761-3150

Tourette Syndrome Association (T.S.A.)
National Office
42-40 Bell Boulevard
Bayside, New York 11361
(718) 224-2999

Tourette Syndrome Association of Georgia
5600 Roswell Road N.E.
North Building, Suite 285
Atlanta, Georgia 30342
(404) 250-4322

Index _____

Order Form

1. Books:

Quantity   Amount

Tourette Syndrome and Human Behavior
_____ 1S Softback $39.95   _____

Search for the Tourette Syndrome and Human Behavior Genes
_____ 8H Hardback $34.00   _____
_____ 8S Softback $29.95   _____

The Gene Bomb   ***Does Higher Education and Advanced Technology Accelerate the Selection of Genes for Learning Disorders, ADHD, Addictive and Disruptive Behaviors?***
_____ 9H Hardback $29.95   _____
_____ 9S Softback $25.00   _____

RYAN — A Mother's Story of Her Hyperactive-Tourette Syndrome Child
_____ 2S Softback $9.95   _____

What Makes Ryan Tick?   ***A Family's Triumph over TS and ADHD***
_____ 10S Softback $14.95   _____

Hi, I'm Adam - A Child's Book about Tourette Syndrome
_____ 4A Softback $4.95   _____

Adam and the Magic Marble
_____ 4B Softback $6.95   _____

Hi, I'm Adam + Adam and the Magic Marble
_____ 4C Both together $11.50   _____

Don't Think About Monkeys - Extraordinary Stories by People with Tourette Syndrome
_____ 6A Softback $12.95   _____

Teaching the Tiger - A Handbook for Individuals Involved in the Education of Students with Attention Deficit Disorder, Tourette Syndrome or Obsessive-Compulsive Disorder
_____ 7A Softback $35.00   _____

A.D.D. Kaleidoscope - The Many Facets of Adult Attention Deficit Disorder
_____ 8A Softback $24.95   _____

Understanding and Treating the Tourette Syndrome/ADHD Spectrum Disorders by Dr. Comings   8 tapes 10 hrs
_____ 11A $75.00   _____

Dysinhibition Syndrome - How to Handle Anger and Rage in Your Child or Spouse
_____ 12A Softback $24.95   _____

Check-up from the Neck-up ***Ensuring Mental Health in the Next Millennium***
_____ 13A Softback $19.95   _____

Subtotal for Books   _____

2. Tax:
California residents please add 8.25% sales tax _____

3. Mailing and Handling:

☐ Fourth Class: $4.00 lst item $1.00 each additional item
☐ U.P.S. Ground: $6.00 lst item $1.00 each additional item
☐ U.P.S. Air: $10.00 lst item $2.00 each additional item _____

Name:_____ **Total** _____

Address: _____

City: _____ State:_____ Zip: _____

Country (if other than U.S.A.): _____

Check Enclosed _____   **or**   Visa ___ Mastercard ___

CC#_____ Expiration Date _____

send to: ☐─○ **Hope Press** P.O.Box 188,
Duarte, CA 91009-0188

or Fill out this form with credit card # and FAX it to 626-358-3520

or Order by phone **1-800-321-4039** — 24 hr service

for more details on each book visit our web site: **http://www.hopepress.com**

Order Form

1. Books: Quantity   Amount

Tourette Syndrome and Human Behavior
_____   1S Softback $39.95   _____

Search for the Tourette Syndrome and Human Behavior Genes
_____   8H Hardback $34.00   _____
_____   8S Softback $29.95   _____

***The Gene Bomb   Does Higher Education and Advanced
Technology Accelerate the Selection of Genes for Learning
Disorders, ADHD, Addictive and Disruptive Behaviors?***
_____   9H Hardback $29.95   _____
_____   9S Softback $25.00   _____

RYAN— A Mother's Story of Her Hyperactive-Tourette Syndrome Child
_____   2S Softback $9.95   _____

What Makes Ryan Tick? A Family's Triumph over TS and ADHD
_____   10S Softback $14.95   _____

Hi, I'm Adam - A Child's Book about Tourette Syndrome
_____   4A Softback $4.95   _____

Adam and the Magic Marble
_____   4B Softback $6.95   _____

Hi, I'm Adam + Adam and the Magic Marble
_____   4C Both together $11.50   _____

***Don't Think About Monkeys - Extraordinary Stories by
People with Tourette Syndrome***
_____   6A Softback $12.95   _____

***Teaching the Tiger - A Handbook for Individuals Involved
in the Education of Students with Attention Deficit Disorder,
Tourette Syndrome or Obsessive-Compulsive Disorder***
_____   7A Softback $35.00   _____

***A.D.D. Kaleidoscope - The Many Facets of Adult Attention
Deficit Disorder***
_____   8A Softback $24.95   _____

***Understanding and Treating the Tourette Syndrome/ADHD
Spectrum Disorders by Dr. Comings   8 tapes 10 hrs***
_____   11A $75.00   _____

***Dysinhibition Syndrome - How to Handle Anger and Rage in
Your Child or Spouse***
_____   12A Softback $24.95   _____

***Check-up from the Neck-up Ensuring Mental Health in the Next
Millennium***
_____   13A Softback $19.95   _____

Subtotal for Books   _____

2. Tax: **California residents please add 8.25% sales tax** _____

**3. Mailing
and
Handling:**
☐ Fourth Class: $4.00 1st item $1.00 each additional item
☐ U.P.S. Ground: $6.00 1st item $1.00 each additional item
☐ U.P.S. Air: $10.00 1st item $2.00 each additional item   _____

Name:_____   **Total** ▬▬▬▬

Address: _____

City: _____ State:_____ Zip: _____

Country (if other than U.S.A.): _____

Check Enclosed _____   **or**   Visa ___ Mastercard ___

CC#_____ Expiration Date _____

send to: ☐─○ **Hope Press** P.O.Box 188,
Duarte, CA 91009-0188

or Fill out this form with credit card # and FAX it to 626-358-3520

or Order by phone **1-800-321-4039** — 24 hr service

for more details on each book visit our web site: **http://www.hopepress.com**

Order Form

1. Books: Quantity   Amount

Tourette Syndrome and Human Behavior
_____   1S Softback $39.95   _____

Search for the Tourette Syndrome and Human Behavior Genes
_____   8H Hardback $34.00   _____
_____   8S Softback $29.95   _____

The Gene Bomb   Does Higher Education and Advanced
Technology Accelerate the Selection of Genes for Learning
Disorders, ADHD, Addictive and Disruptive Behaviors?
_____   9H Hardback $29.95   _____
_____   9S Softback $25.00   _____

RYAN — A Mother's Story of Her Hyperactive-Tourette Syndrome Child
_____   2S Softback $9.95   _____

What Makes Ryan Tick? A Family's Triumph over TS and ADHD
_____   10S Softback $14.95   _____

Hi, I'm Adam - A Child's Book about Tourette Syndrome
_____   4A Softback $4.95   _____

Adam and the Magic Marble
_____   4B Softback $6.95   _____

Hi, I'm Adam + Adam and the Magic Marble
_____   4C Both together $11.50   _____

Don't Think About Monkeys - Extraordinary Stories by
People with Tourette Syndrome
_____   6A Softback $12.95   _____

Teaching the Tiger - A Handbook for Individuals Involved
in the Education of Students with Attention Deficit Disorder,
Tourette Syndrome or Obsessive-Compulsive Disorder
_____   7A Softback $35.00   _____

A.D.D. Kaleidoscope - The Many Facets of Adult Attention
Deficit Disorder
_____   8A Softback $24.95   _____

Understanding and Treating the Tourette Syndrome/ADHD
Spectrum Disorders by Dr. Comings   **8 tapes** 10 hrs
_____   11A $75.00   _____

Dysinhibition Syndrome - How to Handle Anger and Rage in
Your Child or Spouse
_____   12A Softback $24.95   _____

Check-up from the Neck-up Ensuring Mental Health in the Next
Millennium
_____   13A Softback $19.95   _____

                                          Subtotal for Books   _____

2. Tax: **California residents please add 8.25% sales tax** _____

3. Mailing   ☐   Fourth Class: $4.00 lst item $1.00 each additional item
and   ☐   U.P.S. Ground: $6.00 lst item $1.00 each additional item
Handling: ☐   U.P.S. Air: $10.00 lst item $2.00 each additional item _____

Name:_____   **Total** _____

Address: _____

City: _____ State:_____ Zip: _____

Country (if other than U.S.A.): _____

Check Enclosed _____   **or**   Visa ___ Mastercard ___

CC#_____ Expiration Date _____

send to: ☐┬○ **Hope Press** **P.O.Box 188,**
                       Duarte, CA 91009-0188

or Fill out this form with credit card # and FAX it to 626-358-3520

or Order by phone **1-800-321-4039** — 24 hr service

for more details on each book visit our web site: **http://www.hopepress.com**

Order Form

1. Books: Quantity   Amount

Tourette Syndrome and Human Behavior
_____   1S Softback $39.95   _____

Search for the Tourette Syndrome and Human Behavior Genes
_____   8H Hardback $34.00   _____
_____   8S Softback $29.95   _____

***The Gene Bomb   Does Higher Education and Advanced
Technology Accelerate the Selection of Genes for Learning
Disorders, ADHD, Addictive and Disruptive Behaviors?***
_____   9H Hardback $29.95   _____
_____   9S Softback $25.00   _____

RYAN — A Mother's Story of Her Hyperactive-Tourette Syndrome Child
_____   2S   Softback $9.95   _____

What Makes Ryan Tick?   A Family's Triumph over TS and ADHD
_____   10S   Softback $14.95   _____

Hi, I'm Adam - A Child's Book about Tourette Syndrome
_____   4A Softback $4.95   _____

Adam and the Magic Marble
_____   4B Softback $6.95   _____

Hi, I'm Adam + Adam and the Magic Marble
_____   4C Both together $11.50   _____

***Don't Think About Monkeys - Extraordinary Stories by
People with Tourette Syndrome***
_____   6A Softback $12.95   _____

***Teaching the Tiger - A Handbook for Individuals Involved
in the Education of Students with Attention Deficit Disorder,
Tourette Syndrome or Obsessive-Compulsive Disorder***
_____   7A Softback $35.00   _____

***A.D.D. Kaleidoscope - The Many Facets of Adult Attention
Deficit Disorder***
_____   8A Softback $24.95   _____

***Understanding and Treating the Tourette Syndrome/ADHD
Spectrum Disorders by Dr. Comings   8 tapes 10 hrs***
_____   11A $75.00   _____

***Dysinhibition Syndrome - How to Handle Anger and Rage in
Your Child or Spouse***
_____   12A Softback $24.95   _____

***Check-up from the Neck-up Ensuring Mental Health in the Next
Millennium***
_____   13A Softback $19.95   _____

                              Subtotal for Books   _____

2. Tax: **California residents please add 8.25% sales tax** _____

3. Mailing
and   ☐   Fourth Class: $4.00 1st item $1.00 each additional item
Handling: ☐   U.P.S. Ground: $6.00 1st item $1.00 each additional item
        ☐   U.P.S. Air: $10.00 1st item $2.00 each additional item   _____

Name:_____ **Total** ▬▬▬▬

Address: _____

City: _____ State:_____ Zip: _____

Country (if other than U.S.A.): _____

Check Enclosed _____   **or**   Visa ___ Mastercard ___

CC#_____ Expiration Date _____

send to: ☐┬○ **Hope Press** P.O.Box 188,
                Duarte, CA 91009-0188

or Fill out this form with credit card # and FAX it to 626-358-3520

or Order by phone **1-800-321-4039** — 24 hr service

for more details on each book visit our web site: **http://www.hopepress.com**